ENCOUNTERING God

THE LEGACY OF LUTHERAN BOOK OF WORSHIP FOR THE 21ST CENTURY

Ralph R. Van Loon, editor

Kirk House Publishers
Minneapolis, Minnesota

Encountering God

THE LEGACY OF LUTHERAN BOOK OF WORSHIP FOR THE 21ST CENTURY

Cover & design by Karen Walhof

Library of Congress Cataloging-in-Publication Data

Encountering God : The legacy of Lutheran Book of Worship for the 21st Century / edited by Ralph R. Van Loon
     p. cm.
  Includes bibliographic references and index.
  ISBN 1-886513-15-5 (alk. paper)
  1. Lutheran Book of Worship. 2. Lutheran Church—United States—Liturgy. 3. Lutheran Church—Canada Liturgy. I. Van Loon, Ralph R.
BX8067.A3L76 1998
264'.04173—dc21   98-16873
                                                    CIP

Kirk House Publishers, PO Box 39759, Minneapolis, MN 55439
Manufactured in the United States of America

CONTENTS

PREFACE

For Lutherans in North America, the 1970s marked a high point in worship study. *Lutheran Book of Worship* became the focal point of that endeavor. More congregations and individuals were involved in the discussion of worship than at any time in the history of the church. New hymns and music were introduced into Lutheran worship in congregations of all sizes.

Today, as 20 years ago, a purely academic discussion of worship may lead one to conclude that worship is acts and mechanics, style and variety, and that worship is valid as long as it follows some specified order.

The reality is that the order is to lead the worshiper to an encounter with the Triune God—the almighty, all powerful, omnipresent, infinite God, whose presence in the burning bush caused Moses to remove his shoes and before whom the seraphim with six wings hovered.

The recent discovery of hundreds of as yet unknown galaxies speaks tomes about the God we worship, the God of an infinite universe, the creator of all that is, seen and unseen. Worship brings the people to a sense of awe, to a sense of conviction, to a sense of redemption, and finally to a sense of overwhelming peace in their mission.

The object of worship in the 21st century is to bring the people into such an encounter with God. Worshipers will not return Sunday after Sunday for shallow music and flimsy substance. Nor will they return if only good form is being offered. They will return week after week for liturgical worship, in the historical tradition, through which they are **encountering God.** *Lutheran Book of Worship* has ample resources for the form and substance. The planners, the presider, and the preacher are responsible for leading worshipers into an encounter with God.

The Publishers

FOREWORD

Twenty years ago, North American Lutherans were about as excited as Lutherans can ever get. Their excitement was due to the publication of their new books of liturgies and hymns, the *Lutheran Book of Worship* (*LBW*) and its companion volume, *Lutheran Book of Worship:* Ministers Edition.

The excitement was justified. Uniquely, these new books represented a genuine partnership between those who would use the books and the members of the Inter-Lutheran Commission on Worship (ILCW), who prepared them. During the preparation process, worshipers throughout North America participated in testing programs, using and evaluating the proposals that came from the ILCW. Similarly, theologians reviewed the proposed rites and rubrics, that each would be consistent with the confessions and traditions of the church. Musicians and hymnologists, poets and language scholars, parish pastors and lay leaders, biblical and liturgical scholars were also recruited, offering their experiences and talents to provide worship books that would be authentic, timely, and in harmony with Lutheranism's liturgical traditions. Worshipers were confident that the new books of worship would help foster a period of renewal, growth, and unity. At last, Lutherans across North America would be using the same rites and hymns—a long-sought objective was about to be realized. Sadly, though the project was nearing completion, one of the participating churches, the Lutheran Church–Missouri Synod, withdrew its membership from the ILCW in order to prepare its own worship book. Even so, the new hymnal and service books were approved and published in 1978, following 12 long years of studying, researching, testing, revising, and lots of negotiating.

Before the *LBW* and its Ministers Edition were put to use, the ILCW's member churches initiated a continent-wide strategy to introduce and interpret the new books. Hundreds of trained musicians, lay leaders, and pastors were sent out to all the provinces and states to lead day-long workshops, acquainting all congregations with their new worship books. Using films, recordings, presentations, booklets, discussions, and demonstrations, the workshop leaders escorted participants through the *LBW* editions, preparing them to use the books fully and well.

Because congregations had been directly involved in the preparation of the *LBW* and the Ministers Edition, they could claim immediate ownership of the books. Because most congregations attended the introduction workshops and other training events, the new worship books were quickly and widely put to use. Even though their current book, the *Service Book and Hymnal*, was but two decades old at that time, the great majority of congregations chose to use the new *LBW*. Perhaps some made that choice out of denominational loyalty. Perhaps some thought it would help advance Lutheran unity. Others, perhaps most, made the choice out of an awareness that the *LBW* was making the effort to provide rites and rubrics that reflected, proclaimed, and celebrated the richness of Lutheranism's theology and its inherited traditions. These congregations resonated to the books' baptismal accents and the explicit emphasis on shared leadership in the liturgy, full congregational participation, variation in celebration, expanded use of the Bible, more use of music, utilizing all the senses, and the centrality of the Lord's Supper each Lord's Day.

The excitement exhibited and initiated in 1978 was justified. Where the *LBW* was permitted to shape a parish's liturgical and sacramental life, positive differences were apparent and measurable: worship attendance increased, curiosity grew regarding the meaning and content of worship and its ties to mission, lay persons in leadership roles multiplied in number, pastors gained a clearer understanding of their unique tasks as liturgical presiders and preachers, choir members and church musicians accepted the challenges to be liturgical leaders rather than performers, and there was a dramatic increase in the number of parishes celebrating Holy Communion each week. It is fair to say that the publication, introduction, and faithful use of the *LBW* represented something positive and enduring for North American Lutherans.

Now, 20 years after its publication, the *LBW* and its recently approved and published supplement, *With One Voice,* continue to be used in the majority of congregations and prove to be viable and rich worship books and hymnals. Some would not agree. Some congregations have set the *LBW* aside in favor of "alternative" or locally created services and various collections of gospel choruses. Without attempting to question the motives behind decisions to discontinue using the church's liturgies and songs, there are risks involved. First, the Lutheran identity of such congregations may become obscured. After all, the Lutheran church is a liturgical church—that course was set at the time of the Reformation. While there are periods of history that record an estrangement from that course, during the last century and a half Lutherans in North America have consciously sought to reclaim and exercise their liturgical and sacramental inheritance. Opting to discard the church's liturgy in favor of "creative alternatives" simply repeats bleak times in Lutheranism's history and represents a separation from the identity it seeks to achieve and project.

Second, unlike alternative services, those rites and rubrics authored and approved by the church boast the benefit of careful theological review. Since rites and rubrics are liturgical translations, expressions, and celebrations of the church's theology, those who use the traditional, approved liturgies are more likely to grow in knowledge of the faith and deepen their appreciation for Lutheranism's inherited traditions. Similarly, the congregation's theology is shaped quite differently by its use of "alternative" services and music.

Third, alternative services have no future simply because they abandon the past. Such nontraditional services are denied the substantive and enriching liturgical contributions that only centuries of Christian experience can provide.

The arguments for treasuring and using fully the church's inherited and still-relevant traditions are persuasively articulated in the following chapters. They have been written by persons who know, teach, and use the *LBW*. Some of these writers can trace a long history with the *LBW*, having participated in the various working committees and subcommittees of the ILCW. One of the writers, Eugene L. Brand, provided fulltime leadership for the ILCW while he served as its project director. All of the contributors to this volume have been active in ongoing efforts to familiarize worshipers and worship leaders with the liturgical feast that is the *LBW*. However, none of the writers regards the *LBW* as the final and unmatchable worship book and hymnal ever prepared by the church—each knows that an eventual replacement is inevitable as the church engages ecumenical and cultural matters.

In the meantime and until the church sets in motion the preparation of a new book, these distinguished contributors desire to mark and celebrate the 20th anniversary of the *LBW* by addressing its new and current users. The new generation of users will benefit from learning some of the history behind the preparation of the *LBW* as well as the theological and liturgical impulses that gave it shape. Current users will be challenged to recall *LBW*'s stated goals and to discuss their impact on parish life and practice. This volume, *Encountering God,* will serve as a useful resource and handbook for worshipers, worship committees, and worship leaders.

Congratulations to Leonard Flachman and Karen Walhof of Kirk House Publishers for initiating this useful and challenging volume. Both had worked closely with the ILCW through each phase of its work, providing professional guidance in editing and design. Thanks to Kirk House Publishers for publishing *Encountering God*, celebrating the 20th anniversary of a book that continues to assist significantly in renewing the life and mission of the church—the *Lutheran Book of Worship.*

Ralph R. Van Loon, editor

PRESENTATION OF THE AUGSBURG CONFESSION, 1998

AN ECUMENICAL ENTERPRISE

Eugene L. Brand

INTRODUCTION

After two decades of use, the *Lutheran Book of Worship* (*LBW*)—the "green book"—is no longer the "new book." Many of its current users have only faint memories of the *Service Book and Hymnal* (*SBH*)—the "red book." And yet the green book cannot be understood or appreciated without comparing it with its predecessor, the red book, and with the other books American and Canadian Lutherans have used in the past. Though some of those books came to be milestones on the path to Lutheran liturgical convergence in the English language while others now appear more peripheral, they all have left their mark on the manner in which Lutherans in North America worship and how they conceive of their worship.

Lutheran patriarch Henry Melchior Muhlenberg had the dream of uniting all Lutheran congregations "in the North American States," and dreamt that they would express this unity by using the "same order of service (and) the same hymn-book."[1] Successive mergers of churches in North America have come close to achieving the structural part of Muhlenberg's dream, and the *LBW* came even closer to realizing the worship part.[2] The gradual ascendance of English over the various mother tongues of Lutheran immigrants and the inevitable "Americanization" of the churches proved to be inescapable prerequisites for Lutheran unity.

The story of the liturgical convergence has been told several times,[3] and it is not the purpose of this book to tell it yet again. This book is intended to reflect on major themes of concern to the worshipping church in light of 20 years of *LBW* usage and in the face of an uncertain ecclesial future.

Experience shows that the liturgical tradition as Christians relive it Sunday by Sunday, even day by day, influences the content of their faith, shapes their familial and personal devotional lives, contributes to confessional unity, and influences the breadth of their ecumenical vision.

To provide a backdrop for the topics addressed by the other contributors to this book, it is appropriate to review for a new generation of users the impact of the *LBW* and to observe its place in the broader striving for liturgical and structural unity in the church catholic.

ECUMENICAL MATRIX

Liturgical books which have exemplified the classical Lutheran confessional and liturgical heritage have all been ecumenical in character because the Lutheran intention was not to depart from the mainstream liturgical tradition of the Latin church, but to reform it. As with the Anglican *Book of Common Prayer*, the liturgy as Lutherans celebrate it is a reformed version of the Latin rite, not an idealistic effort to restore the worship of the New Testament church. Nevertheless as confessional self-consciousness grew in the several churches of the Reformation, ongoing liturgical revision was carried out largely without consultation with other churches or, especially where the Roman Catholic Church was concerned, sometimes in opposition to them. Thus one came to speak of the *Lutheran liturgy* or the *Anglican liturgy.*

Nineteenth century developments in North America, however, foreshadowed Lutheran participation in the ecumenical consensus of the latter half of the 20th century. In Europe, Lutheran liturgical revision in the various languages of separate national churches has resulted in a *German* Lutheran tradition, a *Slovak* Lutheran tradition, a *Swedish* Lutheran tradition, etc. But immigrant Lutheran churches in North America who transplanted these various traditions found it necessary for pastoral and other reasons to switch to English which had not been a "Lutheran language." This, of course, turned out to constitute the necessary precondition for Lutheran unity across previous linguistic barriers. It also, however, set North American Lutherans irrevocably on an ecumenical course since the English they employed was that of the Anglican *Book of Common Prayer.*[4] Probably without realizing it, an alliance was forged with the English-speaking Christian world which would profoundly influence the liturgical reform of North American Lutherans a century later.[5]

The *SBH* stands as the culmination of a process of liturgical renewal/recovery which began with the *Church Book* a century earlier. It restored

Encountering God

to North American Lutheranism the fullness of its Reformation heritage while, at the same time, opening itself to the riches of other churches. Surely it would serve for decades to come. But clouds of change were appearing on the horizon even before it was published in 1958. It became increasingly clear that, for pastoral reasons, churches needed to abandon the so-called "King James English" of the Prayerbook tradition and adopt a style more consonant with 20th century English. Two events signaled this language crisis, one liturgical, the other cultural. The first event was the instant success of the Revised Standard Version of the Bible published in 1952. Within a short time it replaced the King James version both in church and for personal devotion. Thus the liturgical language of the *SBH* was no longer a mirror of the language of the biblical readings.

The second was the course charted by the Roman Catholic Church in changing its liturgical language from Latin to English. The products of the Roman Catholic International Commission for English in the Liturgy (ICEL) addressed God as "you." Thus the "mother church" of the Latin tradition challenged the liturgical diction of her "daughters," a challenge which could not be ignored because it constituted a pastoral response to a cultural problem: the disparity between 20th century spoken English and the 16th century style of English liturgies. Just as the change to English had been a necessary pastoral accommodation for Lutherans in 19th century North America, so a more contemporary liturgical diction was clearly a necessary pastoral accommodation to 20th century English-speaking countries.

ICEL, aware of the immensity of the task of creating a new liturgical English, was open to cooperation with others. Since most English-speaking churches were becoming aware of the pastoral need to close the cultural gap in language, they were eager to cooperate. Pastoral need also suggested the folly and impracticality of churches approaching the body of common liturgical texts separately. In the United States, some experience with cooperation in text formulation had already been gained through the Consultation on Common Texts (CCT) which had begun its work in the mid-1960s.

It was at this same moment in history that the Inter-Lutheran Commission on Worship (ILCW) began the work which would eventually result in publication of the *LBW*. Though the primary reason for establishing the ILCW was to include the Lutheran Church–Missouri Synod in joint liturgical and hymnological work, from the very beginning it committed itself to full participation in the ecumenical aspects of revising forms of worship. The 1960s and 70s were decades of liturgical revision in virtually all churches in the north. The evolution of the liturgical movement from its restoration phase into its pastoral phase provided a major stimulus for this activity. Another factor was the revision of the liturgical books of the Roman Catholic Church to make them consonant with the *Constitution on the Sacred Liturgy* of the Second Vatican Council. Biblical studies and patristic research had influenced the final decades of the restoration phase of the liturgical movement, and they continued to energize the pastoral phase. Since the issues wrestled with because of the pastoral approach to worship were common issues, it was natural to address them ecumenically. This was uniquely true in the English-speaking world where text reform had a multinational dimension which also fostered ecumenical cooperation. Lutherans were part of that multinational mix which encompassed Australia, Canada, Great Britain, Ireland, New Zealand and the United States.

The International Consultation on English Texts (ICET) constituted itself as an ad hoc group with only informal ties to the churches represented[6] so that the process could proceed quickly with a minimum of bureaucratic structure. This meant that the texts produced would be accepted or rejected on their merits and not because of any official status. In 1969 ICET issued *Prayers We Have In Common* which contained the texts of the ordinary of the mass together with drafts of other commonly used texts. ICET finished its work in 1975 with the publication of the second revised *Prayers We Have In Common* which included texts of the Lord's Prayer, Apostles' Creed, Nicene Creed, *Sursum corda, Gloria in excelsis, Sanctus/Benedictus, Agnus Dei* (a text and a paraphrase), *Gloria Patri, Benedictus, Magnificat,* and *Nunc dimittis.* Having participated in the work of ICET and being committed to the inclusion of its texts in the *LBW*, the ILCW demonstrated its ecumenical commitment.[7] Fortunately other major communions did too so that the ICET texts form a common bond among English-speaking Christians across the globe. Minor deviations have not constituted a major problem.[8]

The ecumenical matrix also contributed other portions of the *LBW*. Use of the King James psalter in the *SBH* had not been a stunning success, and nobody made a case for the inclusion of the RSV psalter in the *LBW*. Neither had been crafted primarily for corporate reading or singing. The ILCW saw no point in creating its own version of the psalms. Much better to use a version also in use by others. After examining the available possibilities it was decided to use the version made by the Episcopalians for

Encountering God

their new *Book of Common Prayer*. This version had been crafted for corporate participation, deliberately retaining the rhythms of the *Coverdale Psalter* previously employed. Furthermore it was decided to point these psalms for singing, something the Episcopalians had not done. To assist it in the work of pointing, the liturgical committees enlisted the help of one of America's leading Roman Catholic scholars. Thus the pointed psalter in the *LBW* is truly an ecumenical product!

A similar process of ecumenical borrowing, also from the new prayerbook, was employed in selecting the *LBW* prayers. Collects prepared by ICEL had been considered, but were thought to be inferior stylistically. A large portion of the collects for the day were given their present form by an ILCW subcommittee.[9]

It is the lectionary for Sundays and feast days which is the most influential of the ecumenical gifts to the *LBW*. Criticism of the so-called historic pericopes goes back at least to Luther himself, because they did not offer an adequate balance of the biblical material and because they included no regular reading from the Old Testament. Yet Lutherans had retained them because of their ecumenical value. But in its revision of the lectionary —*Ordo lectionum missae*, 1969—the Roman Catholic Church, the "mother" of the historic pericopes, made a clean break with the Latin tradition, offering instead a triple cycle of three readings for each occasion.

After researching other lectionary revisions, an ILCW committee recommended the Roman *Ordo* and prepared a revision of it which was subsequently included in the *LBW*. That decision is eloquent testimony to the ecumenical commitment of the ILCW since it meant breaking with sister churches in world Lutheranism. Under the auspices of the Lutheran World Federation a committee had been convened in 1968 and charged with the task of preparing a revised lectionary which would respond to the criticisms of the historic pericopes and which could be adopted by Lutheran churches all over the world.

This committee's work was finally abandoned because of a stand-off between the German and North American churches. The German churches wished to follow their own tradition by retaining the historic pericopes, albeit in revised form, and then supplementing these "reading texts" with additional cycles of "preaching texts," thereby isolating preaching from the liturgy in all years but one. These churches also resisted a full set of readings from the Old Testament. The Americans wished to follow a revised form of the three-year Roman Catholic system for ecumenical reasons—not only would it be used by the majority of the world's

Christians—but it was also being included in their new books by other churches in North America, and because it provided for a fuller coverage of the Scriptures in a manner which kept preaching tied to the readings.

Faced with the choice of being in step with Lutherans in other parts of the world or with the majority of Christians in their own area, the Americans chose the latter. This division of the Lutheran house causes problems not only at global Lutheran events, but also in Africa, Asia, and Latin America whose churches often look to Germany and/or the United States for homiletical materials. By their choice the German evangelical churches have isolated themselves from much of the rest of western Christianity. The former positions may be tempered by the appearance in 1992 of the *Revised Common Lectionary* prepared under the auspices of the CCT in view of experience with the three-year systems and with the goal of reconciling them. This revised pericope system was approved for use both by the Evangelical Lutheran Church in Canada (1994) and the Evangelical Lutheran Church in America (1995).

The ferment of the 1960s and 70s, as indicated above, primarily involved the liturgy. The hymnal portion of the *SBH* would probably have survived longer than the liturgical portion. But the ecumenical matrix for the *LBW* also included a concern for common hymnody. The Consultation on Ecumenical Hymnody (CEH) produced in 1971 a list of hymns and tunes intended to form a common core in the various new hymnals. These would provide not only a symbolic bond among the churches; they would be useful especially at ecumenical services. This core of hymns is included in the *LBW*. In the index to first lines, they are marked with an asterisk. It is unfortunate, however, that the work of CEH did not include common revisions of the ecumenical corpus of hymns. The goal of the project has been hampered by a conflict among the various versions of the same familiar hymn text.

A crucial ingredient in the ecumenical matrix out of which the *LBW* and other liturgical books have come is the development of ecumenical theology over roughly the same period. We cannot consider it here, but neither can it be ignored. Anyone interested in the results of the modern liturgical movement must compare them with such an ecumenical document as *Baptism, Eucharist and Ministry* (1982) from the Commission on Faith and Order of the World Council of Churches.[10]

At the beginning of this section it was asserted that liturgies exemplifying the classical Lutheran confessional and liturgical heritage have always been ecumenical in character because they are reformed versions of the historic Latin rite. That becomes even clearer when the *SBH* Eucharist, which we called the culmination of the recovery phase of the liturgical movement among Lutherans, is compared with the reformed version of the Latin rite contained in the present *Missale Romanum*. The Roman reforms of the 20th century have been no less radical and are even more compatible with the Lutheran and Anglican reforms of the 16th century.

IMPACT

In 1978, Lutherans in North America began to come to terms with the new green book. Fortunately that process had already begun through trial-use materials issued by the ILCW as a means of field testing its work. The ten booklet series labeled *Contemporary Worship* was a foretaste of what was to come. Indeed congregations' feedback had shaped what was to come. Two decades later, what can be said about the impact of the *LBW* on the practice and understanding of worship among Lutherans in North America? Have the goals of the ILCW been realized?

In any attempt to assess the impact of the *LBW*, the book must not be isolated from its context, not in terms of its predecessors, not in terms of the matrix from which it was birthed. Some of the goals could have been and were achieved without the book itself. And yet the book becomes a shorthand way of analyzing Lutheran worship in the period since its publication. With that understanding we proceed.

The ILCW's liturgical goals are listed in the Introduction to the *LBW:*

1. To restore to Holy Baptism the liturgical rank and dignity implied by Lutheran theology, and to draw out the baptismal motifs in such acts as the confession of sin and the burial of the dead.

Nothing points so dramatically to the convergence of ecumenical theology and the ecumenical consensus in worship as this baptismal emphasis. Though the baptismal liturgy is sometimes truncated in ways that betray a lack of understanding of the rite, it has made a difference. Less frequently does one encounter the "we interrupt this service for no more than a few minutes to get this thing over with" syndrome. Where the full thanksgiving over the water is used, it seems immediately to "sell" itself to a congregation. More often there are several candidates for Baptism, sometimes a mixture of infants, older children and adults. Baptizing by immersion or submersion, while still the rare exception, is no longer regarded as revolutionary in Lutheran circles. Progress has been made in "saving" Baptisms for occasions in the church year which have special ties to the sacrament, thus avoiding the impression that Baptism's primary link is to human birth. In new buildings or renovations, fonts are being made more prominent architecturally, are increasing in capacity, and are being filled with running water.

Baptism is being emphasized as the birthing of the church and the foundation of the Christian life with witnessing and moral implications. The Lutheran emphasis that in the confession of sins one daily returns to one's Baptism is clearly expressed for preaching and teaching. The baptismal motif in the burial service is found to be especially meaningful, and funeral palls, symbols of baptismal garments, are being used more frequently. Seeing Baptism as the foundation sacrament of the Christian community is slowly leading to seeing the Eucharist as the birthright of all the baptized.

    2. To continue to move into the larger ecumenical heritage of liturgy while, at the same time, enhancing Lutheran convictions about the Gospel.

The ecumenical matrix of the *LBW* has already been discussed, and its ecumenical influence forms the topic for the final section of this chapter. In both discussions the underlying assumption has been that there is no conflict between liturgical material which is both consonant with the Lutheran theological and liturgical heritage and that which is open ecumenically. The *SBH* had already ventured beyond the strict confines of the 16th century Lutheran Church Orders. With the *LBW* the doors have been opened wide to the fullness of the Latin tradition and to its future evolution.

    3. To involve lay persons as assisting ministers who share the leadership of corporate worship.

Previous Lutheran practice, shared with other "traditional" churches, regarded the liturgy as a dialogue between the pastor (who assumed not only the presidency of the assembly, but all other leadership roles as well) and the congregation in unison. In some places the choir was granted a leadership or representative role too. To put it a bit irreverently, the Sunday service was a one man show. And, unfortunately, both pastor and congregation often conceived of the gathered community as an audience. While "entertainment evangelism" has recently infected some Lutheran congregations, for the most part the audience syndrome has become a thing of the past. Lectors, cantors, ministers of communion, leaders in prayer, choirs, acolytes, ushers—many or all of these leadership roles are today exercised by lay persons. Actually this development is a necessary result of the baptismal emphasis. The *priesthood of all believers* or, more accurately, the *priesthood of all the baptized*, suggests not an audience but a gathering of involved persons engaged together in worship.

This corporate concept is also having its influence on the ordering or reordering of space for worship. The altar is moved out from the wall so that the presiding minister can face the gathering during the Eucharist—a much clearer symbol of the corporate character of the eucharistic feast. The whole space is holy not only because it is the house of God but also because it is the house of God's holy people. Long, narrow naves which tend to separate unduly the congregation from the "holy place" are disappearing. Musicians are brought down from their music room in the west balcony to join visibly the gathered people. Excessively vivid windows or paintings or screens which draw attention away from the corporate action centered at the altar give way to spaces where the worshipping congregation is the chief ornament.

In fairness it must be admitted that these developments sometimes bring with them other problems which continue to challenge congregations. Spaces as described above, while they reflect the emphasis on the eucharistic worship of the baptized community, afford little opportunity for the uncommitted or the partially committed to be present while at the same time keeping their distance. It is more difficult in such a building to create an atmosphere of awe in the divine presence. Indeed the emphasis on corporate action can degenerate into mere conviviality. And, having brought the musicians down from their loft, it is not easy to find an acoustically advantageous place for them.

Surely these are not insoluble problems. The "traditional" nave, aisles, chancel arrangement was perfected over centuries, and the bad examples have disappeared. We must continue to experiment and take the risks of mediocrity.

4. To bring the language of prayer and praise into conformity with the best current usage.

The shift marked by the *LBW* from 16th century English to a more contemporary style has been described above. Here too we must continue to search for the right tone and flow. It is not fair to compare the language of the newer books aesthetically with that of the former prayerbooks which, after all, were the results of several centuries of honing and polishing. The *LBW* did not simply change the address to the divine persons from the archaic "thou" with its necessary archaic verb forms to the more current "you," but it also generally employed gender inclusive language. Since 1978 the problem of God language has come increasingly to the fore. There are theological issues at stake here; the problem is not just stylistic. For the moment solutions which would be both theologically credible and generally acceptable elude us.

    5. To offer a variety of musical styles.

The *LBW* offers three differing and complete settings for the Eucharist together with a variety of psalm tones. In many if not most places this has broken the model of the same setting every Sunday. In fact, the desire for even more options has resulted in several supplementary publications, most recently *With One Voice.* Musical variety can reflect the changing moods of the church year and can also be an antidote for the boredom of too much repetition. On the other hand, too frequent changes in musical settings can distract worshipers from concentrating on the words they are singing and thus from worship itself.

The list in the *LBW*'s Introduction ends here. But two decades of experience suggests the addition of another goal: *to reintroduce among Lutherans the traditional rites of the Triduum.* This material is found only in the Ministers Edition and consists of liturgies for Maundy Thursday, Good Friday, and the Vigil of Easter. Taken together these rites give vivid expression to the indivisible center of the gospel—cross and resurrection— and to God's saving work in creation and redemption. In an incomparable way what Christianity and the church are all about comes to expression in the Triduum, climaxing in the Vigil of Easter. Congregations are discovering how this celebration too draws together Baptism, proclamation, and Eucharist, and sheds light on the entire life in Christ. Without the Triduum the whole liturgical year with its range of celebration has a vacuum at its center.

ECUMENICAL INFLUENCE

The *LBW* has had an influence on the wider Lutheran communion and on relations with other communions. The debts North American Lutherans owe to other communions for what they have contributed to the *LBW* have been already noted in the "Ecumenical Matrix" section above.

The *LBW* is used in other parts of the Lutheran communion both as a resource for liturgical texts and hymns in English and by English-speaking congregations in large cities such as Geneva, London, Oslo, Berlin, Budapest, and Tokyo. Since English has become the second language of much of the world, pastors often require English material for visiting groups, multilingual ecumenical events, etc. They tend to turn either to the *LBW* or to one of the incarnations of the *Book of Common Prayer*. In this way Lutherans in other parts of the world are exposed to and perhaps shaped by the *LBW*.

The *LBW* has also been used as a point of reference by Lutheran churches in other parts of the world. The liturgical commission of the Church of Sweden, for example, took great interest in the *LBW*. Its representatives came to the United States more than once to consult with persons involved in the ILCW. A similar thing happened more recently as the new service book and hymnal for the United Evangelical Lutheran Church in Germany was being prepared. When churches in Hong Kong and Taiwan were preparing a new book for Chinese Lutherans, the *LBW* played an important role in the project. In this way the *LBW* in particular and the liturgical consensus in the English-speaking world in general have exerted an influence beyond North America.

When the late Bishop of Bukoba, Tanzania, Josiah Kibira, became president of the Lutheran World Federation, he requested copies of the *LBW* to use at an English-language Eucharist which he celebrated every Wednesday in his cathedral. The practice has been continued by his successor, Bishop Samson Mushemba. Because of the multilingual situation in Africa, English can become the language of communication among Africans themselves. Thus in the chapel of the university in Harare, Zimbabwe, a largely African congregation gathers every Sunday to worship using the *LBW*. These examples are especially noteworthy because neither is the result of a "foreign" congregation ministering to expatriates or of North American missionaries transplanting the worship book with which they are familiar.

Laudamus, first published by the Lutheran World Federation in 1952 as a trilingual hymnal with minimal liturgical material, evolved by the time of its 5th edition in 1984 into a fuller multilingual service book and hymnal. *Laudamus* was intended primarily for LWF assemblies, but has also been used extensively at LWF meetings and consultations where English or multilingual resources are needed. Liturgical materials are presented in English and German. English liturgies for the Eucharist, Morning Prayer, and Compline were borrowed from the *LBW* as were the English-language psalms and prayers. Through *Laudamus* the *LBW* has had an indirect influence on Lutherans—and especially church leaders—from all parts of the world.

The liturgical materials of the *LBW* have also had an important affect on Lutheran ecumenical relations both in North America and worldwide. In most cases the opinion people from other Christian communions have about Lutheran worship is formed by the *LBW*. And conversely, when Lutherans worship in other congregations the degree to which they feel at home relates to how similar worship there is to the *LBW* liturgies with which they are familiar. The high degree of convergence liturgically primarily between Anglicans (Episcopalians), Roman Catholics and Lutherans, but also among some Presbyterians, Methodists, and Lutherans has prepared the soil for more formal agreements of full communion. If our celebrations of the Eucharist are so similar and if our Baptisms create a common bond, what is it that still requires us to be separated?[11]

Going beyond the creation of a basic ecumenical ambiance, the *LBW* has also figured in at least one formal ecumenical agreement. The 1982 *Agreement* between the Episcopal Church in the United States, The American Lutheran Church, the Association of Evangelical Lutheran Churches, and the Lutheran Church in America in which they formally recognized one another as churches "in which the gospel is preached and taught" and established many forms of common life, provides for "interim sharing of the Eucharist." Paragraph 4.b stipulates: "the eucharistic prayer will be one from the *Lutheran Book of Worship* or the *Book of Common Prayer*." This provision reflects the role of liturgy in mutual recognition between churches.

At the first meeting of the fourth phase of the international Lutheran-Roman Catholic dialogue in Finland in 1995, the opening Eucharist was celebrated by the Lutherans according to the *LBW* (from *Laudamus*). The Roman Catholic partners were in attendance. After the service a Roman Catholic bishop who is a very experienced theologian and ecumenist was heard to say, "So what is the difference between us?" A perfect example of the ecumenical influence of the *LBW*.

Full partnership in the ecumenical efforts toward liturgical convergence in the one holy catholic and apostolic church may indeed turn out to be the greatest legacy of which the *LBW* is the North American symbol.

NOTES

1   From Jacobs, H. E. *A History of the Evangelical Lutheran Church in the United States*, New York, 1893, 337f.

2   Though the Lutheran Church–Missouri Synod participated fully in the preparation of the *LBW* manuscript, the church failed to authorize it, preferring instead to publish its own

version, *Lutheran Worship*. Still, a significant number of Missouri Synod congregations have used the *LBW*.

3   See, for example, Philip H. Pfatteicher, *Commentary on the Lutheran Book of Worship* (Minneapolis: Augsburg Fortress, 1990) and Frank C. Senn, *Christian Liturgy—Catholic and Evangelical* (Minneapolis: Augsburg Fortress, 1997). See also Luther D. Reed, *The Lutheran Liturgy* (Philadelphia: Fortress Press, 1959).

4   As did the 1868 *Church Book*, the Common Service of 1888 employed the diction of the *Book of Common Prayer* and thus set the mainstream tradition of English-speaking Lutherans until the *Lutheran Book of Worship*, 1978, introduced a more contemporary style.

5   See my "The Lutheran 'Common Service': Heritage and Challenge," *Studia Liturgica* 19 (1989).

6   Members were drawn from the following Christian world communions: Anglican, Baptist, Congregationalist, Lutheran, Methodist, Presbyterian, Roman Catholic. The Consultation on Church Union (USA) was also represented.

7   One important result was the restoration of *catholic* for Christian in the Apostles and Nicene Creeds.

8   For example, the *LBW* version of the Apostles' Creed substitutes "he descended into hell" for the ICET "he descended to the dead;" the *Missal of Paul VI* contains the ICET doxology to the Lord's Prayer following the embolism, but uses the traditional English text for the prayer itself; the *Alternative Services Book* of the Church of England substitutes "lead us not into temptation but deliver us from evil" for the ICET "Save us from the time of trial and deliver us from evil" in the Lord's Prayer.

9   On the psalter and collects, see Pfatteicher, op. cit., pp. 131, 318ff and 392.

10 For an analysis of this parallel development see the double issue of *Studia Liturgica* 16/1-2, 1968.

11 On this point see my Berakah Address to the North American Academy of Liturgy published in *Worship* 58 (1984).

WORSHIP AND THE MEANS OF GRACE

Walter R. Bouman

The Christian claim that the saving grace of God comes to human beings through visible means begins with early Christian theology.[1] Article V of the Augsburg Confession continues the tradition. To obtain that faith which receives God's grace

> God instituted the office of the ministry, that is, provided the gospel and the sacraments. Through these, as through *means*, he gives the Holy Spirit, who works faith, when and where he pleases, in those who hear the gospel.[2]

In Article XIII of the Apology of the Augsburg Confession, Philip Melanchthon defines sacraments as "rites which have the command of God and to which the promise of grace has been added" (p. 211). The key terms are "command" and "promise." The rituals of Christian worship are things which the church is commanded to do because there, and there only, are the promises of the gospel to be encountered as available for our trust. Melanchthon continues,

> The genuine sacraments, therefore, are Baptism, the Lord's Supper, and absolution (which is the sacrament of penitence), for these rites have the commandment of God and the promise of grace (p. 211).

To these three rituals Melanchthon adds the Word of God, which "has God's command and glorious promises" (p. 212).

Lutherans, therefore, understand the "means of grace" to be the gospel as it is mediated through the proclaimed Word of God, the Lord's Supper, Holy Baptism, and its life-long continuation in confession/absolution, in other words, Word *and* Sacraments. It is important to stress the connection between them because since the middle of the 18th century, corporate worship in Protestant churches has focused on the Word of God, on preaching.

> The reason is that sacraments have lost out to a rationalistic concept of the Word of God, reducing it to revealed information about divine things, thus leaving nothing useful for the sacraments to do.[3]

All of this has been exacerbated by the American religious context, described as "gnostic" in some recent analyses.[4] Gnosticism was the great adversary of orthodox Christianity in the early centuries of the church's history. The focus in Gnosticism is on knowledge. Salvation comes through saving knowledge. Jesus is the author of this saving knowledge. Gnosticism is highly individualistic and non-sacramental, and thus finds significant support from the American spirit.[5]

Against Gnosticism, whenever it manifests itself, orthodox Christianity has emphasized and affirmed the following: Salvation occurs through specific historical events, namely the death and resurrection of Jesus of Nazareth. Christians share in these historical events through participation in the sacramental means of grace by which the salvation of Jesus is made available. The goodness of creation is affirmed together with the related principle that the finite is capable of being the bearer of the infinite, that creation is capable of bearing both God and the gospel.

Lutheran Book of Worship (*LBW*) contains rites for the administration of the means of grace. These rites will be addressed here in terms of the sequence in which they appear in the *LBW*: The Holy Communion, which includes proclamation of the Word of God, followed by Holy Baptism and the rites for confession/absolution.

THE HOLY COMMUNION

A brief comparison between the *LBW* and its two predecessors, the 1941 *The Lutheran Hymnal* (*TLH*) and the 1958 *Service Book and Hymnal* (*SBH*) is revealing.

The first rite in *TLH* is the service of ante-communion. It uses the traditional order of the first half of the Western rite for Holy Communion: *Introit, Kyrie, Gloria in Excelsis*, Collect, Epistle, Gradual, Gospel, Creed, Sermon, and Offertory. Following the General Prayer, the service concludes with the Lord's Prayer and the Benediction. The second rite is identical with the first, but after the Offertory the rite continues with the

Preface and *Sanctus*, the Words of Institution, the Lord's Prayer and Communion. The sequence indicates clearly that ante-communion is the "normal" worship of the Sunday congregation. Holy Communion was the rite for special occasions.

The *SBH* gives a similar indication. The service is nearly identical with that of *TLH*, except that the *SBH* adds an optional lesson from the Old Testament. After the Offertory and the Prayer of the Church, the rite continues, "If there be no Communion the Minister and Congregation shall say the Lord's Prayer" (p. 8). The rite concludes with the Benediction. By omitting the Lord's Prayer and the Benediction, the rite can continue with the Thanksgiving and the Communion. The clear indication is that the Communion is an *addition* to the "normal" Sunday worship of the congregation.

The *LBW*, by way of contrast, has the Holy Communion as its basic rite. A rubric after the Creed states that "when there is no Communion, the service continues on page 75" (p. 65). One can still conclude with the Offertory, the Prayers, the Lord's Prayer, and the Benediction. But the very arrangement gives a clear indication that the Holy Communion is the normal Sunday liturgy, and if there is no communion something is being omitted.

Thus the *LBW* goes a long way toward restoring the Holy Communion as the normal liturgy for Sundays and Festivals. Weekly communion is, of course, the teaching of the Lutheran confessions.[6] The reason that the Holy Communion is the normal liturgy for Sundays and Festivals goes to the heart of the gospel.

At issue is the identity of the gathering as church. Between gatherings the church is invisible. It cannot be seen. Its members are scattered and cannot be readily identified as members of the church. The church is visible when it gathers. But not all gathering of Christians is church. Christians can gather for instruction, for recreation, for meetings, even for Scripture lessons, preaching, and prayers. But the forms, the rituals, for such gatherings are not distinctively Christian. The gathering of a synagogue congregation is also for lessons, preaching, and prayers. When the Sunday gathering does something other than the Holy Communion, it means that the *form* of the rite is not yet Christian, not yet church. The gathering is using a rite which is pre-Christian, that is, as if the Messiah had not yet come.

The church is the community called into being by the saving event of the crucified and risen Jesus of Nazareth. The church confesses that Jesus of Nazareth is the Messiah of Israel and the world by gathering to participate in the messianic meal, the Holy Communion. That is the unique rite which identifies a gathering as the messianic community.

The Event of Jesus as the Messiah

The gospel of the apostolic scriptures is deceptively simple: Jesus has been raised from the dead! Jesus is the Christ! These are two ways of saying the same thing. The resurrection of Jesus from the dead is the starting point of Christianity.[7]

What the followers of Jesus experienced when they were encountered by Jesus after his execution and burial was not Jesus' resuscitation, but something infinitely more awesome. Jesus had been raised to the *eschaton*, to the final future of the reign of God. That is the significance of Luke's "ascension." Jesus does not go to some "place" in or beyond the cosmos. He ascends into the future, and he is therefore not "gone." He is present with and to his disciples in the power of the future.

When the disciples encountered Jesus raised as the Messiah, they were required to re-appropriate the past. The resurrection of Jesus meant that his claim to embody, represent, and inaugurate the reign of God was indeed valid. His death by execution on the cross was not God's repudiation of his ministry, but rather its affirmation and consummation. His mission to renew Israel, to gather its lost sheep, and to open it to the gentiles was God's mission. His signs pointed to the fact that the reign of God had indeed come among them.[8] Taking up the cross was to be both the way and the consequence of discipleship. Hence the past was to be re-appropriated as the disciple communities retold the stories of Jesus with the "aha" of Spirit-given insight.

But even more radically, they were required to re-envision the future. The resurrection meant that Jesus has death ultimately behind him. "Death no longer has dominion over him" (Romans 6:9). The future belongs to him. He can make unconditional promises, promises not conditioned by death.[9] The reign of God, not the reign and power of death, will have the last word. This led the church to the early confession that Jesus is God. For if "God" means whatever has the last word in history, then Jesus is "God." And because Jesus has been raised from the dead, he now defines and determines what we mean by God. He and the "Abba" whose mission he embodied, together with the Spirit, the one through whom history receives its direction and goal, are now the triune "Name" by which God is finally known.

The Development of Christian Worship

Because of the resurrection of Jesus we can reconstruct the development of the liturgy. The Jewish disciples of Jesus continued to participate in the life of the synagogue and in the rituals of the temple. Simultaneously, however, the disciples of Jesus assembled in homes for that ritual which identified them uniquely: the messianic meal.

> And day by day, attending the temple together and *breaking bread in their homes*, they partook of food with glad and generous hearts, praising God and having favor with all the people (Acts 2:47).

Obviously, not all Jews, not even the majority of Jews, believed that Jesus was the Messiah. But those who did were *identified* by the ritual Luke calls "the breaking of bread," a technical term for the Holy Communion.[10] The meal was understood to be a characteristic of the messianic age. If Jesus was indeed the messiah, and if the messianic age had begun, then they would witness to and participate in this messianic event by being at the messianic banquet table.

By the end of the first century the break between Jesus' disciples and other Jews became complete. The place once occupied by the regular meal in the assemblies of the disciples of Jesus was now filled by a synagogue-type ritual of Scripture and prayer. By the time of Justin (150 C.E.) we have the ritual which he describes (Apol. I, 67):

> On the day which is called Sun-day, all, whether they live in the town or in the country, gather in the same place. Then the Memoirs of the Apostles or the Writings of the Prophets are read for as long as time allows. When the reader has finished, the president speaks, exhorting us to live by these noble teachings. Then we rise all together and pray. Then, as we said earlier, when the prayer is finished, bread, wine and water are brought. The president then prays and gives thanks as well as he can. And all the people reply with the acclamation: Amen! After this the eucharists are distributed and shared out to everyone, and the deacons are sent to take them to those who are absent.[11]

The community of his disciples understands the messianic age to have begun and anticipates its consummation. They are identified as messianic community by their participation in the messianic banquet.

Encountering God

Holy Communion as Messianic Banquet

Such an understanding of Holy Communion as the rite which uniquely *identifies* the communities of Jesus' disciples has its roots deep in the Scriptures of Israel. According to the prophet of the exile, the Lord will feed his people on their homeward journey through the desert (Isaiah 49:9f) as he fed the people of old in the wilderness (Isaiah 48:21). The nations will come to Israel to share in the blessings of the everlasting covenant (Isaiah 55:1-5). Geoffrey Wainwright calls special attention to the passage in Isaiah's apocalypse "which is of particular significance for the eucharist."[12]

> On this mountain the Lord of hosts will make for all peoples a feast of fat things, a feast of wine on the lees, of fat things full of marrow, of wine on the lees well refined. And he will destroy on this mountain the covering that is cast over all peoples, the veil that is spread over all nations. He will swallow up death forever, and the Lord God will wipe away tears from all faces, and the reproach of his people he will take away from all the earth; for the Lord has spoken (Isaiah 25:6-8).

Following the Exile, the meal motif in relation to messianic expectation intensifies. The age to come will be an age of plenty. The God who fed the people with manna in the wilderness will feed his people again (2 Baruch 29:8). Wainwright quotes the Midrash Rabbah: "Just as the former deliverer (Moses) made manna descend, so also the latter deliverer (the messiah) will make manna descend."[13] Strong messianic expectations came to be attached to the Passover by the time of Jesus.[14] According to the Ethiopian Enoch, 62:13-16, "The righteous and elect shall be saved on that day, And with that Son of Man shall they eat and lie down and rise up for ever and ever."[15]

It is now easy to understand why and how the meal plays such an important role in the teaching and activity of Jesus. The feeding of the multitude is a sign of the Messiah (Matthew 14:13-21, Mark 6:32-44, Luke 9:10-17, John 6:1-15; cf. Matthew 15:32-39 and Mark 8:1-10). In John the feeding is the occasion for explicit messianic reflection (John 6:16-59). Central to Jesus' activity is his table collegiality with sinners and outcasts (Luke 15:1-2), and the parables which follow conclude with feasting. Jesus' parables of the reign of God include meal settings (Matthew 22:1-14, Luke 14:16-24). Jesus' sayings pick up expectations of gentiles at the messianic banquet table (e.g., Matthew 8:11). In the last meal with his disciples before his execution, Jesus interprets the bread and cup in terms of his imminent death. But of equal importance, Jesus looks beyond his execution to the coming messianic age. "I tell you I shall not drink again of this fruit of the vine until that day when I drink it new with you in my Father's kingdom" (Matthew 26:29 and parallels).

It is clear, therefore, why the apostolic communities assembled on the "eighth day" (their name for their day of worship)[16] and why, when they assembled, it was for the "breaking of bread." In the resurrection of Jesus the eschaton had begun. They were at the messianic banquet table. Thus they were identified by the Messiah as the messianic community.

The Great Thanksgiving

Already the *SBH* has a prayer of thanksgiving (p. 11). But 40 years later many presiding ministers still act as if the eucharistic prayer (*LBW* rubric 31) is something distinct from what *LBW* rubric 28 calls "The Great Thanksgiving." The eucharistic prayer *is* the Great Thanksgiving. If the congregation uses only rubric 32, the liturgical "words of institution," it has *not* prayed the Great Thanksgiving. The anomaly here is that the people have been invited to give thanks; they have responded that it is right to do so; the preface then gives reasons why the people should give thanks, reasons so awesome that we join the hymn of the angels to welcome Jesus, the Messiah. *But up to this point we have not actually given thanks!*

LBW rubric 32 remains an alternative to giving thanks for reasons which require at least brief historical comments. There is no text for a Christian liturgy in the New Testament. The *Didache* from the early second century has some examples of prayers of thanksgiving. Justin Martyr, writing about 150 A.D., notes that the presiding minister does two things: preaches on the lessons and gives thanks. By 217 A.D. *The Apostolic Tradition* of Hippolytus contains the text of a simple eucharistic prayer, the basis for *LBW* Eucharistic Prayer IV. The practice of giving thanks to the Father, remembering the Son (including the composite narrative of institution), and invoking the Holy Spirit continues in the Eastern church to the present.

However, the medieval mass of the Western church, the text which Martin Luther learned to use, *no longer had a prayer of thanksgiving.* Instead it had a series of prayers, the Canon of the Mass, a fixed text which included the words of Jesus, "This is my body," and "This is my blood of the covenant." According to Ambrose, Bishop of Milan from 374-397 A.D., just these words effected the consecration of the bread and wine. Increasingly it was taught that only an ordained priest could say these words and thus have a "valid" sacrament. This teaching was formally promulgated in the papal bull *Decretum pro Armeniis* of 1439 and adopted by the Council of Trent in 1551. These "words of the Savior" used by the priest "speaking in the person of Christ" were declared to "confect this sacrament."

The medieval prayers clearly stated that the consecration was to be part of an act of offering God a propitiatory sacrifice for the saving benefit of the living and the dead. Luther objected strenuously to the whole idea that the mass was such a propitiatory sacrifice. In his reforms of the liturgy he removed all prayers of sacrifice so that only the composite liturgical words of institution remained. In 1526 he directed that the priest was to say these words facing the people from behind the altar. Most Lutheran churches followed Luther's proposal of omitting everything but the words of institution, although they did not say them to the people.

In the biblical and liturgical scholarship of the 20th century, scholars made clear that the command, "Do this," must be understood in terms of the Jewish context. "Do this," (1 Corinthians 11:24-25) cannot refer to eating and drinking, because there is no such command in this earliest liturgical tradition. It must refer instead to giving thanks, which Jesus does in taking up the bread and the cup. A Jewish/Christian prayer of thanksgiving is a way of *receiving* a blessing from God, not a way of trying to manipulate God through some sacrifice we offer (Luke 17:16; Colossians 3:16-17).

The Apology, Article X, quotes approvingly the tradition of the Greek church in which "the priest clearly *prays* that the bread may be changed and become the very body of Christ" (p. 179). A prayer of thanksgiving does not make the Eucharist our work instead of God's gift. In Article XXIV the Apology elaborates on the sacrifice of thanksgiving.[17]

When the Inter-Lutheran Commission on Worship (ILCW) proposed a number of eucharistic prayers, there was insistent objection. *LBW* rubric 32 was included as an option for those Lutherans who did not find the historical, confessional, and theological reasons for a eucharistic prayer persuasive. But the words of institution alone are neither the thanksgiving prayer of which the Apology speaks nor are they the giving of thanks with which the messianic salvation is received and celebrated. The danger of using the words of institution alone is that they come to be regarded as effecting the consecration, the very thing which the Formula of Concord, Article VII, rejects (p. 482).

The eucharistic prayers of the *LBW* follow the classic trinitarian structure: *Praise and thanksgiving addressed to the Father*, firmly anchored in the salvation experience of Israel, from whom comes *the history of the remembered Son,* Israel's Messiah, who inaugurated the messianic reign of God with his death and resurrection, and who gave his disciples the meal of his life-giving sacrifice as an anticipation of the messianic banquet, concluding with *invocation of the Holy Spirit,* who is the guarantee that the reign of God will finally be victorious.

The prayer of thanksgiving should not be hurried, for here something of the utmost importance is taking place. Our Lord is pleased to use *our* words and *our* eating and drinking as the means through which he gives us forgiveness for our past, hope for the final future of the reign of God, and courage for our mission in the present.

Participation in the Holy Communion

From the beginning, only the baptized were allowed to participate in the Holy Communion.[18] At the time of the German Reformation, the evangelical churches retained the custom of confession prior to sharing in the Holy Communion.[19] Children were normally admitted to participation in the Holy Communion at age five or six. Later Lutheran practice made participation in the Holy Communion dependent on confirmation, which was administered at ages 13 to 15. After extensive studies on confirmation and first communion reported to the churches in 1969, most Lutheran congregations in North America began to admit children to participation in the Holy Communion prior to confirmation, at about age ten.

The Evangelical Lutheran Church in America recently adopted a new statement on the practice of Word and Sacrament entitled *The Use of the Means of Grace.* This statement continues to recognize the principle of the 1978 *A Statement on Communion Practices* (re-affirmed in 1989) that "admission to the Sacrament is by invitation of the Lord, presented through the Church to those who are baptized" (p. 24). The 1978 statement concluded, however, that the participation of baptized infants in the Holy Communion is precluded. The 1997 statement draws a different conclusion.

While recognizing that customs vary from one congregation to another, the 1997 statement takes into account the fact that some congregations share the Holy Communion with very young children and even with infants at their Baptism. On the basis of historical studies of the early church and following the example of the Evangelical Lutheran Church in Canada, the 1997 statement permits the participation of baptized children in the Holy Communion

> at a time determined through mutual conversation that includes
> the pastor, the child, and the parents or sponsors involved, within
> the accepted practices of the congregation" (p. 25).

Encountering God

The statement also permits infants and children to "be communed for the first time during the service in which they are baptized." (p. 25) All congregations are admonished to accompany participation in the Holy Communion with catechesis appropriate to the age of the child.

The Word of God

The emphasis on and the recovery of the weekly celebration of the Holy Communion must not ever be understood as taking place at the expense of the proclamation of the Word of God. Lutherans regard the proclamation of the Word of God as sacramental, for God is present in the proclamation of the Word, according to the Apology, Article XIII, par. 12 (p. 212).

The strongest statement on the Word of God in the Lutheran confessions is made in a polemical context directed against the emphasis placed on human traditions.

> Certainly the statement, "He who hears you hears me" (Luke 10:16), is not referring to traditions but is rather directed against traditions. . . . It is a testimony given to the apostles so that we may believe them on the basis of another's Word rather than on the basis of their own. For Christ wants to assure us, as was necessary, that the Word is efficacious when it is delivered by men and that we should not look for another word from heaven. "He who hears you hears me" cannot be applied to traditions. For Christ requires them to teach in such a way that he might be heard, because he says, "hears me." Therefore he wants his voice, his Word to be heard, not human traditions (Apology, Article XXVIII, pars. 18-19, p. 284).

When Christians proclaim the gospel of the forgiveness of sins, God is actually forgiving sinners. When Christians announce the gospel of the reign of God, the reign of God is actually present in the midst of the reign of sin and death. God's "hidden victory" over sin and death is actually on the scene. The proclamation of the Word of God is the vehicle for the Holy Spirit, the "down payment" on the messianic age (2 Corinthians 1:22; Ephesians 1:13-14). The gift of the Holy Spirit in the proclamation of the Word of God empowers Christians to live in the reality of the reign of God.

There is, therefore, a direct connection between the proclamation of the Word of God and the messianic meal which follows in the liturgy. Because Jesus is risen death no longer has power over him (Romans 6:9). He is present in the messianic community as the power of the future. Since death does not have the last word, there is more to do with our lives than to protect and preserve them at whatever cost to others. Our lives can be offered in service to the reign of God, in service to the gospel.

Therefore, the *LBW* has introduced two offertory prayers after the proclamation of the Word of God and as the table is about to be set for the messianic meal. In these prayers, we offer "our selves, our time, and our possessions." With the gifts of money we "offer ourselves to your service and dedicate our lives to the care and redemption of all that you have made" (pp. 67-68).

With the bread and wine Jesus the Messiah comes to us with his own self-offering, his body and blood offered on the cross. There he makes us his body for the world. St. Paul rehearses the liturgical tradition of the Lord's own words at the meal on the eve of his betrayal and death to make clear to the selfish and self-protective Corinthians that their selfishness means that they are eating and drinking of the bread and cup "in an unworthy manner," that they are not discerning the Lord's body, which was offered for the world (1 Corinthians 11:17-32).

The proclamation of the gospel, that the messianic reign of God has come, that Jesus is the Messiah (Mark 1:14-15; Luke 4:16-21), frees us to offer ourselves, to place ourselves on the table with the gifts of bread and wine. There the Messiah gifts us with the power of his offering, makes us his body for the world, and sends us in the power of the Holy Spirit. Thus the proclamation of the Word of God and the celebration of the messianic meal are inseparably linked in the liturgy, the Holy Communion.

HOLY BAPTISM

Holy Baptism is the church's sacrament of evangelism. Walter Brueggemann writes about the church's need to renew the rite for Holy Baptism so that it can once again be experienced as the church's sacrament of evangelism.

> We must recover the focal drama of Baptism, which is a subversive act of renunciation and embrace. The claims of the gospel of God's hidden, decisive victory are fully voiced in our language and in our Baptism. We are, however, mostly so kept and domesticated that we cringe from the very news given us. We find ways to skew our language and trivialize the sacrament so that there is nothing left for us except accommodation to cultural expectation.[20]

The first goal identified in the Introduction to the *LBW* was "to restore to Holy Baptism the liturgical rank and dignity implied by Lutheran theology." The contrast with previous books is evident. *TLH* had no order for Holy Baptism at all. The *SBH* had an "Order for the Baptism of Infants" in a section entitled "Occasional Services" following the prayer offices, psalms, canticles, collects, and prayers (pp. 242-244). Congregational participation is limited to responding to the prayers. The *LBW* rite for Holy Baptism follows immediately the settings of the Holy Communion (pp. 121-125). It becomes evident at once that responsibility for the administration of Holy Baptism belongs to the congregation which is constituted by its celebration of Holy Communion. Holy Baptism is to be administered in the midst of a congregational Eucharist on four days when the very character of the liturgy is baptismal: the Vigil of Easter, The Day of Pentecost, All Saints' Day, and The Baptism of Our Lord.

There is a single rite for the Baptism of both children and adults. It is once again evident, as it has always been when the church understands its missional character, that Holy Baptism is normally for adult converts, and that children or infants may also be baptized. The rite is structured as a *congregational* activity with a congregational sponsor for each candidate, congregational confession of the creed, and congregational representatives leading the congregation in welcoming the newly baptized members. Because the *congregation* has the responsibility to make sure that the sacraments are administered, the presiding minister and actual administrator of Holy Baptism is the ordained pastor of the congregation.

Because "Christians are made, not born" (Tertullian), Holy Baptism is at the very center of the church's mandate to "*make* disciples of all nations." Because all candidates are presented by sponsors, sponsors are key persons in the church's ministry of evangelism. The rubrics for Baptism (*LBW* Ministers Edition, pp. 30-31) suggest that "when infants are baptized, the presentation and the responses may be said by one of the parents instead" because "parents will, as a matter of course, assume responsibility for the spiritual nurture of their children baptized in infancy." In the case of older candidates, sponsors accompany them "through the instruction period, through the rite of Baptism, and into the life of the congregation. Their presentation of the candidates implies endorsement and the pledge of support by prayer and example."

The rubrical admonition that "sponsors *should* be practicing Christians" suggests that we may have lost much of the connection between Baptism and evangelism, that sponsorship is no longer regarded as a responsibility and mission of members of the congregation, and finally that Baptism itself is no longer understand as the congregationally administered "sacrament of initiation into the community of faith." So we are in real danger that this "subversive act of renunciation and embrace," as Brueggemann calls it, is being trivialized.

Aidan Kavanagh writes that Holy Baptism originally included what eventually came to be called "confirmation," that is, invocation of the Holy Spirit with the laying-on-of-hands.[21] The *LBW* rite has once again made a significant effort to reunite these two separated parts of Holy Baptism. After the washing with water in the triune name, the rubric prescribes: "The minister lays both hands on the head of each of the baptized and prays for the Holy Spirit." Then "the minister marks the sign of the cross on the forehead of each of the baptized. Oil prepared for this purpose may be used" (p. 124). What was once termed confirmation has been renamed *Affirmation of Baptism* in the *LBW* (pp. 198-201).

We can summarize what takes place in Holy Baptism under three headings.

1. We are embraced by the God of the gospel. A christening does indeed take place. But that does not mean giving the candidate her/his name. When we are baptized into the name of the Father, and of the Son, and of the Holy Spirit, we are being given the name of God which is grounded in the very gospel itself: Jesus is the Messiah, the Christ! We are identified with the Christ; we belong to the Christ. Whatever happens to the Christ happens to us. We are put to death with Christ. We are raised with Christ to newness of life (Romans 6:1-11). That is what it means to be embraced by the God of the gospel.

Because Jesus is raised from the dead, we know that his cross has happened to God. Jesus, the Son, and his Father have suffered ultimate alienation, taken it into the very being and history of God. So there is now no ultimate alienation, no God-forsakenness, no place which the Son, his Father, and their Holy Spirit have not encompassed in their being and history. Therefore the reign of God has begun; the messianic age is underway. God the Holy Spirit, the "down payment on God's future," is now opening up the possibilities of life and hope for everyone, everything.

2. We are initiated into the community of the messianic age, the church. That is why the *congregation* baptizes and its pastor *presides*. Hence, no matter how many other sponsors there are, the parent or sponsor who presents the candidate is a member of the baptizing congregation. Having a sponsor means that the candidate is an "apprentice," learning what it means to believe and live in the gospel from one who is already a Christian.

Encountering God

It is the ministry of the sponsor to initiate the candidate for Holy Baptism into the congregation's liturgy of Holy Communion, to share with the candidate the church's teaching of the gospel, and to be a model or guide in the Christian life of the candidate.

There is a renunciation which the congregation witnesses because the congregation is the communal renunciation of "all the forces of evil, the devil, and all his empty promises." In the midst of the rite the congregation prays and confesses the faith. Representatives of the congregation present symbols of Baptism. And finally the whole congregation welcomes the new members of the community.

3. In Baptism we are set into the struggle between the messianic age and the "old age." Between Christ's resurrection and the final consummation of the reign of God the baptized are called to live in the conflict between the messianic age, the era of God's peace and justice and compassion, and the "old age," the era in which the powers of sin and death still reign. The language of dying and rising with Christ (Romans 6:1-23), of being "born anew" (John 3:1-21), reflects both the transition and the conflict. Hence Colossians, which initially speaks of one being "transferred" from the rule of darkness to the rule of the Son (Colossians 1:14), describes the struggle in powerful terms (Colossians 3:1-17).

CONFESSION / ABSOLUTION

When we sin, we have given up the struggle. Forgiveness means that we are restored to the struggle. That is why Holy Baptism continues to be experienced throughout the lifetime of the Christian in sacramental absolution and confession. In the Large Catechism, Martin Luther writes:

> Here you see that Baptism, both by its power and by its signification, comprehends also the third sacrament, formerly called Penance, which is really nothing else than Baptism (p. 445).

Because we are simultaneously saint and sinner, the struggle against sin will continue until our final "baptism," our death and burial to await God's final victory.

Therefore the *LBW* includes baptismal rituals for absolution and confession. Although we are absolved on the basis of our confession, it is actually the absolution, the forgiveness, which frees us to make confession.

> Sin is something for which we need divine forgiveness. This can mean nothing to the philosopher of morality but everything

to the believer. It is an insight reserved for the believer because the believer alone knows what forgiveness is and, therefore, the believer alone knows what sin is.[22]

Confession is never the condition for the granting of absolution. Rather, *because we are forgiven*, we are free to confess, to struggle with sin, to make amends where appropriate, to want admonition, to seek appropriate witness to the coming kingdom. When the church accepts the call and commission to administer Baptism it accepts the freedom and responsibility to surround those whom it baptizes as a community of redemptive love. "God forgives everything and condones nothing."[23]

When an individual trusts God's grace in Baptism in the context of the redemptive community s/he is free to want admonition, free to live a life of repentant confession and servant witness. It cannot be stressed too much that it is forgiveness which frees for confession. Because we are forgiven in the context of the Messianic age, we are free to give up our defenses and our despair. The truth of God's forgiveness frees us to give up the lies of self-justification or despair behind which we live.

Herbert Girgensohn has identified six forms of confession in the life of the church.

1. *Secret confession* of the heart, that is, confession which occurs in the privacy of one's thoughts, in which sins are acknowledged before God because God's forgiveness is believed.
2. *General confession*, such as that which occurs before the liturgy or before the meal within the liturgy.
3. *Reconciliatory confession* of hostile parties. "The wrong that stands between persons must be removed and the relationship restored by acknowledging the fault and being forgiven."
4. *Public confession* of public guilt, betrayal of witness to the coming kingdom.
5. *Corporate confession* of corporate guilt, e.g., *communal* racism or sexism.
6. *Individual confession* before one who speaks for God and the community.[24]

There are three rites for confession and absolution in the *LBW*. The general confession (*LBW*, p. 56) is not always necessary both because other confessional opportunities are to be encouraged and because the Eucharist serves identity and mission (being the body of Christ for the world). The general confession should be used especially during the seasons of Advent and Lent, probably not during the seasons of Easter and Christmas/Epiphany, with pastoral discretion determining the use during the Pentecost season.

The form for individual confession (*LBW*, p. 196) grows out of Luther's Small Catechism. It is not a substitute for counseling, and vice versa. Individual confession requires pastoral instruction. Thomas Oden has suggested that the pastoral call is the Protestant equivalent of the Catholic confessional.[25]

The rite for corporate confession (*LBW*, p. 193) has three uses, and the rite needs to be adapted to these uses. The first is reconciliation of parties in conflict. Both the forgiveness and the confession will be particular to the individuals involved. The second is individual forgiveness with laying on of hands. This is the use of the rite which requires the least adaptation. There is a sermon or address on the freedom of the gospel for confession. After a general confession, individuals are invited to receive individual absolution. The third is corporate confession of corporate sin. This requires the greatest pastoral sensitivity. The congregation is invited to hear from groups or individuals who are being oppressed and/or afflicted, who are being sinned against. But the congregation cannot be coerced into confession. It must be free for its own way and time to take ownership, to take responsibility, to make its confession. This is the most difficult form of corporate confession to administer.

So, as long as the powers of death and sin are still on the scene, there is no respite from the struggle against sin for the baptized. The powers of death and sin do not hand out privileges to those who have been adopted by the enemy. But there is a hidden advantage (Colossians 3:3): We are caught up in the great battle on the side of the final victor. For Christ is the first of the "all" who shall "be made alive" (1 Corinthians 15:20-28). We are engaged in the adventure of discipleship. There is nothing to compare with that.

NOTES

1   J. D. N. Kelly, *Early Christian Doctrines* (New York: Harper and Brothers, 1960), pp. 193-199. Kelly begins his discussion of early views of the sacraments with the summary statement: "The Church's sacraments are those external rites, more precisely signs, which Christians believe convey, by Christ's appointment, an unseen sanctifying grace."

2   *The Book of Concord*, edited by Theodore G. Tappert (Philadelphia: Muhlenberg Press, 1959), p. 31. Further references to the documents in the *Book of Concord* will simply be indicated by the page number in parentheses.

3   Carl Braaten, *Principles of Lutheran Theology* (Philadelphia: Fortress Press, 1983), p. 88.

4 Harold Bloom, *The American Religion* (New York: Simon and Schuster, 1992); and Philip J. Lee, *Against the Protestant Gnostics* (New York: Oxford University Press, 1987).

5 Frank Senn, "What Has Become of the Liturgical Movement?" *Pro Ecclesia*, Vol. VI, No. 3 (Summer 1997), p. 321.

6 See the Augsburg Confession, Article XXIV (pp. 56-61) and the Apology, Article XXIV (pp. 249-252).

7 Guenther Bornkamm, in *The New Testament: A Guide to Its Writings* (Philadelphia: Fortress Press, 1973), pp. 23-24, writes: "The Gospels and the Jesus tradition they enshrine are rooted in the certainty of the resurrection of Christ. . . . It may sound like nonsense, but we venture to say that the gospel story begins with its end. For Jesus' Jewish opponents and for the Roman occupying power, there could be no doubt that his end on the cross was the annulment of his story. For the disciples, on the other hand, the appearances of the risen one and their experience of his presence in the Spirit meant that his end was a new beginning, in the sense of a final and absolute act of God for the salvation of the world. Men had condemned Jesus, but God turned their no into a yes. In that yes God committed himself to the world that rejected him." Cf. Robert Smith, *Easter Gospels* (Minneapolis: Augsburg Publishing House, 1983), who writes on p. 199: "The Gospels are Easter books not only because they end as they do. They are Easter books from beginning to end, penned by people who in various ways — not in the same way — knew Jesus as raised from the dead, forever alive, and mighty." Cf. also James D. G. Dunn, *The Evidence for Jesus* (Philadelphia: Westminster Press, 1985), Chapter 3 and the bibliography on p. 109, and Gerald O'Collins, *Jesus is Risen* (New York: Paulist Press, 1987).

8 Gerhard Lohfink, *Jesus and Community* (Philadelphia: Fortress Press, 1982), pp. 7-20.

9 Robert Jenson, *Story and Promise* (Philadelphia: Fortress Press, 1973), pp. 48-61; Eric W. Gritsch and Robert W. Jenson, *Lutheranism: The Theological Movement and Its Confessional Writings* (Philadelphia: Fortress Press, 1976), pp. 36-44.

10 Joachim Jeremias, *The Eucharistic Words of Jesus* (Philadelphia: Fortress Press, 1966), p. 120.

11 Quoted from Bard Thompson, *Liturgies of the Western Church* (Cleveland: The World Publishing Company, 1961), p. 9.

12 Geoffrey Wainwright, *Eucharist and Eschatology* (London: Epworth Press, 1971), p. 21.

13 *Ibid.*, p. 22.

14 *Ibid.*, p. 23.

15 *Ibid.*, p. 24.

16 Willy Rordorf, *Sunday: The History of the Day of Rest and Worship in the Earliest Centuries of the Christian Church* (Philadelphia: Westminster Press, 1968), p. 277 *et passim*; cf. Samuele Bacchiocchi, *From Sabbath to Sunday: A Historical Investigation of the Rise of Sunday Observance in Early Christianity* (Rome: The Pontifical Gregorian University Press, 1977), pp. 278-302.

17 We are perfectly willing for the Mass to be understood as a daily sacrifice, provided this means the whole Mass, the ceremony and also the proclamation of the gospel, faith,

prayer and thanksgiving. Taken together, these are the daily sacrifice of the New Testament; the ceremony was instituted because of them and *ought not* be separated from them (pp. 256). The principle use of the sacrament is to make clear that terrified consciences are the ones worthy of it, and how they ought to use it. There is also a sacrifice, since one action can have several purposes. Once faith has strengthened a conscience to see its liberation from terror, then it really gives thanks for the blessing of Christ's suffering. It uses the ceremony itself as praise to God, as a demonstration of its gratitude, and a witness of its high esteem for God's gifts. Thus the ceremony becomes a sacrifice of praise (pp. 262-63). Piety looks at what is given and at what is forgiven; it compares the greatness of God's blessings with the greatness of our ills, our sin and our death; and it *gives thanks.* From this the term "Eucharist" arose in the church (p. 263).

18 Kelly, *op. cit.*, p. 193.

19 See Augsburg Confession, Article XXIV, par. 6 (p. 56); Article XXV, par. 1 (p. 61); Apology, Article XXIV, par. 1 (p. 249); Large Catechism, Part Five, par. 2 (p. 447); and Large Catechism, Brief Exhortation to Confession, par. 29 (p. 460).

20 Walter Bruggemann, *Biblical Perspectives on Evangelism* (Nashville: Abingdon Press, 1993), page 45.

21 Aidan Kavanagh, *The Shape of Baptism* (New York: Pueblo Publishing Company, 1978), pp. 46-50. Kavanagh quotes a magnificent fifth century inscription found in the baptistery of St. John Lateran in Rome:

> Here is born in Spirit-soaked fertility
> a brood destined for another City,
> begotten by God's blowing
> and borne upon this torrent
> by the Church their virgin mother.
> Reborn in these depths they reach for heaven's realm,
> the born-but-once unknown by felicity.
> This spring is life that floods the world,
> the wounds of Christ its awesome source.
> Sinner sink beneath this sacred surf
> that swallows age and spits up youth.
> Sinner here scour sin away down to innocence,
> for they know no enmity who are by
> one font, one Spirit, on faith made one.
> Sinner shudder not at sin's kind and number,
> for those born here are holy.

22 Werner Elert, *The Christian Ethos* (Philadelphia: Muhlenberg Press, 1957), p. 154.

23 C.S. Lewis, *The Problem of Pain* (New York: Macmillan, 1973), p. 46.

24 Herbert Girgensohn *Teaching Luther's Catechism*, Vol. II (Philadelphia: Muhlenberg Press, 1959), pp. 63-64.

25 Thomas Oden, *Pastoral Theology* (San Francisco: Harper and Row, 1983), pp. 169-185.

HOW AWESOME IS THIS PLACE!

The *Lutheran Book of Worship* and the Encounter with God

Gordon W. Lathrop

HOLY BETHEL

According to the Genesis narrative (Genesis 28:11-22), when Jacob put his head upon the stones at Bethel, he dreamed that the place where he lay was filled with God and the signs of God. A stairway or ramp—a Mesopotamian *ziggurat*, most likely—extended between earth and heaven. On it the angels of God were ascending and descending, making Bethel the very center of a kind of commerce with the divine. Jacob could see this commerce, this series of exchanges that, according to many religions, takes place invisibly at temples and holy shrines. But the imagery of the narrative was also unlike the expectations of many shrines. God, whom we would expect to find at the top of the ramp, housed in the hut which was closest to heaven and receiving the intermediary angels was, instead, standing "beside" Jacob (28:13), promising presence and blessing without intermediary. The angels had become indicators of the importance and holiness of the place, not commerce-bearers. When Jacob awoke, he proclaimed, "How awesome is this place! This is none other than the house of God, and this is the gate of heaven." Such awe belongs conventionally to holy places. Here, however, the awe is heightened because of the surprising character of this God: "Surely the LORD"—not just any deity—"is in this place—and I did not know it!" (28:16).

Of course, the story was one foundational cult-narrative of a particular Israelite shrine, the "house" or temple at Bethel. This cult-center, which may have had a Canaanite pre-history, played an important role in many Old Testament stories, being associated with Abraham (Genesis 12:8), Jacob, Deborah (Judges 4:5), Samuel (1 Samuel 7:16), and finally the northern kingdom of Jereboam (1 Kings 12:29-33). Then, it was to Bethel that Amos came (cf. Amos 7:13) to proclaim again a surprising view of God and of worship: "Even though you offer me your burnt offerings and grain offerings, I will not accept them. . . . Take away from me the noise of your songs. . . . But let justice roll down like waters" (Amos 5:22-24).

It is fascinating to set the surprising proclamation of Amos next to the surprise already present in the narrative of Jacob's dream: God is not captured in our cult, not manipulated by our cult-conceptions, not resident at the top of our ladder of sacred exchange. Rather God is far more awesome than we thought, present in promise to the littlest and most wretched ones, and transforming our holy places to be places of the encounter with God's presence, promise, and justice, in ways we had not expected.

But the surprise is not over. This very story of Bethel, the "house of God" and its unexpected critical turns, hovers behind a passage found in John's Gospel. In the narrative of the gathering of the first disciples, Nathanael has already confessed that Jesus is "Rabbi" and "Son of God" and "King of Israel." Jesus responds to this series of holy titles with an even more astonishing assertion. "You will see greater things than these," he says. "You will see heaven opened and the angels of God ascending and descending upon the Son-of-Man" (John 1:49-51). For the Fourth Gospel, Jesus is himself Bethel. In him is the gate of heaven, the awesome place, the holy exchanges, the very presence of God beside the poor and wretched. He is the one at the bottom of the ladder, overwhelming yet accessible to needy humanity. What humanity has longed for in shrines and temples is found in an utterly new way in him.

This very idea of Jesus as the holy place recurs in the Gospel of John, with ever new surprise: Jesus' body, crucified and risen, is the new temple (John 2:19-22). The Father is to be worshipped, not on the Samaritan Mt. Gerizim nor the Jerusalem temple-mount, but wherever the Spirit is poured out in the presence of the truth of the Son (4:19-26; cf. 14:6). The water which is to flow from the temple to water the wilderness is the Spirit and water from his heart (7:37-39). And all of this is said of the crucified-risen one, for he is that "house" or "dwelling place" (12:32; 14:3), the source of water and the Spirit (19:28-37; 20:22). Wherever the community gathers in his presence, it will have its conception of God and of holy places radically transformed, in a way that accords with the great biblical tradition of Bethel. The community will encounter the holy Trinity, will be drawn into its very life, and will discover how this one God is "for us," standing with the wretched and needy, and drawing us all out of death into ways of justice and life.

Christian liturgy, at its best, has continued this tradition of Bethel. The liturgy has held Leviticus and Amos together, the enacting of sacred signs of God together with the prophetic denunciation of worship without justice, worship without awe. The liturgy has been a place where ordinary expectations of God have been invited into the surprise and transformation of grace, where our god-projections have been met by the judgment, the grace, and the life of the Holy Trinity, where our attempts at exchange with the deity have been invited instead to become occasions to give ourselves to our neighbor. The liturgy has depended on the sense that the holy place occurs wherever the community gathers around the crucified and risen Christ, present in Word and Sacrament. The liturgy has seen the reading and preaching of the Scriptures and the celebration of the Eucharist as Bethel-stones, as awesome places of the presence of the triune God who gathers all fearful Jacobs into promise and life. The liturgy has understood the angels as hovering about these "places" of Word and Sacrament, not as intermediaries but as markers of the centrality and holiness of the place: we indicate this presence by our song together with the angels in the *Gloria in excelsis* of the Word-service and in the *Sanctus* at the table. The liturgy has welcomed participants into this Bethel-assembly by immersing them in the water and Spirit which come from the crucified, by bringing them to the new birth of Baptism. And because of the unexpected grace of the God of this Bethel—the way this God is present in the world, at the bottom of the ladder—the liturgy has turned its participants toward God's beloved, wretched world: in intercession, in sending food and money to those in need, in sending the community itself to be body-of-Christ for the world.

We may rightly ask ourselves if the liturgy we are celebrating in our Sunday assemblies is such a Bethel, such a "house of God." The question will not only be an inquiry about how much awe is experienced in the meetings of our congregations, though that will not be a bad start. It will also be whether or not our conceptions of God are undergoing a transformation by the encounter with the surprising grace and truth of the Trinity. When our worship services have instead become conventional ways of "going to church," with *our* anthems and sermons and offerings and stained-

Encountering God

glass windows and membership procedures as the accented center of the event, they may run the risk of being more like Mesopotamian *ziggurats* than like Jacob's surprising Bethel. The same may be true if our services are romantic pageants of the ways we imagine the Middle Ages to have been or, more likely in our day, consumer gatherings for entertainment and for the sales of North American religion, dealt with as if it were a commodity.

But if the Word and Sacraments of Christ are received with hope and humility as the heart of our assemblies, if they are there as if they were indeed Bethel-stones, full of the presence of the triune God, and if these things and the community around them are constantly calling our god-conceptions into conversion to faith in the biblical, triune God, then we will know the surprise of Bethel. And how awesome is this place!

THE *LUTHERAN BOOK OF WORSHIP* AND THE ENCOUNTER WITH GOD

At the 20th anniversary of the *Lutheran Book of Worship* (*LBW*) it is very useful to remember with gratitude the ways in which that book—and the liturgical movement it summarized and represented—has helped to enable such assemblies. Among the many gifts of the *LBW* which we should reconsider in this present time, the book's concern for the transforming, faith-creating encounter with God is one of the most important. Such a concern can be seen explicitly in the *LBW*'s interest in the centrality of Word and Sacrament, in its thoroughgoing use of trinitarian language, in its recovery of biblical imagery, in its fresh sense of thanksgiving or *eucharistia* at the center of the liturgy, and in its call for multiple leadership as the community gathers in the mercy of God.

Some of these gifts we have come to take for granted; others we have neglected. We will be assisted in recovering the Bethel-character of our assemblies if we look again at the explicit intention of these characteristics of the *LBW*, strengthening them in our actual practice. But we will also be inhabiting the movement of which the *LBW* is such an important witness, if we ask how the trajectory of these characteristics of the *LBW* may continue into the future of our parish liturgical life.

But, we might ask, what does the *LBW* have to do with the encounter with *God*? It is just a book, with a recent human history. We may even know some people who worked on it, and they are not God! In the first place, that should not surprise us. The biblical God makes use of books—Bible-books and hymnbooks and prayerbooks—along with bread and wine and water and real people and actual places and times to meet, as surely as God at Bethel made use of stones and the memory of *ziggurats*. Our encounter with God is in the midst of a quite material world, the world God created and loves.

But, in another sense, the *LBW* is not "just a book" at all. It is better regarded as the fragments and records of the ways many assemblies of Christians have done things, summed up as much as that is possible in print, and passed on as a gift to our present local congregation. The *LBW* is a concrete means of communication and communion between congregations through history. It represents a whole series of actions that cannot be put in print: people gathering, singing, praying, reading the Scriptures, preaching, baptizing, holding the supper, and, in these things, encountering God, coming to faith, going in mission. The gift from the other congregations to our present congregation needs to be put in motion in each place. It needs to be inhabited, experienced, enacted in a lively way with the book as resource. That liveliness will be the clearer—will be more like Bethel—if the central characteristics of the *LBW*-gift are borne in mind.

The first and most important of these characteristics is this: for us, in the Christian congregation, *Word and Sacrament* are our Bethel-stones. We have no other place to put our head. Or if we do, we will probably dream mostly of ourselves or of fear and death. The greatest gift of the *LBW* is the call to congregations to place Word and Sacraments in the very heart of our assemblies. So, the *LBW* envisions the Holy Communion being celebrated every Sunday, as the principal service of the congregation. It provides a strong lectionary, immersing congregations in "richer fare" from the table of God's Word than we might otherwise know. It proposes that Baptisms always take place in the presence of the assembly and especially at the great festivals of the church. It provides patterns of daily prayer intended to recall and support the Sunday assembly around Word and Sacrament through the course of the week. It does this, not because of some arbitrary decision, obedient to inscrutable medieval rubrics, but because of its interest in the encounter with God. Jesus Christ is Bethel for us, and he is known there where he gives himself away: in the word he opens our minds to understand beginning with Moses and all the prophets (Luke 24:27), in the bread he breaks (Luke 24:31), in the Baptism into his death which is the beginning of sharing his resurrection (Romans 6:4). There where we meet him, crucified and sharing our death, risen and pulling us all up to life, we do so in the power of the Spirit, and so we are drawn to be before God in the very life of the Trinity. Indeed, what Christians mean by "the Trinity" is that God who is known and encountered in all richness through Word and Sacraments held side by side in the midst of our needy lives.

Such is the lively and central gift which comes from the earliest Christian communities, from the congregations of the Reformation and from more recent times, and which is embodied in the *LBW*. Of course, there are ways of negating this gift. We can minimize the reading of the Scriptures in our assemblies, making them of little account, not paying attention, even reducing the number and length of the readings to one or two verses. We can refuse to take the readings seriously in our preaching or our planning of music. We can make Baptisms private again, or deal with them perfunctorily in the assembly. We can refuse to celebrate the supper every Sunday, in the very heart of our meetings. But, then, what will come to stand in the center instead will most likely be ourselves and our own religious projections and proposals. No Bethel. No surprise. No call to faith.

On the other hand, the movement toward the continual centrality of Word and Sacraments, the movement so strongly represented by the *LBW*, is not a static thing. The *LBW* itself is misused if it is understood as an unchangeable law-book instead of the record of a common and lively tradition. For example, the *Revised Common Lectionary* (RCL), so widely used in Canada and in the United States and approved by two of the Lutheran churches of North America, is thoroughly in keeping with the accent of the *LBW* on the centrality of Word and Sacrament. This lectionary is a rich collection of readings for the Sunday Eucharist, held in common with many other congregations as gift, enabling a wider communion, only slightly revising the lectionary recorded in print within the pages of the *LBW*. Similarly, the catechumenal process and rites, which have been developed in a renewed cooperation between leaders of the Evangelical Lutheran Church in Canada, the Lutheran Church–Missouri Synod and the Evangelical Lutheran Church in America (a current form of the same cooperation which produced the *LBW* itself!), adds more than is available in the actual print of the *LBW*, but accords profoundly with the *LBW* accent on the centrality of the means of grace. So does the use of the ancient *ordo* or shape of our liturgy (see *With One Voice*, pp. 8-9) as a way to interpret and organize all the resources which can be used in the assembly, including the *LBW* itself as well as other books which may supplement the *LBW*. Understand the *LBW* as pointing toward and serving the stones of Bethel, and these trajectories developing our use of Scripture and Baptism and liturgical shape fall into place.

To make clear the purpose of the centrality of Word and Sacraments, the *LBW* gave us the further gift of surrounding their celebration with a strengthened use of dynamic *trinitarian language*. The most obvious example is the wonderful greeting with which the Holy Communion begins: "The grace of our Lord Jesus Christ, the love of God, and the communion of the Holy Spirit be with you all." Drawn from the greeting with which Paul concluded his second letter to the congregation at Corinth (2 Corinthians 13:13), a salutation full of apostolic authority and conjoined with the greetings of all the other churches and the encouragement toward mutual love, this is a strong word with which to begin our meetings. It means to convey what it says. It means to communicate what the whole meeting is about, especially in its central actions of Scripture and meal. And it means to do so mutually: the assembly greets the presider in return, speaking the same word to her or to him. All the assembly is now to be enveloped in the grace, love and communion of the triune God. Because of the Word and Sacraments, this assembly is that participation in the Holy Spirit which, by the grace of Jesus Christ, draws us into the very love of God.

Then this dynamic proclamation of the God who is turned toward humanity, who is for us, is repeated elsewhere in the liturgy. Wherever the Matthean form of the trinitarian name ("In the name of the Father and of the Son and of the Holy Spirit"[Matthew 28:19]) occurs, especially in that return to Baptism with which the liturgy may begin, the *LBW* makes it clear that this is the name in which we were baptized, inviting us to sign our own bodies with the cross-sign that claimed us, and so calling us into the active meaning of the name: God for us through the crucified that we might come to faith and the community of faith. Then older traditional liturgical uses of trinitarian language, continued by the *LBW*, come into clearer focus: The *Gloria in excelsis* repeats the praise of this triune God at the beginning of the Word-service. So does the thrice-holy of the *Sanctus* at the table. In these two central moments, we are gathered by the Spirit into the encounter with Christ's death and resurrection and so into the truth about the triune God. The creed confesses the triune faith as does the eucharistic prayer. And the blessing establishes at the end what the apostolic greeting intended at the beginning: the whole event has been the face of the triune God turned with shining grace toward all things.

Again, recent experience has shown that, contrary to the spirit and the concrete proposals of the *LBW*, we can refuse this gift. We can eliminate the trinitarian greeting or simply minimize it, not understanding its key interpretive importance to the whole liturgical event. We can seldom use the creed, the *Gloria in excelsis*, the *Sanctus*. "Trinity" can remain a sterile intellectual mystery, beyond us, not encountering us. And our conceptions of "God" can remain unchallenged.

Encountering God

But the *LBW* intends Bethel, as the dynamic address of the apostolic greeting makes clear. It is as if all the members of the assembly are invited to turn to each other in love and mutual honor, saying, "This acting, present triune God be with you all." Here, again, the *LBW* is best understood as the record of a movement, a trajectory toward a richer understanding of the Sunday event as a trinitarian event. Congregations will be inhabiting that trajectory as they, for example, strengthen their trinitarian catechesis and welcome fresh trinitarian hymnody, as they see their Baptisms as entry into the life of a community of the triune name. The *LBW*'s dynamic use of trinitarian language is a good place for that catechesis to begin and a good grounds for the evaluation of that hymnody. In the process of baptismal renewal, all the churches which make use of the *LBW* could do well to pay attention to the counsel of the 1997 Statement on the Practice of Word and Sacrament, adopted by the Evangelical Lutheran Church in America (*The Use of the Means of Grace*, p. 24b):

> It is in the crucified Jesus that we meet the God to whom he entrusted all, who raised him from the dead for us, and who poured out the Spirit from his death and resurrection. Washing with water in this name is much more than the use of a "formula." The name is a summary of the power and presence of the triune God and of that teaching which must accompany every Baptism. Without this teaching and without the encounter with the grace, love and communion of the triune God, the words may be misunderstood as a magic formula or as a misrepresentation of the one God in three persons, equal in glory, coeternal in majesty. What "Father" and "Son" mean, in biblical and creedal perspective, must also be continually reexamined. The doctrine of God teaches us the surprising theology of the cross and counters any alleged trinitarian sanction for sinful inequality or oppression of women in church and society.

Such a recovery of teaching and of the encounter with the dynamic Trinity belongs to the trajectory of the *LBW*. So does a vigorous ongoing discussion of the ways orthodoxy must always be about responsible change: to say a thing the same way in a new situation is inevitably to misspeak. To speak of the Trinity faithfully in prayer will call for such responsible and communally discussed change, perhaps along the lines indicated in the eucharistic prayers of *With One Voice* (*WOV*) and in the lectionary *Readings for the Assembly.* The question itself—how do we speak the biblical triune God as the God who encounters us?—belongs to the movement of the *LBW*.

Similar things can be said about other gifts of the *LBW* which assist a liturgical assembly in the surprising, faith-creating encounter with God. At the time of the book's publication, one of the new characteristics of the *LBW* which was most frequently and gratefully noted was its widespread use of *biblical imagery* in texts of prayer and proclamation, rather than language of conceptual and dogmatic formulation. One has only to compare the baptismal rites of earlier agendas and manuals to the rite in the *LBW* in order to feel the strength of this change. That we have so widely come to see Baptism as our participation in Noah's survival and Israel's exodus is partly due to this shift in the language of our principal book of worship. The shift, however, had everything to do with the encounter with God. It is biblical imagery, its concrete earthiness and its gracious surprises, which are among the most appropriate media for the transformation of our current cultural and personal conceptions of God into faith and trust in the God who acts to give life to the dead and call into existence the things that do not exist (Romans 4:17).

But this biblical imagery is especially exercised in prayers of thanksgiving, in the *eucharistia* which is so important to both the letter and the spirit of the *LBW*. These prayers—the eucharistic prayers at the table, but also the "flood prayer" which gives thanks at the baptismal font, the thanksgiving for light at Vespers, and the Easter proclamation (the *exultet*) of the Vigil of Easter—are especially filled with a recitation of biblical images for the acts of God and biblically formed expressions of the hope for God. Indeed, the very act of thanksgiving itself is a kind of biblical image, a recovery of the biblical stance before God which is made possible for us as the grace spreads also to us (2 Corinthians 4:15). And this recovered *eucharistia* has to do with the encounter with God. It is addressed to God, through Jesus Christ, in the power and communion of the Holy Spirit. *Eucharistia* is participation in verbally expressed trinitarian faith. And such communally expressed proclamation has the possibility of calling our conceptions of God to conversion.

A similar possibility may accompany the signal *LBW* characteristic of *multiple leadership.* It may very well be that a liturgy led by one lone authority, exercising ministry in a hierarchically arranged building, had some difficulty in challenging a conception of God as the one who stood at the top of the angelic ladder. The leadership envisioned by the *LBW*—a strongly participating assembly, many assisting ministers, a choir supporting the voice of the congregation and its action, a serving presider—may not automatically counter such an idea of God, but it creates a space in which the surprising God of Bethel may be encountered. At the foot of the *ziggurat,* among fearful and dying humanity, God's own triune and life-giving being is itself communal!

TRAJECTORIES OF FUTURE REFORM

According to the Genesis narrative, Jacob came back to Bethel, to encounter and worship the God of promise there (Genesis 35:1-7). So do we, again and again, every Sunday. We see that many of the characteristics of the *LBW,* received again as gifts and practiced with an intentional appropriation of their importance, can assist us to find that our assemblies for worship are like Bethel. Such characteristics include the accent on the centrality of Word and Sacrament, the use of dynamic trinitarian language, the recovery of biblical imagery, the importance of *eucharistia,* and the presence of many serving leaders.

Of course, as we have seen, these gifts can be ignored, even by congregations which think that they are "using the green book." The absence of catechesis—in preaching, in baptismal preparation or in adult education—can make the use of biblical imagery in the liturgy seem like a bizarre foreign language. Presiders can still think they are "consecrating the ele ments," without the slightest sense of the biblical and communal depths of beautiful and proclamatory *eucharistia.* The thanksgivings for light at Evening Prayer or at the Easter Vigil can be never used if those liturgies are never used. And, most commonly, a single presider can exercise all the leadership roles, blithely ignoring the immensely important Ⓐ and Ⓟ of the book. The saddest thing about all of this is not its ignorance of the *LBW.* It is, rather, the kind of God such poorly-planned liturgies suggest.

But then, the most remarkable trajectory forward, in many places, would be for these gifts of the *LBW* to be received and inhabited, profoundly, lovingly. Not because it is required. It is not. In North American Lutheran circles, no one requires anything of us. And even if it were, one can do the "required" in a perfunctory way. Or one can do the "required" as if one were mounting up on "Jacob's ladder," alongside the angels. No. It is better to say that the real intention of the gifts of the *LBW* is the surprising encounter with the God of Bethel, at the foot of the ladder, in the gospel of the crucified and the life of the Trinity.

Still, "inhabiting the movement" of which the *LBW* is a witness will also involve a sense that, especially in these centrally important matters, the trajectory continues into the future, beyond the letter of the book itself.

That does not mean that "anything goes." The same mutual consultation, the same communion with many congregations of the Christian past, the same fidelity to trinitarian faith as marked the *LBW* itself will need to mark such trajectories. By those criteria, we can say that these things rightly belong to the *LBW*: the importance of the *ordo* of Christian worship; the use of the *Revised Common Lectionary*; the recovery of baptismal catechesis and the rites which may mark baptismal process; a richer use of trinitarian language; a stronger use of biblical imagery in hymnody and prayers; a growing collection of prayers of thanksgiving at the table and the font; and a deeper understanding of servant leadership.

But perhaps the most important trajectory forward for all of our congregations is this one: *mission*. That is where the encounter with God leads. When Amos came to Bethel, he inveighed against worship that omits doing justice. When Jesus Christ discloses the surprise of Bethel, we discover that God is already present in promise to the poor, the godless, the sinful, the wretched, the dying. Granted what we have seen and heard and tasted, the *LBW* liturgy rightly sends us away: "Go in peace. Serve the Lord." That dismissal was also a old inheritance from the historic congregations of Christians, but a new gift to North American Lutherans who began to use the *LBW*. It is a gift still in need of development. A trajectory forward here will also do well to listen to the ELCA's *Use of the Means of Grace* (51a,b):

> Baptism and baptismal catechesis join the baptized to the mission of Christ. Confession and absolution continually reconcile the baptized to the mission of Christ. Assembly itself, when that assembly is an open invitation to all peoples to gather around the truth and presence of Jesus Christ, is a witness to the world. The regular proclamation of both Law and Gospel, in Scripture reading and preaching, tells the truth about life and death in all the world, calls us to faith in the life-giving God, and equips the believers for witness and service. Intercessory prayer makes mention of the needs of all the world and of all the church in mission. When a collection is received, it is intended for the support of mission and for the concrete needs of our neighbors who are sick, hurt, and hungry. The holy supper both feeds us with the body and blood of the Christ and awakens our care for the hungry ones of the earth. The dismissal from the service sends us in thanksgiving from what we have seen in God's holy gifts to service in God's

Encountering God

beloved world. In the teaching and practice of congregations, the missional intention for the means of grace needs to be recalled. By God's gift, the Word and the Sacraments are set in the midst of the world, for the life of the world.

Such reflections also belong to the trajectories of the *LBW*. Congregations engaged in such mission are also inhabiting the movement to which the *LBW* is witness.

Of course, "Bethel" is only one biblical narrative symbol for the encounter with God. There could be many, many others. But "Bethel" is a good one, one used by many North American Lutheran congregations when they sought to find a name for their assemblies to put upon their doors. But the contention here has been that all of our assemblies are invited to be that house of God. Understood in this way, the *LBW* invites us to lay our lives down upon the stones of Word and Sacrament. We will find our conceptions of God challenged, our world transformed: "Surely the LORD is in this place—and I did not know it!"

THE BLOOD IN OUR VEINS

Lutheranism's Liturgical Lineage

Philip H. Pfatteicher

The history of liturgy is of more than antiquarian interest. Sometimes, in our modern preoccupation with the present moment, with "what's happening now," we think that what was done before is irrelevant. Henry Ford spoke for many when in 1919 he said bluntly, "History is bunk." If history and tradition are stones that pull us under the tide of events, if they are chains that keep us from moving ahead, then we are well rid of them. But it need not be so. Properly understood, history is the foundation on which all present construction builds. Without a clear sense of history, we build on sand.

We need to know where we came from in order to know where we are going, for the past is never finished and over. It flows within us, like the blood in our veins, whether we are aware of it or not. Every living creature carries within itself the influence of its own ancestors who have made it what it is. So it is also with the liturgy.

ANCIENT ORIGINS

To understand worship as we have it today, it is helpful to begin in the New Testament with two familiar stories. First, consider Luke 2:22-40, the Gospel for The Presentation of Our Lord in the temple (February 2). In the Orthodox churches this feast is called "the Meeting," that is, the meeting of God with humanity. The meeting takes place in the temple, and it tells a good deal about the way God and people encounter one another. The focus of the action, although he is only an infant 40 days old, is Christ, in whom

God came among us. In him the two natures meet: he is God and he is at the same time human, God and man together in one person. Moreover Christ is the effective sign of God's fatherly love; he is God come to us. Jesus is a man who lives as he was intended, as we are intended to live. Further, as many modern theologians like to say, Jesus is *the Sacrament*; St. Augustine said, "There is no other sacrament except Christ." Christ is, in the description of a sacrament given in the *Book of Common Prayer*, "an outward and visible sign" that paradoxically veils and reveals God's splendid glory, bringing into effect a divine reality. In Jesus Christ is found, as St. Paul says (Colossians 2:9), the fullness of the gospel, for he *is* the Good News of grace and reconciliation.

This wonderful passage near the beginning of Luke's Gospel also shows that Christianity is primarily a gift. It is not something that we discover on our own; it is not our decision. It is a gift given to us in our blindness and ignorance and unworthiness.

Liturgy, the ordered worship of God by the church of Jesus Christ, is the supreme experience of that reality. It dramatizes the sources of Christianity's vitality. Liturgical acts re-present the original experience in order to stoke the fires of memory, and "to remember" in the biblical understanding is to bridge the gap of time, to call into the present those events that we might think are finished and done with. To "remember" in the biblical and in the liturgical sense is to make the past and the present and the future contemporary with one another.

The story of the Meeting sets the tone for Christian worship. A second and even more mysterious Gospel sets the basic order of Christian worship. It is the report of the encounter of the risen Lord with two disciples near Emmaus on Easter evening. Jesus, as yet unrecognized, walks with them and to clarify their confusion and bewilderment about "the things that have taken place in Jerusalem in these days . . . beginning with Moses and all the prophets . . . interpreted to them the things about himself in all the scriptures" (that is, in the Old Testament, the Hebrew Bible). Then, as a further dimension of this interpreting, he himself at table with them "took bread, blessed and broke it, and gave it to them." And only then "their eyes were opened and they recognized him; and he vanished from their sight." The actions of taking, blessing, breaking, and giving the bread call to mind the celebration of the Lord's Supper as the church has done it ever since. Moreover, we can discern here the two-fold pattern that has characterized Christian worship since that time: first interpreting the Scripture (reading lessons and preaching) and then the sharing of a meal at which Christ himself is the host, unseen and yet recognized by his disciples.

In the New Testament there is little evidence of actual, specific worship practices. The first Christians continued the practices they knew as Jews, and the influence of the synagogue on Christian worship was clear: a weekly holy day (that came eventually to replace the sabbath), daily prayer especially in the morning and in the evening, the elements of reading the Bible and preaching, some influence on the eucharistic prayer of thanksgiving. In Acts 2:42 we read that the converts to Christianity on the day of Pentecost "remained faithful to the apostles' teaching [doctrine] and fellowship [community], to the breaking of bread [the Lord's Supper] and the prayers [the traditional hours of daily prayer]." St. Paul condemns certain errors in connection with the celebration of the Lord's Supper and gives what is probably the earliest New Testament evidence for the Holy Communion—even older than the Gospels—in his report of the narrative of the institution of the Holy Supper (1 Corinthians 11:23f). In the Revelation of St. John the Divine we with the seer glimpse the heavenly liturgy, replete with priests [elders, presbyters] and lamps and incense and angels and crowns and thrones and the glassy sea and all the rest of that picture made familiar by the popular hymn, "Holy, holy, holy, Lord God almighty" (*LBW hymn* 165). This picture of the heavenly liturgy, some say, may have been inspired by worship in the church at the turn of the first century (ca. A.D. 100).

We do know that the early Christian practice was to observe both the Sabbath (Saturday) and Sunday (the Lord's Day), honoring both the third commandment and the experience of the resurrection. The developing Eucharist has a relationship with the yearly celebration of the Passover, an evening meal, but the celebration was moved to the morning to emphasize the resurrection which took place before dawn. Moreover, Sunday was a work day, and in the age of persecution meeting in the morning was safer for it aroused less suspicion.

Ca. 112 Pliny, governor of Bithynia in Asia Minor, wrote to the Emperor Trajan,

> Christians meet on a fixed day, before dawn, sing in alternate
> verses a hymn to Christ their God, and bind themselves by oath
> not to do wrong.

Exactly what that means is unclear, nor can we be sure how perfectly the pagan governor understood what Christians in fact did.

An ancient document of the same era (ca. 100) gives more reliable information. In 1874 a Greek parchment manuscript was discovered in Constantinople that contained a document called the *Didache*, "The Teaching of the Apostles." It shed light on the period immediately following the apostolic age and gives what may be the oldest "eucharistic prayer" in the Christian tradition. The prayer contains lovely passages as the document directs the Christian community in worship.

With regard to the Eucharist we give thanks in this manner.

First, for the cup:
> "We thank you, our Father, for the holy vine of David your servant which you have revealed to us through Jesus your child. Glory be yours through all ages!"

Then for the bread broken:
> "We thank you, our Father, for the life and knowledge which you have revealed to us through Jesus your child. Glory be yours through all ages!"

The prayer continues,
> "Just as the bread broken was first scattered on the hills and then was gathered and became one, so let your Church be gathered from the ends of the earth into your kingdom, for glory and power are yours through all ages."

Finally, "when your hunger has been satisfied, give thanks":
> "We thank you, holy Father, for your holy Name which you have made to dwell in our hearts, and for the knowledge and faith and immortality which you have revealed to us through Jesus your child. Glory be yours through all ages."

Moreover, this ancient document explains that the day of the Lord is set aside for the celebration of the Supper of the Lord. Indeed, the name for Sunday, "the Lord's Day," probably derives from the celebration of the Lord's Supper on that day as the weekly memorial of the resurrection.

A second ancient document gives a more complete picture of early Christian worship. Not long after the earthly life of Jesus was completed, a man was born in Galilee in a Roman city built on the site of ancient Shechem. The man's name was Justin. After an earnest search for truth through the various schools of Greek philosophy he at last met some Christians and found what he had been searching for. He made his way to Rome where he opened a school and where, about 156, he died a martyr's death. He has been known ever since as St. Justin, Martyr. In his *Apology* (that is, a defense of Christianity) he has left us a precious document which describes Sunday worship in Rome in the middle of the second century (ca. 150). On Sunday the Christian community gathers and listens to readings from the apostles or the prophets, after which the presiding minister preaches and exhorts them "to imitate the splendid things we have heard." Prayers are then offered "for all people everywhere." After the exchange of the kiss of peace, "bread and a cup of wine mixed with water are brought to him who presides." The presider then "prays and gives thanks according to his ability," and the people give their assent to the prayer with the "Amen." The gifts of bread and wine are distributed, and "everyone shares in them while they are also sent by means of deacons to those who are absent." Finally, those who are able make contributions to care for those in need.

A third document, a half-century or so later, gives a more detailed description of how the Christian church in Rome celebrated the Eucharist. The work, by Hippolytus of Rome, is called *The Apostolic Tradition* (A.D. 215), and it is the richest source we have for understanding of the liturgy in the church in Rome at the beginning of the third Christian century. It is, indeed, the only text we have from this early period. By means of this document we are in contact with the Eucharist as celebrated in Rome early in the third century.

Whereas Justin in his desire to preserve the tradition gives only an outline of what Christians did on Sunday, Hippolytus gives a full text of the central prayer of thanksgiving (while leaving intact the freedom of the presiding minister to improvise). The prayer begins with the verses still in use to this day:

> The Lord be with you.
>> And also with you.
> Lift up your hearts.
>> We lift them to the Lord.
> Let us give thanks to the Lord our God.
>> It is right to give him thanks and praise.

The prayer then gives thanks for Christ, the Word through whom God has created all that exists, who was born of the Spirit and the Virgin, who in obedience to God's will and to win for God a holy people stretched out his arms on the cross. When he was about to give himself voluntarily to suffering to set us free from suffering, he took bread and said, "This is my body"; he took the cup and said "This is my blood." Remembering his death and resurrection, the presider prays on behalf of all the people, "We thank you for having judged us worthy to stand before you and serve you." Prayer for the Holy Spirit follows to bring together in unity those who receive the Sacrament, and a doxology concludes the prayer.

Two things are noteworthy about this ancient prayer: the vigor of its swift phrases and the absence of the *Sanctus* ("Holy, holy, holy"). The song

Encountering God

of the seraphim in God's presence, derived from Isaiah 6:1-3, apparently had not yet entered into the great prayer of thanksgiving. The prayer Hippolytus gives is still in use today; it is preserved in the Ministers Edition of *Lutheran Book of Worship (LBW)* as Eucharistic Prayer IV (Ministers Edition, pages 226, 262, 298).

DEFORMATION OF THE LITURGY

Hippolytus wrote in Greek, then a dying language. Within a few decades of his writing, by the middle of the third century the church in Rome for its worship had changed from Greek to the language of the people, Latin. Gradually the text of the eucharistic prayer became fixed, and from the sixth century onward it is used without change or improvisation. The entrance rite developed into the rather elaborate form we still use: Introit (today we use the entrance hymn or psalm), *Kyrie, Gloria in excelsis*, collect. The texts of the Eucharist and the propers for the use of the celebrant were collected in books called sacramentaries. The oldest of these is the Leonine or Verona sacramentary; the material in it is from the fifth and sixth centuries, but the manuscript in which it survives is from the early eighth century. The Gelasian sacramentary, a manuscript of the mid-eighth century, is the oldest known Roman sacramentary in which feasts are ordered according to the church year. The Gregorian sacramentary, actually a family of sacramentaries, contains elements by Gregory the Great (bishop of Rome 590-604). Classic material from all these ancient books continues in use in the propers, especially in many prayers of the day, in the *Lutheran Book of Worship*.

In 754, King Pepin decreed that the Roman liturgy was to be adopted throughout his kingdom of Gaul (France). Nonetheless the Roman rite varied in different provinces and dioceses, mostly in ceremonial matters, and it was not until 1570 in response to the Reformation that the Roman rite was established "universally" in what had become the Roman Catholic Church.

During the late Middle Ages, confession was moved from the sacristy to the foot of the altar at the beginning of the mass. Offertory prayers developed. From a modern perspective, the most serious deformation of the mass was the obscuring of its communal character. Latin was retained even when it was no longer the language of the people. In the 13th century the chalice was no longer given to the laity (at their request for fear of spilling the blood of Christ). Most of the eucharistic prayer, the canon, was said silently by the celebrant. The consecration of the bread and wine rather than the eating and drinking was seen as the climax of the celebration. The long-standing problem of infrequent communion grew (as early as the fourth century John Chrysostom had complained that communion was not frequent enough), and the once-a-year minimum became the standard and indeed the maximum. The Holy Supper was becoming a spectacle to be watched. The liturgy clearly was in need of renewal.

REFORMATION DECISIONS

Luther's principal concern in his challenge to the church was biblical. He wanted what he had found to be the heart of the gospel, justification by God's grace alone received by faith alone, to stand out clearly and inform all that the church did and taught. Only reluctantly did Luther set his hand to liturgical reform. His knowledge of liturgy was limited to his experience of the mass of his time, the Roman mass in its medieval use; he knew little of the development of the liturgy or of its use in the Eastern churches.

Luther's first attempt at revising the mass so that it would not contradict the gospel was his *Formula Missae* of 1523. The full title is significant: "An Order of the Mass and Communion for the Church at Wittenberg." One of his concerns was to restore communion to the celebration of the mass, and he did not imagine that he was proposing his form for the whole church to use. It is simply "an Order."

> It is not now nor ever has been our intention to abolish the liturgical service of God completely, but rather to purify the one that is now in use from the wretched accretions which corrupt it and to point out an evangelical use. We cannot deny that the mass, i.e., the communion of bread and wine, is a rite divinely instituted by Christ himself. . . (*Luther's Works* 53:20).

Luther's Latin mass is more of a commentary than an actual text or liturgy. He retained as much as he could of the historic mass—the Latin language, the choir elements (introit, *Kyrie, Gloria*, gradual), the lectionary, vestments. His radical surgery was reserved for what was understood to be the heart of the mass, the consecration.

> What I am speaking of is the canon, that abominable concoction drawn from everyone's sewer and cesspool. . . . From here on almost everything smacks and savors of sacrifice. . . . Let us, therefore, repudiate everything that smacks of sacrifice together with the entire canon and retain only that which is pure and holy, and so order our mass (*Luther's Works* 53:21, 26).

The great prayer—which in the Roman rite of the time was a series of pieces rather than one coherent unified prayer—throughout, as Luther saw it, spoke of sacrifice rather than of God's gift to us. Moreover, the words of institution had long been understood as the moment of consecration, the essential element. So in his impatience, Luther took an easy route—he excised all the prayers of the canon surrounding the words of institution and left only the biblical words of Christ to stand alone as sufficient, sung in the same tone in which the Lord's Prayer is chanted.

The parts Luther omitted were all said silently by the priest, and so the people did not miss them. Luther retained the traditional gestures however, with the result that the people would not notice anything unusual in the celebration and would not be disturbed. What they saw looked like the mass they had always known. Following the words of institution Luther had the choir sing the *Sanctus*, and while the final part, "Blessed is he who comes in the name of the Lord," is sung, Luther directs, "Let the bread and cup be elevated according to the customary rite."

The Lord's Prayer is sung, followed by "The peace of the Lord be with you always," which Luther called "the true voice of the gospel." While the *Agnus Dei* is sung the priest communes "first himself and then the people." The benediction concludes the mass.

For weekday services Luther retained the use of Matins, the minor hours (prime, terce, sext, none), Vespers, and Compline.

Luther's second and more radical revision of the Eucharist was his *Deutsche Messe*, the German mass of 1526. He did not intend this to replace the Latin mass but to be used for "the unlearned lay folk." In this Mass Luther removes all the choir elements and replaces them with congregational hymns. The spirit of this service is preserved in *LBW*, the Chorale Setting (p. 120). In the course of his commentary, Luther suggests that the altar be moved away from the wall so "the priest should always face the people as Christ doubtlessly did in the Last Supper."

A hymn begins the service followed by the three-fold *Kyrie* in Greek and a collect. Then the Epistle is chanted, after which a German hymn is sung, and then the Gospel is chanted. The congregation then sings a German hymn version of the Nicene Creed, "We all believe in one true God" (*LBW* hymn 374). The sermon is preached, concluding with a prayer derived from the Lord's Prayer. With no further introduction the words of institution are chanted and the sacrament is distributed to "the women after the men." An excellent post-communion prayer of thanksgiving is provided, one still in use—prayer 241, pages 74, 94, 117), and the Aaronic benediction, which Luther had suggested in the Latin mass, is required as the conclusion to the German mass.

The *Deutsche Messe* was a meager and unsatisfying liturgy. Nonetheless, it at least made the mass intelligible to those who did not know Latin, and it helped to restore communion and gave impetus to congregational hymns. Luther was under no illusion that this German mass alone would revive the church.

> For those who itch for new things will soon be sated and tired of it all, as they were heretofore in the Latin service. There was singing and reading in the churches every day, and yet the churches remained deserted and empty. Already they do the same in the German service (*Luther's Works* 53:89).

As defective as the service now seems, it had enormous influence on emerging Lutheran liturgical practice.

Luther's reforms of worship spread throughout central and northern Europe in the form of Church Orders, directions for the government of territorial churches and their worship. Between 1523 and 1555, 135 church orders appeared. They set forth in the context of worship the evangelical teachings and their implications. The orders varied considerably, but all kept the Eucharist central, continuing the unbroken tradition of the whole church. The sermon was required, as was not the case in the Roman mass of the time, and the people had their part in singing hymns and responses. The Reformed churches in contrast preferred monologues by the minister.

DIVERSIONS FROM TRADITION

The Thirty Years' War (1618-1648) in which German Protestants fought against German Catholics and in which forces from Sweden, France, and Spain later joined, established a centuries-long hostility between Protestants and Roman Catholics. Moreover, the war caused widespread destruction and impoverishment of churches and thus of their liturgical life. The books that had preserved the treasures of liturgical music and chant, the existence and use of which the church orders had assumed, were damaged or destroyed. Church buildings were looted of their plate and metal and wood furnishings.

The age of Lutheran orthodoxy saw a hardening of positions on the various sides of the Reformation and a fixing of liturgical forms. In reaction to what was perceived as a dry and decaying rigidity, the movement called Pietism began under Philip J. Spener who, beginning in 1670, held devotional meetings stressing Bible study and the practice of Christian belief. The aim was to place the living spirit above the letter of doctrine. Such a movement that emphasized the individual and the emotional response to the Bible found little of value in the inherited forms of liturgical worship. The liturgy became extraordinarily barren.

The 18th century philosophical and cultural movement called Rationalism further undermined the strength of traditional liturgy. All that was not in accord with reason was rejected as unworthy of human concern. Thus the miraculous features of the Bible were questioned and then rejected by many. Christianity was adapted to mechanistic science, and the body was viewed as a machine within which was a reasonable soul with its principal seat in the brain. This emphasis on reason influenced all the arts (painting, sculpture, architecture, music, literature) as well as philosophy and religion. Mystery was banished. Symbolism was suspect. The emphasis was on clarity. The surviving remnants of liturgical worship disappeared and were replaced with wordy services with lengthy exhortations to morality. There was little participation by the congregation.

Liturgy—and theology with it—therefore suffered greatly, and the effects were long-lasting. One example may serve to show what happened. In *A Collection of Hymns and A Liturgy* prepared by the Ministerium of New York in 1850, the collection of hymns comes first in the book, showing their importance. The collection has no relation to the church year whatsoever. In the back of the book "A Liturgy" is included (notice that it is not called "The Liturgy"), but it is hardly a liturgy in any usual sense of the term. It is merely a collection of suggested prayers for use by the pastor. The formula provided for the distribution of Holy Communion is "Jesus said, Take, eat; this is my body." The inclusion of "Jesus said" weakens the absolute commitment to the real presence and introduces a note of skepticism, as if to say, "Jesus is reported to have said this, but we know rationally that this cannot be meant quite literally." A representative prayer shows the influence of a dying pietism:

> O forbid that I should ever make shipwreck of faith by not holding fast a good conscience. Preserve me from the smallest degree of that spirit, which works in the children of disobedience. Preserve me from proving faithless to my vows, and from bringing reproach on the Christian name. Help me to follow the Lamb whithersoever he goeth, to abide in him the true vine, and to stand fast in the liberty wherewith he hath made his disciples free.

There is no clear shape or direction or purpose. The prayer excludes any sense of the community and is just a string of pious phrases for an individual to say.

There were exceptions. In the time of Johann Sebastian Bach (1685-1750) in Leipzig the morning service retained the traditional form. The service began with the *Introit* sung in Latin, followed by the *Kyrie* and *Gloria* sometimes in Latin by the choir and sometimes in German hymns by the congregation. The collect was chanted in Latin, the Epistle chanted in German followed by a hymn and the intoned Gospel. The Nicene Creed was intoned in Latin. After it a cantata, a principal feature of the service, was sung by the choir. Then the German hymn version of the creed was sung. Another German hymn introduced the sermon, and the sermon concluded with prayers and intercessions, announcements, and stanzas from an appropriate hymn. If the cantata was divided, the second part would be sung next. The preface and *Sanctus* were sung in Latin, followed by the Lord's Prayer and the words of institution in German, and the distribution of the sacrament. The liturgy concluded with a collect and the benediction. Although the service was in the traditional form, the Eucharist was in large measure the occasion for choir performance.

In North America, Henry Melchior Muhlenberg, the patriarch of the Lutheran Church in America, together with Peter Brunnholtz and John Handschuh in 1748 prepared a liturgy in German for use in the churches of the Ministerium of Pennsylvania. It followed the traditional order: hymn, confession, *Kyrie*, versified *Gloria*, collect for the day, Epistle, hymn, Gospel, versified creed, sermon, prayer of the church, offering, The continuation of the celebration of the Holy Communion was optional. This is in part a reflection of the frontier conditions under which many of the churches labored. There were no trained choirs and few trained musicians; pastors were in short supply. Muhlenberg's liturgy was never printed but was copied by hand by each man who served in the Ministerium.

In 1786 a revision of Muhlenberg's liturgy was printed, and it was an indication of the decline in interest in preserving the traditional forms. The *Gloria* was omitted altogether, the collects were dropped, the creed was omitted, a prayer for the word was inserted before the benediction. When English books began to appear in the next century, they take their style from the surrounding Protestant groups with long monologues by the minister, no congregational responses, all in language often borrowed or adapted from the *Book of Common Prayer*. Liturgy and theology, the twins of orthodoxy, were in decay, and the Lutheran church in its desire to be like the

Protestant groups around it and in order to look and be "North American," had lost most of its distinctive tradition and heritage.

RECOVERY EFFORTS

In the middle of the 19th century, however, a renewed interest in Lutheran confessional theology and worship began to make itself known, and the deformation of the historic liturgy began to be reversed. In 1860 the Ministerium of Pennsylvania published an English liturgy based on the work of Wilhelm Loehe in Germany. In 1867 the General Council of the Evangelical Lutheran Church in America was formed and in 1868 the *Church Book* was published by the General Council. It restored to Lutheran use the liturgy of the German Church Orders following Luther's *Formula Missae*: confession, introit, *Kyrie*, *Gloria*, collect, Epistle and Gospel, creed, hymn, sermon, offertory, general prayer, preface, *Sanctus*, Lord's Prayer, words of institution, *Agnus Dei*, distribution, thanksgiving, and the Aaronic blessing. Noteworthy in this liturgy is the provision for the optional use of an Old Testament lesson before the Epistle (an innovation not picked up until the *Service Book and Hymnal* of 1958), a proper preface for each season of the church year, an exhortation to communicants between the *Sanctus* and the Lord's Prayer that gives the sense of the themes of a eucharistic prayer, and the rubric directing the minister to extend his hands over the bread and wine while praying the Lord's Prayer. The hymnal which followed the liturgical section of the book is arranged according to the church year. A complete lectionary giving the Epistle and Gospel for each Sunday and festival of the year is provided as part of the propers. German Bibles had usually included a table of the traditional appointed Epistles and Gospels for the church year, but their use in worship was not always consistent. This book is therefore the first truly adequate and representative liturgy of the Lutheran church in North America.

Twenty years later Lutheran cooperation had advanced to such a degree that three principal bodies—the General Council, the General Synod, and the General Synod South (a remnant of the Civil War)—agreed to work together on a common form of service they could all use. The result was an extraordinarily influential work, the Common Service of 1888. The guiding rule in the work, laid out in the preface to the Common Service, was "the common consent of the pure Lutheran Liturgies of the Sixteenth Century, and when there is not an entire agreement among them, the consent of the largest number of those of greatest weight." The liturgists could declare with confidence and pride,

> The Common Service here presented . . . is no new Service, such as the personal tastes of those who have prepared it would have selected and arranged; but it is the old Lutheran Service, prepared by men whom God raised up to reform the Service, as well as the doctrine and life of the Church.

The 16th century orders, moreover, the preface goes on to note, "were not new and original works, created by the Reformers" but were revisions of the Latin service of the church. The principal achievement and glory of the work of 1888 is that "the whole outline and structure of the service of the Western church for a thousand years before the Reformation is preserved." "Of the Sunday Collects, there are but few which have not been in continuous use for more than twelve hundred years." They are used in the Roman church, in the Lutheran churches of Germany, Denmark, Norway, Sweden, and the United States "and wherever scattered throughout the world," and throughout the Anglican communion. "Here indeed is a Communion of Saints." This service with its ancient roots, the preface boasted correctly, "can lay claim, as no other Order of Service now in use can, to be the Common Service of the Christian Church of all ages."

The Common Service was incorporated in the *Common Service Book* of 1917 which in addition to the liturgy, enriched with proper Graduals for each Sunday and festival of the church year (to be sung by the choir between the Epistle and Gospel), provided in the same volume a hymnal arranged according to the church year. The adoption of the book led to the merger of the cooperating churches into the United Lutheran Church in America. The Common Service made its way into the service books of other Lutheran groups—the Missouri Synod as well as the various Scandinavian bodies in America (the Norwegians, however, generally ignored the Common Service)—and became a truly common service for Lutherans in North America.

In 1958, as a prelude to the mergers which formed the Lutheran Church in America and the American Lutheran Church, the *Service Book and Hymnal* was published. It continued the Common Service with but few modifications, notably the inclusion of the peace litany from the Eastern Orthodox liturgy ("In peace let us pray to the Lord") as an alternative to the threefold *Kyrie* of the Common Service. "The rich treasury of ecumenical hymnody" was employed in the creation of the hymnal portion of the book. The use of the word "catholic" in the creeds was restored, replacing "Christian", which remained in a footnote as an alternative use. The most significant introduction in this book was the inclusion of an remarkably well crafted prayer of thanksgiving within which the words of institution were set. (Provision was also made for the use of the unadorned verba for those who desired to retain what to them was the traditional Lutheran use.)

The *Service Book and Hymnal* was still new when work began on the next influential book, *Worship Supplement* of 1969, prepared by the Lutheran Church–Missouri Synod. "A modern experiment," it began as a revision of *The Lutheran Hymnal* of 1941. The language was revised, certain materials such as the Greek *Kyrie eleison* were restored, and new material was introduced (three eucharistic orders, forms of intercession, the eucharistic prayer; offices for Prime [mid-morning], Noon, and Compline in addition to Matins and Vespers.)

When this supplement was published, work had already begun on the next service book for Lutherans in North America. The Inter-Lutheran Commission on Worship (ILCW) worked from 1968-1978 to produce the present book, the *Lutheran Book of Worship* (1978). As the *Service Book and Hymnal* (1958) began tentatively to look to other traditions besides continental Lutheranism for inspiration, the *LBW* carried the process still further. A fortuitous conjunction of events made it possible for the ILCW to make use of the newly-revised Roman rite (1970) and the concurrent work of the Episcopal Church in revising its *Book of Common Prayer* (1976, 1979). The result of the reform of the rites of the Roman, Lutheran, and Episcopal churches is a remarkable convergence of liturgical traditions resulting in services that are in many ways nearly indistinguishable between the three churches. Increasingly, the liturgical convergence is to be found in Methodist and Presbyterian churches as well.

The present Lutheran book is thus the inheritor and continuation of a long line of liturgy that stretches back not only to the Reformation period but back beyond that to the apostolic age itself. Such is the blood that flows in its veins.

WORSHIP: THE CENTER
OF PARISH LIFE

Frank C. Senn

Three words in the title of this chapter require comment. The word "worship" means "ascribing worth." Specifically in terms of Christian devotion it suggests "ascribing worth to God." Christians ascribe worth to God in their praise and prayers, both personal and communal, as well as in their doing of God's will in their lives. "Worship" has this sense, then, of what the individual or the community of faith offers to God. The word "liturgy" is both a more precise term for what we are discussing and a more expansive one since it means "the representative public work of the people," and therefore comprehends both corporate devotion to God and the public witness of the worshiping community to the world. The kind of worship described here can be called "liturgical worship" in that it is both a corporate and a representative activity; it is both a service of the congregation rendered to God and a public enactment of the church's faith and life.

The word "parish" also requires comment. In its strict sense "parish" is a kind of ecclesiastical geography that hardly applies to the American situation. In the voluntary character of American church life people seem not to feel obligated to attend their "parish church"—the church in whose geographic "boundaries" (if such even exist) they live. It is not unusual for people to drive pass several churches to get to the "parish" they have decided to join. The usual designation of the local assembly of God's people in Lutheran documents is "congregation" (which was Luther's preference in the Large Catechism), but if we used this term we would still have to distinguish between "local congregation" and other "congregations" such as synod and churchwide assemblies because "congregation" is really a synonym for "assembly"or "gathering." This being the case, it is easier to call the ecclesiastical entity with which we are dealing "parish" since that is commonly understood to mean the local congregation.

The third term deserving comment is "center." Parishes engage in many kinds of activities, and most of them have some value. But according to the Augsburg Confession, article 7, the church is visible only when it is assembled (actually "called out of the world"—-that's what *ekklesia* means) for the proclamation of the Word of God and the administration of the sacraments of Christ. The church lives from the means of grace, not from its good works. And the Holy Spirit works through the means of grace to create faith "when and where he chooses" (Augsburg Confession, article 5). So other activities of the parish derive from and feed into this liturgical assembly for Word and Sacrament, and in this sense worship may be called the "center" of parish life. This shall be demonstrated during this chapter's section on worship planning.

ON THE LORD'S DAY IN THE LORD'S HOUSE AT THE LORD'S TABLE

Every Sunday, the first day of the week, is a day of rest and recreation for most people in Western society. On this day many Christians wake up earlier than their non-church going neighbors and make their way to "church." What their neighbors do not know, and what many Christians themselves do not realize, is that this is really the eighth day of the week, an anticipation of the Day of the Lord at the end of history, and already now the Lord's Day in consequence of the resurrection of Jesus Christ from the dead on the first day of the week. These Christians are on their way to become the church, the people of God, the body of Christ in the world. They become the church by assembling with fellow believers in an assembly called out of the world, the *ekklesia*. The whole enterprise is saturated with eschatology: the church called, gathered, enlightened, and sanctified by the Holy Spirit through the preaching of the gospel and the celebration of the sacraments of Holy Baptism and Holy Communion is a new creation gathered in the presence of the crucified, risen, and ascended Lord Christ who will come again to judge the living and the dead. The church tangibly receives her Lord in the eucharistic meal in which Christ gives himself to his people in his body and blood just as he gave himself for the life of the world on the cross.

The people who make their way to become the church also make their way to the place of assembly. Most places of assembly can be called "church" because the assembly holds title to the facility, although assemblies of the Lord's people on the Lord's Day have taken place in a wide variety of settings. The church building is not a temple, as if God would be present in it apart from the gathering of the people of God around the Word of God and the Sacraments of Christ. But since Christ promised to be present "wherever two or three are gathered in my name," and since he is the head of the body, which is the church, the facility may be called the "Lord's house."

The parish desires to have its own building in order to have a facility that has been specifically designed to accommodate the proclamation of the Word, the celebration of Holy Baptism, and the sharing of the Lord's Supper. Focal points of action in the assembly are ambo or pulpit, font or pool, table or altar. There should be ample space for the community's ministers of Word and Sacrament to function in these places. There must also be ample space for the people to gather to hear the word, to celebrate Holy Baptism, and to receive Holy Communion. For this people has been constituted in Baptism as a "royal priesthood" (1 Peter 2:9). Whose priests are these baptized people? They are not the church's priesthood because the church as a whole is a priesthood. They are the world's priests who offer the world to God in a sacrifice of love and praise.

Being priests of the world was humankind's original God-given vocation. Man and woman were to be the icon, the image, of God in the world. The image was effaced, and the vocation was rejected in the "fall." So it is precisely the mark of redeemed humanity to embrace once again the priestly vocation of bearing God's image to the world and offering the world to God. The building provides space for the royal priesthood to assemble for its public work of proclaiming the word and administering the sacraments. Its acoustics must facilitate singing and speaking and provide places from which the community's musicians and choirs can effectively lead congregational singing. The space will be decorated with essential symbols of the faith, such as the cross, but also with portrayals of Christ according to his human nature. This is appropriate since Christ is "the image of the invisible God" (Colossians 1:15) and the ruler of the universe ("all things") for the sake of the church, his body (Ephesians 1:22-23). Pictures of the saints who have been Christ's servants may also adorn the worship space, since they serve as examples for the present generation of believers. The iconic presence of Christ and his saints will suggest that the act of worship in this place takes place between heaven and earth and that it unites the past, the present, and the future. The parish is gathered into nothing less than this cosmic worship of heaven and earth.

The essential action of the royal priesthood is to give thanks. Thanksgiving is an acknowledgment of gifts received and of the giver who gives them. Fallen humanity does not acknowledge God as "the giver of every good and perfect gift." Only redeemed humanity gives thanks as their "duty and delight," and thereby acknowledges God's largess and interaction with his creation. Therefore, the climactic moment in Christian worship is the Great Thanksgiving, in which the royal priesthood of the redeemed world offers to God what God has already given, specifically bread and wine which earth has yielded and human hands have made, in remembered acknowledgment of God's acts of creation and redemption through Christ. Christians will implore the Holy Spirit to manifest these gifts of bread and wine to faith as the body and blood of Christ, according to Christ's word, and the community of faith will receive these "holy things for the holy people."

Celebrating the Lord's Supper, also called the Eucharist, is the unique act of worship on the Lord's Day. This is because the presence of the coming one in this meal makes it a "foretaste of the feast to come," an anticipation of the messianic banquet in the kingdom of God and therefore the appropriate rite for the eschatological eighth day. The Orthodox theologian, Alexander Schmemann, called the whole liturgy a journey into the dimension of the kingdom of God. The kingdom is symbolized, brought together ("symbol," *sum-ballein* means "to bring together" two realities), in the gathering of the church and the celebration of the Eucharist because the kingdom is where the Father's reign is mediated through the Son in the Spirit. The kingdom is where the world has been reconciled with God and brought into unity with God. From time immemorial reconciliation and unity have been sealed by meal hospitality. The world's reconciliation with God has been accomplished by Christ's sacrifice of atonement, and this is gratefully remembered as the core content of the eucharistic memorial— not just in words but also in the acts of eating and drinking the Lord's body and blood (1 Corinthians 11:26).

The full service of word and meal is essential to the full experience of the Lord's Day, and the *Lutheran Book of Worship* (*LBW*) has affirmed this principle. The *LBW* moved beyond previous Lutheran service books by providing the Holy Communion (the name of the chief service) in its full, uninterrupted order as the full service of Word and Sacrament, and provided a rubric for what to do "when there is no Communion" only at the end of this order. The worship book itself witnesses to the fullness of the church and its liturgy in its very layout. This surely has made some contribution to the retrieval of eucharistic life in the church at all its levels of expression. But the reason for desiring the eucharistic life is that in the Eucharist the church enters into the life of God by receiving Christ himself in his body and blood into the individual lives of the body of Christ.

THE COMMUNITY GATHERED AROUND WORD AND SACRAMENT

We have called such an act of worship as described above "liturgical worship." Deriving from ancient Greek usage, "liturgy" means a public and representative work, such as legislators do in a legislative assembly or such as the priests of Israel did in the tabernacle and temple. Both uses of the term are found in New Testament and early Christian usage. In 2 Corinthians 9 and the book of Acts the gifts collected in the Macedonian and Greek congregations for the relief of the poor in Jerusalem constituted the "liturgy" or representative work of these congregations—-in this case their gesture of fellowship and good will. Paul was the "liturgist" or official representative of these Gentile congregations who brought these gifts to Jerusalem. The second meaning of the term is applied to the work of Christ himself in the Letter to the Hebrews. Christ fulfilled the sacrifices of the old covenant in his once for all offering of himself on the cross for the sins of the world. Now he eternally offers this sacrifice before the Father in heaven on behalf of his sisters and brothers on earth. In this sense Christ is the church's liturgist or representative before the Father in heaven, and the church may appeal to Christ's sacrifice and mediation as the confident basis on which to approach God's throne of grace with its own "spiritual sacrifices" of praise, prayer, and thanksgiving.

In the church's liturgical assembly representative work takes place in several directions. The royal priesthood of the baptized represent the world before God by offering to God gifts from the creation and their prayers on behalf of the world in a sacrifice of love and praise. This has been called the sacrificial dimension of worship. The royal priesthood will also represent God to the world when they are dismissed from the liturgical assembly to their vocations in the world. In their daily lives and responsibilities the royal priesthood serve as sacramental signs of Christ's presence in the world by being, in Luther's words, "little Christs to their neighbors." Within the liturgical assembly, however, the ministers of the Word and the Sacraments represent Christ to the people gathered, both faithful and seekers, in the acts of preaching and presiding at the table. Therefore, both the ordained and the laity have representative liturgical roles. The church's ordained ministers are liturgists who represent Christ in preaching his gospel and administering his sacraments. The royal priesthood of believers are liturgists who pray for a world that cannot pray for itself and who offer the gifts of creation for God's use. The clergy alone are not the church, with lay spectators, and the laity alone are not the church which hires employees who happen to be ordained. Clergy and laity each have a liturgical role, and the full liturgy of the church requires that both roles should be exercised.

One of the greatest contributions of the *LBW* is that it provided for this differentiation and mutuality of roles. The little designations 🅿 and 🅰 — presiding minister (ordained) and assisting minister (lay person)—indicate the proper roles of the apostolic ministers of Word and Sacrament and the royal priesthood of believers. Both roles are needed for liturgical worship. The presiding minister, in the presiding role, extends the apostolic greeting and offers the collect or prayer of the day, but the assisting minister offers the bids of the Kyrie-litany. The congregation and choir (🅲) render the canticle of praise. The Scriptures belong to the whole people of God and it is appropriate that lay persons read them publicly. The act of preaching, however, is reserved to those who are regularly called (according to the Augsburg Confession, 14). The thanksgivings and intercessions of the prayers of the church belong to the people exercising their priestly role of praying for the world, and the presiding minister should not usurp the assisting minister's role in offering these prayers. The assisting minister offers these prayers as the representative of the people, but ways must be found by which the people can contribute their petitions. To the lay priesthood also belongs the offering of gifts; hence the direction that representatives of the people (e.g. the ushers or designated gift-bearers) bring the bread and wine to the ministers at the table. But the Great Thanksgiving is reserved to the ordained presiding minister who proclaims the words of Christ and acts in the stead of Christ at the Lord's Supper. The ministration of the sacrament is shared by both presiding and assisting ministers. The presiding minister gives solemn blessings, such as the communion blessing and the benediction. But the assisting minister offers the people's thanksgiving for the gift of the sacrament in the post-communion prayer and dismisses the congregation.

It should also be noted that Holy Baptism is celebrated in the context of the service of Holy Communion, and is also noteworthy for its differentiation of liturgical roles. Baptism is identification with Christ in his death and resurrection; it is also initiation into the body of Christ in the world. Theologically speaking, the Word of God calls one to faith, and the Bible has served as the textbook of the catechumenate. The liturgy of the Word has been called the liturgy of the catechumens. Incorporation into the community of faith is sealed by inclusion in the eucharistic fellowship, and the liturgy of the eucharistic meal has been called the liturgy of the faithful. This is why the rubrics in the *LBW* locate the celebration of Holy Baptism after the liturgy of the Word (i.e. of the catechumens) and before the liturgy of the eucharistic meal (i.e. of the faithful). But Holy Baptism is totally integrated into the Holy Communion. The intercessory prayers and the confession of faith of the service (the Apostles' Creed in interrogatory form) occur within the order for Holy Baptism. The assembly's gesture of welcome is the greeting of peace which serves as the transition into the liturgy of the eucharistic meal. As our churches move with more assurance to the communion of all the baptized, in order to affirm that initiation into the fellowship of the church is incomplete without inclusion in the eucharistic fellowship, the sacramental economy is already in place in this order.

Less assuredly in place in the sacramental economy is the practice of confession and forgiveness which serves to preserve the spiritual integrity of the eucharistic fellowship. The Brief Order for Confession and Forgiveness is a kind of purificatory rite of preparation for worship (hence the inclusion of the collect for purity). Yet the *LBW* also provides orders for Corporate and Individual Confession and Forgiveness by which holy absolution, as a divinely-instituted means of grace, may also be received by the congregation as a whole and by individual members. These are historic ways of preparing for the celebration of Holy Communion by doing that which restores the integrity of the church and by returning its individual members to the forgiving and reconciling grace of Baptism.

GROWING IN FAITH AND KNOWLEDGE

The Holy Spirit works through the means of grace—the preaching of the gospel, Holy Baptism, Holy Communion, holy absolution—to create and nurture faith. This faith is a trusting and obedient relationship to God the Father made possible by the saving work of the suffering Servant-Son of God who has become the head of his body, the church. This faith relationship also implies what kind of knowledge it is important for Christians to grow into: the knowledge of God. We are not talking here of knowledge "about" God. The church is not a school for those who want to take courses in religion, theology, ethics, or values. The church is a community created by the Holy Spirit in the image of God the Holy Trinity to be a community of love, willing to suffer in the world for the sake of God's kingdom, and sanctifying those aspects of the world which come into the orbit of one's daily life by offering them to God in a sacrifice of love and praise. But while the church is not a school, it has a school by which its members can grow in such knowledge: the liturgy.

The liturgy of the word has been called the liturgy of the catechumens. It is the explicitly instructional part of the service. Week by week the faithful, catechumens, and seekers hear the Bible read in substantial portions, including readings from the Old Testament, the New Testament epistles and gospels, and the psalms which serve as devotional songs and responses to the readings. These readings are arranged in a sequence that follows the life of Christ during the so-called "festival half" of the church year and, at least as far as the epistles and gospels are concerned, are read continuously during the "ordinary" time of the church year (e.g., the Sundays after the Epiphany and after Pentecost). The sermon is to grow out of the these readings and comment on them. The interpretative key to all the readings, and to many of the festivals and days of devotion, is the gospel story of Jesus. But the epistles also proclaim Christ and his relevance to Christian life in the world and the Old Testament readings provide the context for the Christ-event in salvation history rather than in myth. In the Lutheran tradition the hymn of the day also amplifies the proclamation. It is often a reflection on the gospel of the day and has been wrapped around the preaching— sometimes before the sermon, sometimes after. In historical practice, the stanzas of the hymn were sung as the preacher ascended into and descended out of the pulpit, which was often located at some distance from the chancel and altar. The church cantatas of the Baroque period, culminating in those of Johann Sebastian Bach, were based on the hymn of the day and were placed around the sermon. This is a clear statement that church music in the Lutheran tradition is a form of proclamation of the Word.

We hear in the readings, the sermon, and the hymns the essence of the Christian faith. This faith is also summarized in the creed and distilled in the Great Thanksgiving of the Holy Communion. It may also be evoked in pictures, images, and symbols—in icons and stained-glass windows, on vestments and paraments, and in the cross located at some focal point in the worship space. In all these ways we are exposed to the good news of what God has done for us in Christ, and we build a relationship with God that is strengthened by constant exposure to Scripture and repetitive responses.

Often overlooked is the role that the daily prayer services of the church can play in nurturing this faith and knowledge of God. These services cluster around the pivotal times of sunrise and sunset. The rhythms of daily prayer remind us that we are part of the natural world, that we experience a fresh start every morning (Morning Prayer or Matins), that we have a need to wind down at the end of the day (Evening Prayer or Vespers), and that we need rest and sleep at the end of the day (Prayer at the Close of the Day or Compline)—but that all of this occurs in the grace and providence of God. The daily prayer services are based on large chunks of the Bible: psalms, readings, and gospel canticles. The two-year daily lectionary in the *LBW*, pp. 179-192) is designed for use with the daily prayer offices, as is the table of "Psalms for Daily Prayer" (p. 178). Again, these prayer offices form us in the knowledge and love of God, and the church's leaders have been remiss in not providing regular opportunities to gather for daily prayer as Christians have done for centuries. Providing opportunities for praying the daily public prayer of the church may require some creativity in scheduling, but just so it also requires knowledge of and commitment to the spiritual discipline of daily prayer and meditation using the church's historic forms.

GROWING IN MISSION AND SERVICE

The reason why members of the parish must grow in faith and the knowledge of God is directly related to the mission of the parish: It is to communicate the life of God to the world, as that life is known to us in Jesus Christ. The life of God in Christ is made known in the Scriptures, explicated in the sermons, conveyed through the sacraments, and manifested in the life of the parish itself. All kinds of good works are performed in the parish. Chief among them, although this is seldom considered, is providing, maintaining, and supporting a round of liturgical services that offers the world what it needs, even if it is not what the world wants—forgiveness of sins and reconciliation with the creation's Creator. Indeed, since God's mission is to "reconcile the world to himself" (2 Corinthians 5:18-19), and we are assured by God's promises that this happens in the preaching of the gospel and the administration of the sacraments. By providing the divine service as an integral and central aspect of its mission, the parish is participating directly in God's mission. There should be no lack of confidence that the mission and service of the parish is the mission and service of God.

It has been observed that today most people who are looking for a new "church home" or who are simply "unchurched" come into contact with the church primarily by attending public worship. Some of these visitors may become members of the parish; some may not. But the mission of the worshiping community is to provide both proclamation of the gospel in Word and Sacrament and exposure to and opportunities for people to express *orthodoxia*—"right praise" or "true worship." True Christian worship is worship of the Holy Trinity. The service of Holy Communion and the other orders in the *LBW* are trinitarian from beginning to end. There is no guarantee that orders of worship made up by the pastor or purchased from liturgical entrepreneurs can provide this degree of orthodoxy. Much of what passes for evangelical worship, as that has been influenced by the evangelical revivals and expressed in various contemporary "alternative liturgies," is imbued with a heavy dose of unitarianism of the second person in its expressions of devotion to Jesus. The "friend we have in Jesus" is also the Lord of heaven and earth—the *Kyrios*—who, by this title, is identified with the Yahweh of Israel; who, by his ascension to the right hand of God the Father, is assumed into the Godhead, and who, by the sending of the Holy Spirit, creates and unifies a new community on earth that is his body in the world.

Whatever else the image of the parish as a "body" may suggest, it certainly conveys the idea of an organism rather than an organization. It is a thing with life and with life's possibilities for growth and propagation. But this life is not generated from the membership; it comes from God the Holy Spirit who calls, gathers, enlightens, and sanctifies the whole church on earth (Small Catechism, II, 3). The Pelagian idea that good works are what builds the church—e.g. the parish's friendliness, its care for one another, its involvement in the neighborhood, notwithstanding the value of such efforts,—is devastating, because it puts human beings in the place of God. The apostle does not urge his readers to do good works, but to "walk worthy of the vocation to which you have been called" (Ephesians 4:1). Our calling in Holy Baptism is nothing less than "to live to the praise of God's glory" (Ephesians 1:6, 12, 14).

There is nothing more winsome to the Sunday visitor than to experience a congregation that puts itself into its worship "with hearts and hands and voices." St. Augustine testified in his *Confessions* that the sight of the people at worship, the vigor of their singing, and also the persuasiveness of the preaching of Bishop Ambrose of Milan were powerful factors in his own conversion to faith and life in the true God. Music is a powerful stimulus to devotion—not the music that is performed by polished choirs such as one can hear at concerts, but canticles and hymns that are sung lustily by the congregation. But certainly the preeminent instrument of the mission of God is the preaching of the Word of God. In the sermon the preacher has the opportunity to open up the Scriptures and apply them to the lives of the faithful, catechumens, and seekers alike, and to the mission of the church in the world. Such a sermon can only be prepared if the pastor spends sufficient time in the study consulting commentaries and consulting with the people concerning their experiences of faith in the world.

The life of God in the parish implies that the members of the congregation will support the liturgical worship of the church according to their abilities and competence. A fully celebrated liturgy requires presiding and assisting ministers, acolytes and other servers, ushers and greeters, other readers and communion ministers, choirs and musicians, altar guild servers and visual artists. The parish council and congregation will also see that the parish's liturgical services are adequately funded in the operating budget. The center of the parish's life is not the place to cut corners.

The liturgical stewardship of the people comes together each Lord's Day in the weekly celebration of the service of Holy Communion. The best introduction to this weekly rhythm of Word and Sacrament in parishes where this has not been the pattern of worship is simply to do it. The frequency with which the sacrament of the altar is celebrated cannot be put to a vote. Some amount of pastoral teaching should be devoted to the eucharistic mystery anyway, especially during the Sundays of Easter each year when the bishops of the ancient church explained the mysteries to the newly-baptized. Perhaps that is the most appropriate season in the church year to move into the rhythm of the Lord's Supper every eighth day, if that is not yet the parish's pattern.

While Holy Communion personalizes the grace of God, just as Holy Baptism and absolution do, the reasons for celebrating the Eucharist should not be based only on an appeal to individual need and benefit; it should be based on the church's need to participate in the mission of God. God acts through the means of grace to reconcile the world to himself through Christ; through these means the Holy Spirit gives faith to whom the Spirit chooses. The condition for any of this to happen is for the church to provide what Christ instituted. The church's ordained ministry serves the Word and the Sacraments, and the parish cannot be telling its pastor not to offer the Word and the Sacraments. The parish's responsibility is to protest a pastor who does not offer this ministry.

If the right worship of the true God is at the center of the parish's life and mission, and if the parish's mission is to communicate the life of God to the world, then the God who enters the life of the parish through the

preaching of the Word and the administration of the Sacraments will have some influence on the rest of the parish's activities. Youth and adult catechumens will be taught and formed in the faith, and the parish will ensure that sufficient time and energy are devoted to this task. If the parish prepares church suppers, they will be for or at least include the poor of the community. The members of the parish will visit or otherwise communicate with those for whom they pray. They will turn their pockets (and their investments) inside out to invest in the mission of God through the work of the parish.

IMAGINATION AND FLEXIBILITY
IN WORSHIP PLANNING

The *LBW*, in promoting true liturgical worship that is a corporate activity of the whole people of God and in providing options that made it possible to tailor the liturgy to particular times and places, also required a greater degree of planning than had previously been the case if worship were to be done with imagination, creativity, flexibility, and integrity. The worship and music committee deliberates on the broad principles of parish worship, such as customs related to the church year, the adequacy and appointments of the worship space, and budgeting for worship and music needs in the parish's general or operating fund. In addition the committee gives advice and feedback to the pastors and musicians who have primary responsibility for worship planning, and addresses the concerns of groups with particular areas of responsibility such as the altar guild, the ushers, and the acolytes. The committee also attends to the needs of worship education in the parish (e.g., by providing information in the parish newsletter). The chief concern of the worship and music committee is to enable the congregation to participate in its worship knowledgeably and logistically.

The pastors and staff musicians (e.g., choir directors, organists) meets regularly to select hymns and choir music that relate to the propers of the liturgy and the character of the liturgical day or season. The services of assisting ministers, acolytes, ushers, and altar guild members are scheduled and appropriate training and review sessions are provided.

Consideration may be given to having a parish liturgical arts committee that can arrange for designs and banners that will highlight the emphases of the church year or special commemorations. In many parishes there are persons who do embroidering and are willing and able to make paraments and vestments. They would profit from consultation before

embarking on major projects, including from the pastor who is regarded as an "expert" in biblical images and liturgical symbols.

Those parishes that have used the *LBW* in its fullness have provided a round of liturgical services that offer a variety of expressions within a stable order. These variations have been observed to a greater or lesser extent in different parishes. The following schema illustrates some of the possibilities for ordering the service of Holy Communion that have been observed generally in congregations I have served over the last 20 years, and now at Immanuel Lutheran Church in Evanston, Illinois, by using the options provided by the musical settings and rubrics.

- Musical setting 1 is used during the Christmas and Easter seasons and on special festive occasions; setting 2 is used on Sundays after the Epiphany and after Pentecost; setting 3 is used from All Saints Day through Advent and during Lent; the chorale setting is used on Reformation Sunday and on other occasions when the Lutheran heritage is celebrated.
- The Brief Order for Confession and Forgiveness is usually used before the service. It is conducted at the location of the baptismal font. It is omitted during the Christmas and Easter seasons, since the seasons of Advent and Lent have a penitential character in preparation for these festivals; a prayer of confession is then included among the petitions in the prayer of the church.
- The Entrance Hymn is chosen for its strength of text and tune and its suitability to the season of the church year. On occasion a psalm is used in place of the Entrance Hymn.
- The *Kyrie* is omitted on Sundays after the Epiphany and after Pentecost other than lesser festivals, but is sung without the canticle during Advent and Lent.
- The canticle, "Glory to God," is sung during the Christmas, post-Epiphany, and post-Pentecost seasons. The canticle, "Worthy is Christ," is sung during the Easter season, on lesser festivals that are saints' days, and on All Saints Day (Sunday).
- At spoken services (e.g., perhaps during the summer), the *Kyrie* and Hymn of Praise are omitted and the order of service goes directly from the apostolic greeting to the Prayer of the Day. We generally omit at spoken services all the canticles that would be sung.
- In my current congregation, the psalmody is usually sung antiphonally by half-verses (to observe the pattern of Hebrew

poetry) between the two sides of the congregation (with the choirs also divided to support the two sides of the congregation), using the psalm tones provided in the *LBW*. In this regard, we depart from the *LBW* rubrics which direct the psalms to be sung antiphonally or responsively by whole verses. Sometimes the choir sings a setting of the psalm text. Sometimes a hymn versification of the psalm is sung by the congregation.

- The Alleluia Verse or Lenten Verse are usually sung by all; sometimes the choirs sing the proper verses for the Sundays or festivals; sometimes a gradual hymn is sung by the congregation during a gospel procession.
- The Sermon is usually preached after the Gospel and is based on the Gospel, but with reference to the other readings as often as possible. Certainly the purpose of evangelical preaching is to proclaim Christ, according to the mysteries of faith celebrated in the church year and with reference to the Christ who is present among his people in the sacraments. Preaching at the eucharistic liturgy should frequently point toward the act of receiving communion.
- It is important to note that the churches that most universally use the *LBW*—the Evangelical Lutheran Church in America and the Evangelical Lutheran Church in Canada—have approved the use of the *Revised Common Lectionary*, which supplants the three-year lectionary in the *LBW*. While there are many common choices of readings between these two lectionaries, there are differences that will affect the choice of the Hymn of the Day.
- The Hymn of the Day is usually sung after the sermon. Sometimes it is sung before the sermon. Sometime it is split with stanzas sung before and after the sermon. Sometimes the choir and congregation sings a concertata setting of the hymn. Sometimes the choir sings a Bach cantata, which surrounds the sermon as the cantatas frequently did in St. Thomas Church in Leipzig during Bach's time.
- The Nicene and Apostles' Creeds are used according to the rubrics; the Athanasian Creed is recited on The Holy Trinity Sunday.
- Some petitions for the prayer of the church are prepared in advance by the pastor or assisting minister. They include not only pastoral concerns but also the concerns of committees

within the congregation regarding special issues and parish programs. Worshipers are invited to write down prayer requests on a sheet of paper in the narthex as they enter for worship and then to light a votive candle on the votive candle stand. These requests are collected by the assisting minister before the entrance procession and are integrated into the appropriate category in the prayers. On occasion, worshipers have been invited to mention aloud or quietly names and concerns during spaces allotted for this in the prayers.

- The greeting of peace is always enacted.
- There is always music during the offering: an organ or instrumental voluntary, a choir or solo anthem, or a congregational hymn. The offertory responses printed in place in the *LBW* are used unless the choir sings a proper offertory. During Lent the congregation sings "Create in me a clean heart" in place of "Let the vineyards be fruitful" or "What shall I render to the Lord." At the offertory, ministries of the congregation are recognized (e.g., church school teachers on Rally Day, choir members and instrumentalists on Church Music Sunday [Fourth Sunday of Easter], and the installation of church council members and officers).
- The Great Thanksgiving is used according to the five options provided in the *LBW* Ministers Edition. Among the options, I seldom use rubric 33, "Blessed are you, Lord of heaven and earth." Eucharistic Prayer I (the "Rose" canon) is used on many Sundays; Eucharistic Prayer II is used from Christmas Eve through Epiphany and from Easter Eve through Pentecost; Eucharistic Prayer III is used during Lent and on some lesser festivals; Eucharistic Prayer IV (Hippolytus) is used at spoken services when the *Sanctus* would not be used, although it also makes an appropriate prayer during Advent. I never use the words of institution apart from their context in a eucharistic prayer. I admit that I have experimented with the use of eucharistic prayers from the authorized worship books of other churches with which my church (ELCA) has had official relationships of eucharistic sharing or full communion (not limited to North American denominations, and including member churches of the Lutheran World Federation). Additional eucharistic prayers have been provided in the leaders edition of

With One Voice, but in comparison with the Great Thanksgivings in the *LBW* and some other authorized prayer books, I do not find them to be satisfying.

- Both versions of the Lord's Prayer are used, alternating uses from week to week.
- Communion has been administered to communicants kneeling at the communion rail, standing at the communion rail, or processing to a communion station.
- The "Lamb of God" is usually sung, as well as other hymns and songs during communion.
- The *Nunc dimittis* is sung after communion during the Advent and Christmas seasons through The Epiphany of Our Lord, as well as on The Transfiguration of Our Lord, Reformation Day, All Saints' Day and Christ the King; otherwise "Thank the Lord" is sung or some other post-communion hymn. During Lent our post-communion canticle is *LBW* canticle 13, "Keep in mind that Jesus Christ has died for us."
- At the altar the presiding minister indicates to the assisting minister which post-communion prayer to use. In addition to the three prayers provided in place, the alternate prayer of the day for Maundy Thursday (rubric 38) or prayer #209 ("Almighty God, you provide the true bread from heaven") are occasionally used.
- The service usually ends abruptly with the benediction and dismissal. However, on major festivals and during the Easter season we use a closing hymn after the benediction and before the dismissal. When the organist plays a postlude, the people listen courteously or leave quietly.
- Announcements are always a problem because parish leaders think they are important while most worshipers, other than those with a vested interest in the activities being publicized, regard them as an unwanted intrusion on worship. It is best not to have any. If they cannot be avoided, notices should be kept to a minimum and given at locations where they make sense. When something special is happening in the service that might "throw" the congregation, the worshipers are alerted to this before the service begins—as briefly but as clearly as possible. Notices of deaths in the parish are given before the prayer of the church. Notices of parish events, such as special ser-

vices during the week, are given before the dismissal. In my current parish, introductions and announcements are made at the sit-down coffee hour following the service. Greeters encourage visitors to remain for this fellowship hour.

So-called "traditional worship," by which many mean that which uses the *LBW* as its principal resource, has been criticized in recent years as opaque to many non-Lutheran visitors and therefore as standing in the way of "church growth." Sincere criticism should always be taken to heart, but the source of criticism should also be considered. Liturgical celebrations derided as ritualistic, didactic or propagandistic may indeed be just that. Instead of experiencing the life- and world-changing presence of the crucified and risen one who comes again as Lord and Judge of the nations, worshipers may have been subjected to unvarying routine, manipulated by unskilled liturgy planners, or harangued by pressure groups. These situations often result from a lack of knowledge of and sensitivity to the true character of the church's liturgy on the part of worship planners and leaders. Many critics of "traditional worship" assert that those who plan and lead worship need to know first of all the parish and its community. Liturgically sensitive critics will agree with that and also assert that worship planners and leaders need to appreciate the meaning and dynamics of liturgical worship and learn how to get out of its way. Liturgical worship that is done well—at the center of the parish's life, rendered by the whole people of God under competent ministerial leadership (ordained and lay)—is its own best evangelization, catechesis, and conveyor of moral vision, because the one encountered in the liturgy is none less than the Author of life, the Savior of the world, and the Sanctifier of God's people. There is no guarantee that the same orthodox vision of God will be communicated in "alternative" forms of worship, nor that worship leaders who are uncomfortable with "traditional" worship will lead "alternative" forms of worship with any greater degree of competence, since their disease is often with public ritual as such and not just the kind of ritual it is. All things considered, the *Lutheran Book of Worship* remains a reliable and sturdy asset for the parish and will continue to provide a resource for the church's public work and spiritual renewal. Its riches need to be discovered anew.

THE PRAYERS
OF THE COMMUNITY

Mark P. Bangert

INTRODUCTION

Far more than a collection of materials for Sunday eucharistic assemblies, the *Lutheran Book of Worship (LBW)* provides a variety of resources for personal and corporate daily prayer and praise.

While "Petitions, Intercessions, and Thanksgivings" (*LBW*, pp. 42-53) are meant primarily to be a resource for assisting ministers, this collection of materials also offers prayers for daily use by individual worshipers. Corporate eucharistic requirements determined the selection of psalms in the pew edition of the *LBW*, and yet, many of these psalter texts (e.g. 23, 116, 130) originated as personal prayer and are still very fit to carry the deepest sighs of faithful individuals. Or, in the well-worn path of Lutheran spirituality, worshipers—individually or together—can find riches for their prayer lives among dozens of hymns from the *LBW* (e.g., hymns 188, 224, and 324).

Lest we think that the poles set up here are between Sunday corporate worship and daily individual worship, the *LBW* sets out to supply liturgical resources for groups of Christians throughout the week. This comes as no surprise for those who have traditionally used Morning Prayer (Matins) as a substitute or alternative for Sunday assemblies or have employed Evening Prayer (Vespers) for parish midweek Lenten or Advent services. The Service of the Word also fills a need for corporate worship during the week.

Yet, the vision behind Morning Prayer and Evening Prayer gives these prayer offices a profile much more profound than occasional services designed for special weekday parish worship. Here, to understand that vision and to explore it anew we

1. take a look at how Morning Prayer and Evening Prayer have become serviceable liturgies for facilitating parish worship needs formerly centered in their parallels in both the *Service Book and Hymnal (SBH)* and *The Lutheran Hymnal (TLH)*
2. restate the vision behind *LBW* Morning Prayer and Evening Prayer
3. explore that vision in the present context

As these explorations unfold, Prayer at the Close of Day (Compline) presents a special case. Its inclusion in the *LBW* similarly derives from the desire to provide daily prayer for groups of Christians, but in contrast to Morning Prayer and Evening Prayer, Compline's own history locates its development in monastic settings. Nevertheless its beneficial use among Christians of all traditions today indicates that its particular ability to express rest, reflection, and hope at the end of increasingly busy days suggests continued availability. Compline's form in the *LBW* is traditional, showing little change from previous versions. Its music is not new but rather represents tonal formularies centuries old. The decision to include it in the *LBW*, in retrospect, is justified by its relative popularity. Yet, in comparison with Morning Prayer and Evening Prayer, Compline provides nothing new or challenging—it retains its simple, ancient form. In what follows, therefore, attention will be given primarily to Morning Prayer and Evening Prayer with only occasional references to Compline.

NEW WINE IN OLD SKINS

If received as collections of new translations, new musical settings, and slightly revised orders, Morning Prayer and Evening Prayer from the *LBW* easily served to give a new look to previous forms of Matins and Vespers as used in Lutheran parishes across North America. They could give the impression of continuity — an important benefit for those uneasy about a whole new book of liturgies and hymns. Using the new models in this way had other benefits. Worshiping groups soon discovered to their delight some of the refreshing changes proposed by these new orders.

For those who saw the older Matins and then *LBW* Morning Prayer as alternative services for the Sunday assembly, the lessons and psalm appointed for a Sunday or feast day found places in these orders quite easily, though the requirement for the hymn after the psalmody in Morning Prayer created some difficulties. Even the sermon could find its way into the Morning Prayer order, though by preference moved from its former place following lessons to a position at the end of liturgy, where it may be preceded by an offering and a hymn and followed by one of three prayers—examples of the new gems contained in these services. Having a place for a Sunday sermon in Morning Prayer fulfilled a desire close to Lutheran hearts, though turning these liturgies into opportunities for proclamation diverted questions about the nature and purpose of both daily corporate prayer and every Sunday Eucharist.

The following table makes some of this clear.

SBH	*TLH*	*LBW*
	Hymn (M and V)	
Versicles	Versicles	Versicles(MP only)
		Service of Light (EP only)
Venite (M only)	*Venite* (M only)	*Venite* (Ps. 95, MP only)
		Psalm 141 (EP only)
Hymn (M only)	Hymn (M only)	
Psalm(s)	Psalm(s)	Psalm(s)
Lesson(s)	Lesson(s)	
Responsory/hymn	Responsory/hymn	Hymn
		Lesson(s)
Offering(V only)	Offering	
Hymn (V only)	Hymn (V only)	Responsory/hymn
Brief address	Sermon	
Canticle	Canticle	Canticle
Te Deum	Te Deum	Benedictus
Benedictus	Benedictus	Te Deum
Magnificat(V only)	*Magnificat*(V only)	*Magnificat*(EP only)
Nunc Dimittis(V only)	*Nunc Dimittis*(V only)	
Prayer	Prayer	Prayer
Kyrie	*Kyrie*	Prayer of the Day
		(MP only)
Our Father	Our Father	Others(MP only)
Collect for the Day	Collect for the Day	Litany(EP only)
Others	Others	Grace or Peace Prayer
Collect for Grace/Peace	Collect for Grace/Peace	Our Father
Bless we...	Bless we...	Let us bless...
Blessing	Blessing	(Blessing)
		(Offering)
		(Hymn)
		(Sermon)
		(Prayer)
		Blessing

For those parishes or groups of parishes that desired a more festive evening service, the *LBW* Evening Prayer actually proved to be a attractive advancement over predecessor liturgies. It seemed only right to follow the lead of the "Notes on the Liturgy"[1] which make provision for the use of festive vestments such as the cope, and make room for the use of incense if for no other reason than to give fuller expression to the refrain which accompanies Psalm 141 ("Let my prayer rise before you as incense"). The Service of Light from Evening Prayer offers an opportunity for processions with a large candle and/or the lighting of lights held by individuals — a ceremony many parishioners already knew from more elaborate Christmas Eve services. At the time of the psalms and at the place for lessons, Evening Prayer rubrics encourage the use of multiple psalms and lessons, giving musicians the opportunity to insert choral psalm settings and responsories. Finally, the sung Litany at the conclusion lifted up the corporate nature of prayer in a more prolonged and festive manner. All of these features, though novel to most worshipers 20 years ago, seemed to flow easily from the Vespers order predating the *LBW*.

For those in specialized worship situations, such as diaconal or deaconess communities, parish staffs, churchwide staffs, seminaries or in the home, Morning Prayer and Evening Prayer make it a little easier to expand the two services with larger portions of the Scriptures and of the psalms. A two-year lectionary (*LBW*, pp. 179-182) makes it possible to read sections of the Scripture in sequence and a seasonal psalm table (*LBW*, p 178) offers a pattern of reading the psalms which acknowledges both time of the day and time of the church year. Silence after the psalms and after the lessons invites time for meditation which in the case of the psalms leads to prayer. These represent refreshing nuances for those who look to such liturgies for their communal prayer day by day, and these variations can be utilized without upsetting patterns of worshiping through the older orders of Matins and Vespers.

Finally, those who wished for a way to use Matins and Vespers as the framework for a fuller personal worship life, including the employment of edifying materials from the saints of old and from the gifted of today, Morning Prayer and Evening Prayer came fitted for amplified usage.

In fact, even before the *LBW* came to print, Brian Helge (who died prematurely in 1991), Philip Pfatteicher, and others from the drafting committee for Morning Prayer and Evening Prayer began to investigate how these two services as well as Compline might grow into a kind of Lutheran breviary for pastors and others interested in a daily routine of prayer. Not that the *Minister's Prayerbook* of John Doeberstein[2] or *The Daily Office* by

Herbert Lindemann[3] were no longer viable for such goals. Their roots in pre-*LBW* days and their limited resources seemed rather to call for a more substantial collection of materials not easily exhausted after continued use. This goal now has been met in *For All the Saints*,[4] which contains—together with *LBW* Morning Prayer, Evening Prayer, Compline, and supporting materials—a vast compilation of readings and prayers for the daily praying of these services. In all these ways, for all these needs, *LBW* Morning Prayer and Evening Prayer offered enough of what was new to bring Matins and Vespers into a shape and mode of delivery still recognizable, but also outfitted with signs of having made significant liturgical change. Along the way there were further surprises. Using the *LBW* psalter with its system of psalm tones placed the psalms as sung offerings back into the mouths of all the worshipers. Both Morning Prayer and Evening Prayer were given new musical settings. In certain places the new music made reference to some of the melodies from setting one of the liturgy for Holy Communion. The music provided "through-composed" (not based on formulary tones such as the Anglican-style chants for the canticles both in *SBH* and *TLH*) settings much better suited to the non-metrical texts of the fixed psalms and gospel canticles of both Morning Prayer and Evening Prayer. Those worshipers who ventured into the music for the *Te Deum* in Morning Prayer found a singable, if not challenging, song which attempted to accomplish what the canticle invited.

Directions for antiphonal singing in some of the pieces from these services made it possible to represent musically the dialogical nature of corporate prayer, a feature prominent in daily worship from the earliest of times.

Finally, the two-year lectionary offered a systematic way of reading the Scriptures while honoring the progression of longer narratives, a method neither required by nor possible in the Sunday assembly. These added benefits still reside in Morning Prayer and Evening Prayer, awaiting discovery by many and offering rewards which are considerable.

Yet, trying to pour the new wine of *LBW* Morning Prayer and Evening Prayer into the old wineskins of Matins and Vespers has had its downside. Too often the leader Ⓛ role of these services was filled by a pastor, as was the habit of old, simply because the role called for a sermon. Missed in this transformation was the significance of lay leadership for these services.

Again, rubrical options, the precedent of floating hymns in old Matins and Vespers, and perhaps also the newness of the through-composed settings of the gospel canticles especially have led either to the deletion of these canticles altogether or to their replacement by unrelated hymns. Unfortunately such developments prevent worshipers from regular contact with those magnificent songs of Zechariah and Mary from Luke 2. Such a fate has also come upon the *Te Deum*—that creed-like praise song held dear without a break since the earliest centuries of the church.

Perhaps the greatest problem of all with current usage of Morning Prayer and Evening Prayer derives from Luther's reforms of these services in the 16th century. On the one hand his inclinations to restructure portions of the monastic course of prayer for all the people led him to single out two daily liturgies from the required eight, all of which he regularly used. In retrospect his restructuring invites criticism of a fussy sort. Yet it is worth noting his desire to make daily prayer available to all the people. On the other hand, his zeal for the Word and his desire to make the basic teachings of the church known and loved led to a use of these services chiefly for didactic purposes. That signaled a momentous switch in purpose. Such designs tend to linger by habit, especially when Morning Prayer and Evening Prayer serve only as opportunities for preaching. New wine in old wineskins offers little promise for the new vintage. Indeed, the most profound characteristics of these *LBW* services continue to beg for wider understanding, acknowledgment, and implementation.

NEW WINE IN NEW WINESKINS

Among the many concerns and desires which shaped Morning Prayer and Evening Prayer for the *LBW*—such as the need for a fresh translation of the psalter, new music, and an ample, workable supply of variable elements (antiphons, etc.)—three guiding principles emerged to shed light on the many decisions which needed to be made along the way. First, these services were to reflect less the monastic ideal of prayer and more the goals and purposes of the so-called "cathedral office." Second, the solar rhythm of the day was to be manifested in the shape of these services and in their content. Finally, they were to be constructed in such a way so as to provide for use under a variety of circumstances.

Cathedral Office

Acquaintance with the development of monasticism teaches us that regular daily prayer is at the heart of monastic life. Monastics of both genders, singing their daily prayer offices, capture our interest, and the supposed tranquillity of cloistered life beckons the hassled citizens of today's culture with nearly irresistible attraction. At the center of contemporary imaginings about monasticism lies the daily prayer routine and it is there

—in monastic prayer that we suppose daily liturgies of communal prayer to have their roots.

In fact, the origins of Morning Prayer and Evening Prayer lie as much in the development of lay-inspired "cathedral" prayer, so called because it likely came to life in the bishop's church of urban centers located both in the east and the west. Evidence points to the regular daily gatherings for prayer by all the people—bishop, clergy, and lay alike. Meeting in the morning and in the evening, such assemblies drew strength from the freedom newly enjoyed by Christians and made possible by the legalization of the faith in the beginning of the fourth century.

These services were comparatively simple. They made space for a spectrum of ministries—readers, psalmists, bishop, presbyter, deacon. They provided for ceremony and symbol as ways to appeal to all the people and were designed to be sung and prayed by heart. The liturgies remained the same from day to day so that the people could concentrate on movement and their own prayer.

A service of Evening Prayer in the cathedral style included these elements:

> Lamplighting rite
> Hymn of light with short prayer
> Psalm 141 with incense and prayer
> (Sometimes, other psalms and a lesson)
> Intercessions and concluding prayer
> Blessing
> Dismissal[5]

A service of Morning Prayer regularly included these elements:
> Opening Psalm (either Psalm 51 or 63)
> (Sometimes other psalms and lesson)
> Old Testament Canticle
> Psalms 148-150 (the Hallel psalms)
> Hymn of Light
> *Gloria in excelsis* (Glory to God in the highest)
> Intercessions
> Blessing
> Dismissal

Because of recurring materials and the simplicity of these services, all the people could participate without having to find their way through lengthy sessions of psalmody or to follow long readings from the Scriptures. Expanded psalmody and large selections of Scripture both developed in and are typical of monastic orders beginning to evolve about the same time. After several hundred years the cathedral and monastic versions began to merge.

It seems clear that some form of the cathedral pattern of daily prayer could benefit the church of today. In the *LBW* forms of Morning Prayer and Evening Prayer, the cathedral and monastic forms are merged and acknowledged so.[6] Usage, however, particularly if steered by Lutheran inclinations to didactic purposes, tends to dampen the more popular ceremonial aspects in order to fuel ingrained monastic habits. The cathedral ideal is worth further attention.

Rhythm of the sun

In the morning and in the evening they gathered, those urban Christians from the fourth century, and they did so without clerical pressure or injunction.[7] The habit of gathering at these hours apparently has roots in pre-Christian times when it was tied to work patterns, but more than anything else, the morning-evening rhythm of daily prayer gave opportunity to fill the edges of the day with signs and words which shaped the community of Christ. Given the strong faith of early Christians in the imminent return of Christ, day by day immersion in his victory over death provided the faithful with a way to nurture and sustain their hope.

Light or its absence is integral to apprehending Christ's death and resurrection. Great darkness covered the earth on the day of Christ's death, and dawn opened the space for the proclamation of the resurrection message. Eager to be impressed by Christ's own death and resurrection, Christians soon saw in the edges, in the poles of the day, those strong images which could carry the gospel message.

In the fully developed monastic cycle of daily prayer, the two polar services, Lauds (later to be known as Morning Prayer) and Vespers still displayed muted recognition of light and in their structure revealed characteristics not found in the other services. With almost uncanny perception Luther separated out these two services for use again by all the people. Luther's restructuring, now strengthened by what we know of the patterns of daily prayer by the first Christians, continues to have life in Morning Prayer and Evening Prayer of the *LBW*. Because of the favored profile given to Morning Prayer and Evening Prayer, Compline remains a case by itself and is best received as a vestige of monastic patterns of prayer, albeit a compelling example of late night prayer for small groups, family or the individual.

Light imagery persists across the centuries. In Morning Prayer the question is asked, as it were: What does it mean to have the dawn awaken one for the day to come? In Evening Prayer this question: What does it mean to go *into* the night? In Compline: What does it mean to be *in* the night?

In Morning Prayer, the dawn awakens us from silence, so our first utterance is "O Lord, Open our lips." Within seconds our mouths "give glory to God our *light* and our life." Creation awakens as well and the whole of the universe gives praise in the so-called Hallel psalms (Psalms 148-150), specifically programmed for Morning Prayer. In Simeon's song, "Blessed be the Lord," worshipers sing that the "dawn from on high shall break upon us," and the promise of the day to come gives them opportunity to pray for the needs of all. In the Paschal Blessing (a kind of expanded form of "Let us bless the Lord") Baptism and the resurrection of Jesus are linked, giving birth to the parent of all praise hymns, the *Te Deum*.

In Evening Prayer approaching darkness is prepared for with the lamplighting rite, its utilitarian aspects soon superseded with the faithful declaration that "Jesus Christ is the Light of the world."

Coming into the presence of God fresh from the day's rigors leads one to confession in Psalm 141. Approaching darkness makes one aware of death and the long watches of those who come near to death. In the peace of the Risen One intercessions pour out of the hearts of the community as the rhythm of the sun leads inexorably to another sunrise and to the final dawn of each of the faithful.

Irregular use of these services diverts attention away from their wide-spread anchorage in the sign of light. Artificial light, together with late night work and show, deflate the power of the sign. Yet, fear of the night persists among the very young and those who live in urban centers, just as the joy of daylight cheers the hearts of all. The rhythm of the sun is still with us. In Morning Prayer and in Evening Prayer we have assembled for us a powerful collection of words and actions, which can shape and mold us for daily "dying to sin and rising in Christ."

Prayer for every occasion

In our time Christians pray daily under a variety of circumstances. In the *LBW* a way is provided to assist people in entering Morning Prayer and Evening Prayer according to their own personal and communal needs. The rubrics describe how small red circles in the margins of these liturgies outline a form of prayer for households or personal use. Responding to other circumstances, the service as presented in place gives an order for normal parish gatherings and an augmented form, shaped by liberal employment of many options, yields a form for festive worship by a large assembly.[8]

These options and a range of possibilities in between show their faces from time to time in some parishes, in seminaries, and among those people who yearn for some structure of daily prayer. Behind these suggested versions, however, lies a deeper vision which aims to break down some of the walls which are perceived to exist between personal prayer and "formal" liturgical prayer. The red-circle version of Morning Prayer and Evening Prayer yields other useful insights. In its motivation to provide a shortened form, the red-circle versions unveil skeletal structures, which can serve as the shape of daily prayer in a variety of cultures and groupings. That shape is quite simple:

Psalm
Hymn
Lesson
Gospel canticle
Intercession

Other ingredients, such as versicles, antiphons, greetings, and blessings only serve to make the rough places plain. The shape is simple and can be made even simpler for personal prayer:

Psalm
Lesson
Intercession

As daily personal or small group prayer the psalm in this compact order might be (at least at first) the same every day, or it might consist of only one verse from a psalm, such as "Let my prayer rise before you as incense." A single verse from a lesson, perhaps with a moment of meditation, yields the intended benefits of daily Scripture, and intercessions in this plan can be as simple or as lengthy as time and group permits. Expansion derives from the addition of perhaps one verse from the appropriate canticle: "The dawn from on high shall break upon us," or "My soul magnifies the Lord." Joining oneself to the daily prayer of the parish results in the experience of the shape in amplified form, and all can be seen as the church's prayer across a flexible continuum. The five-part shape also provides a pattern for those wishing to exercise their own gifts to create alternative orders for special groups and circumstances.

Recent resources for household prayer assist worshipers to experience the continuum of prayer in yet other ways. In *Praying with the Church*, Philip Pfatteicher outlines a seven-step process for developing the habits of daily prayer,[9] the first of which is to pray the Lord's Prayer three times a day. Each step of the process brings one closer to the shape outline above.

In *Welcome Home*, household prayers for the morning evolve from the shape, and editors provide worshipers with those materials that help to make prolonged usage seasonal in nature.[10] Lessons, perhaps more than any other element, help one to sense these seasonal shifts, so the weekly readings suggested in *Between Sundays*[11] constitute a distinct contribution to the fleshing of the shape for any occasion of daily prayer.

The need for diverse patterns of daily prayer is, if anything, more acute today than 20 years ago. That Christians day by day still pray at all is a wondrous and blessed gift of the Spirit. Should they learn to employ the shape which emerges from Morning Prayer and Evening Prayer at every opportunity for prayer, they would begin to perceive how all their prayer is linked and joined to the church's outpourings in the Spirit. At the same time that shape shows the way to a life which daily receives the imprint of Christ's death and resurrection which alone can satisfy the current hunger for spirituality.

OLD WINE IN NEW WINESKINS

The three principles that helped to shape the services of Morning Prayer and Evening Prayer in the *LBW* are both "new wine" and "old wine." They are new because their full impact has yet to be discovered by those who use the services as well as by those who seek to devise their own patterns of daily prayer. But they are also old, simply because of their compelling advantages and authenticity.

Yet, this age with its pressing theological agendas brings to any practice of daily prayer a whole new set of concerns. These concerns cannot and must not be avoided. Neither can contemporary prayers afford to overlook what from prolonged use appear to be inhibiting weaknesses of the *LBW* services for daily prayer, especially as these shortcomings are juxtaposed with the current condition and its apparent concerns. New wineskins here needs to mean new incarnations of Morning Prayer and Evening Prayer which, responding to current yearnings, grow either from more creative use of the services themselves or from attaching new flesh to the skeletal shape. Such new incarnations of Morning Prayer and Evening Prayer may actually come about by returning to the guiding principles of 20 years past—now the old wine. But before such explorations, here are four concerns.

First, contemporary popular culture lifts up the casual as the authentic mode of living. Structure and form slip into that category of things to be avoided if not distrusted. Naturally, according to this way of thinking, written prayer is to be discarded since anything composed by another, it is assumed, cannot express the innermost yearnings of another. When this cultural inclination is connected to theological traditions which have long disdained liturgical form because of its supposed connection to (Roman) catholic hierarchical control, then the urge to run for your life overcomes any other consideration of prepared prayer. Critics propose an alternative, and that is to pray freely each day as the Spirit moves. If that works, such prayer deserves high praise. But such freedom can also lead to repetitive prayers which show boring contentment with and exaltation of the beauty of the day or with intercessions for one's close circle of friends and family. The challenge is to provide a form which both induces formation beyond one's own imagination and embraces those personalized expressions of care and anxiety invariably brought to community prayer.

Second, the ritual expectations of Morning Prayer and Evening Prayer in the *LBW* may be regarded as too complex for some. In Morning Prayer, for instance, if one chooses to use additional psalms and an Old Testament canticle, does the canticle require a kind of "psalm prayer"? If so, where is it located; if not, why not? Ritual complexity derives from the attempt to merge in these services both the cathedral style and the monastic style of daily prayer. The services were constructed to accommodate the needs of those who might want to pray daily using all the possible variations created precisely for such a desire. Resulting rubrical complexity, surely an innocent issue 20 years ago, may represent a challenge for some assemblies as these services are being planned.

Third, worshipers who are alert to the importance of gender-sensitive language frequently discover texts that rely upon male imagery. A considerable number of such texts are found in the appointed psalms from the *LBW* psalter and the translations of major canticles. In the past decade poets and biblical scholars have created a host of new materials and translations which make possible the consideration of prayer language rich with alternative metaphors.

Finally, there was a desire 20 years ago to provide new music for those liturgies appearing for the first time in the *LBW*. But that desire put the committees who chose music for the book in a precarious position, for the success of a musical setting ultimately rests on prolonged usage by the people. It is said that "you win some, you lose some." Whether one judges the music for Morning Prayer and Evening Prayer as "good" or "bad" is not the point. Rather, there are those who regard the music as too difficult for their congregation and make no effort to use it. Therefore, through no fault of the composers, many of the settings for the canticles and psalms have inadvertently hindered the use of these services in some congregations. Concerns are challenges, and these challenges can be met in part by deploying the principles of design used to shape the daily prayer of the community in the *LBW*.

Old wine refreshes the taste buds even of the young. The old desire to let the cathedral style point the way for daily community prayer yields some important observations. It is recalled that such fourth century communal prayer relied upon repetition, simplicity, and appeal to the senses. Repetition is still at the heart of any life lived in culture. One need only note the routines of sporting events, the widespread participation in Taizé prayer mantras, and the table prayers, for instance, of my grandchildren. The supposed absence of ritual repetition among today's worshipers ought not to go unchallenged. By necessity simplicity arises from repetition and carries with it its own caution to minimize nonessential elements in the services. Movements invited by the lamplighting rite and the paschal blessing rightly serve as attractive correctives to the didactic characteristics of long lessons and recitations of psalmody. Basic signs of light and darkness need our help to unleash their power for calling forth the deep relationships everyone has with these rhythmic barlines of our lives. Simple, singable but durable musical settings of the new gender-sensitive texts may encourage some to develop a renewed interest in daily community prayer. These factors help to explain the popularity of the so called "St. Olaf Morning Prayer"[12] and "Holden Village Evening Prayer."[13]

These new musical settings might also suggest much more serious attention to developing simple, repetitive, sense-responsive services. The old wine that recognizes the solar rhythms of the day offers new challenges. Not that the edges of the day have been declared sacred; rather, these moments of dawn and dusk, these times of transition, serve in a striking way to encase the eschatological, definitive victory of Christ intended to be repeated in us daily until the end of time.[14] A daily imprint begins a process known for centuries as spiritual formation. Light consciousness in the morning calls forth praise in union with the creation, which itself awakens with us, making worshipers conscious of the interdependence they share with the fragile earth. One cannot come away from Morning Prayer without seriously attending to the cautions and exhortations of those lovers of God's "caverns of the earth and the heights of the hills." The approach of darkness elicits thoughts of death in a way which doesn't shy away from the horrors of the news, from the battles waged with terminal diseases, nor from the prospect of growing old robbed of mind and memory. Evening Prayer at dusk embraces fears, anxieties and pain, "in peace." There is room for that kind of prayer on a daily basis. And, as some grow into the desire for more of the "right words," found, as Pfatteicher suggests, in the psalms,[15] the richness of that prayer book can arrive with a new freshness through more gender-sensitive translations, such as that prepared by the International Commission on English Liturgy.[16] The old wine that aims to bind together a continuum of prayer across all stations and circumstances of life provides inspiration to today's liturgical architects. A focus on the shape of Morning Prayer and Evening Prayer encourages one to lift up those ingredients that support simplicity, sense-conscious ceremony, and responsiveness to the edges of the day. Even more, the shape permits us to test how we use the Scriptures in these services, whether as opportunity to imitate monastic regulations for hearing all that was ever written, or whether as a moment for hearing a simple, life-giving word for each day. In spirit the shape may ask that a one-paragraph meditation on a sentence of the Scriptures supersede lengthy pericopes meant more for Sunday exposition. Then too, the shape gives away a fifth of its structure to intercession. While Morning Prayer in the *LBW* encourages the inclusion of the psalmodic style of prayer as contained in Responsive Prayer 1 or the use of the great litany, both are models of community prayer. But daily times of intercession are also meant for worshipers, one by one, to commend their individual days to God, invoking the Spirit upon their baptismal lives in their various callings. The current rubrics, of course, encourage all these paths of intercession. That is the point. How powerful it would be for a young child to know that her prayer stands alongside the great litany. That sense of continuum awaits full implementation.

There are undoubtedly a host of reasons to give up on communal daily prayer, and their power to convince has increasingly overcome blessed habit and masked desire. But we Christians are a "together" as Robert Taft has written,[17] and our prayer is always with the church on earth and the hosts of heaven. Morning Prayer and Evening Prayer still provide the best opportunity for a "daily celebration of the [victory of Christ which] will patrol the corridors of our mind, waking up one by one a throng of truths and perceptions which we have the incredible inclination to forget."[18] These venerable liturgies commend themselves to the church yet again.

NOTES

1 *Lutheran Book of Worship: Ministers Edition,* "Notes on the Liturgy," (Minneapolis: Augsburg Publishing House and Philadelphia: Board of Publication, Lutheran Church in America, 1978), p. 15. Hereafter *LBW* Ministers Edition.

2 John Doeberstein, ed., *Minister's Prayer Book* Philadelphia: Muhlenberg Press).

3 Herbert Lindemann, ed., *The Daily Office* (St. Louis: Concordia Publishing House, 1965).

4 Frederick J. Schumacher, ed., *For All The Saints: A Prayer Book For and By the Church,* 4 vols. (Delhi, New York: American Lutheran Publicity Bureau, 1994).

5 Robert Taft, *The Liturgy of the Hours in East and West* (Collegeville: The Liturgical Press, 1986), p. 212.

6 *LBW* Ministers Edition, p. 14.

7 Paul Bradshaw, *Daily Prayer in the Early Church* (New York: Oxford, 1982), 150.

8 *LBW* Ministers Edition, p. 15.

9 Philip Pfatteicher, *Praying with the Church* (Minneapolis: Augsburg Fortress, 1995), p. 55.

10 *Welcome Home,* e.g. *Year of Mark,* ed. Samuel Torvend and Kari Kloos (Minneapolis:Augsburg Fortress, 1996), pp. 20-22.

11 Gail Ramshaw, *Between Sundays: Daily Bible Readings Based on the Revised Common Lectionary* (Minneapolis: Augsburg Fortress, 1997).

12 Kevin Vogt, *An Order for Morning Prayer: St. Olaf Service* (Chicago: G.I.A., 1993).

13 Marty Haugen, *Holden Evening Prayer* (Chicago: G.I.A., 1990).

14 Taft, p. 338.

15 Pfatteicher, p. 19.

16 *The Psalter* (Chicago: Liturgy Training Publications, 1995; copyright held by International Committee on English in the Liturgy, Inc., 1994). A new translation of the canticles is included in *Psalms for Morning and Evening Prayer* (Chicago: Liturgy Training Publications, 1995), pp. 261-267.

17 Taft, p. 342.

18 George Guiver, *Company of Voices: Daily Prayer and the People of God* (New York: Pueblo, 1988), p. 13.

A VISION OF WORSHIP LEADERSHIP

In the Liturgical Assembly

Paul R. Nelson

Any evaluation of the achievements of *Lutheran Book of Worship* (*LBW*) must acknowledge its important work of recovery and integration of classic forms of liturgy, not only into the areas of language and music, but also into the patterns of leadership in the assembly. In this respect it builds on the Lutheran books which preceded it. It also breaks new ground. There is a transforming power to its vision of differentiated and shared leadership roles cooperating in the assembly for worship.

Since the 1960s liturgical scholarship in many Christian churches has attempted to recover a vision of the assembly for worship that is an expression of the ancient meaning of "liturgy"—work of the people. In many churches in the Western world this has become a working principle and a conviction that underlies many of the directions that worship has moved. This conviction is consistent with biblical studies of the same period which also rediscovered themes that focus attention on the assembly for worship as a people gathered and ordered, where many lead according to their gifts and call.

St. Paul says in Roman 12:

> For as in one body we have many members, and not all the members have the same function, so we, who are many, are one body in Christ, and individually we are members one of another. We have gifts that differ according to the grace given to us: prophecy in proportion to faith; ministry, in ministering;

the teacher in teaching; the exhorter in exhortation; the giver, in generosity; the leader, in diligence; the compassionate, in cheerfulness (NRSV Romans 12:4-8).

This vision of a body with many and diverse members but ordered for ministry to and by the whole body is a hallmark of Paul's theology. It occurs, in slightly different forms, again in 1 Corinthians 6 and Ephesians 4.

This biblical vision is not the only perspective on leadership in the New Testament. Service is at the heart of the vision of Christian leadership in the New Testament. This is Christ's admonition to his disciples to understand his unique vision of leadership in his community.

So Jesus called them and said to them, "You know that among the Gentiles those whom they recognize as their rulers lord it over them, and their great ones are tyrants over them. But it is not so among you; but whoever wishes to become great among you must be your servant, and whoever wishes to be first among you must be slave of all. For the Son of Man came not to be served but to serve, and to give his life a ransom for many" (NRSV Mark 10:43-45).

This pattern of servant-based leadership is a Christological affirmation—not merely a matter of leadership style or political correctness.

The Inter-Lutheran Commission on Worship (ILCW) was a proponent of this vision of leadership in the liturgical assembly even before *LBW* was published in 1978. With the publication of *Contemporary Worship 2: The Holy Communion* in 1970 the vision of the ILCW was articulated in unmistakable terms.

The service should never be led by one minister alone. The presiding minister is always ordained, but should be assisted by others both clergy and lay. Otherwise, the symbolism of a truly corporate action is blurred. The core of the presiding minister's role is the Great Thanksgiving.[1]

The ILCW built this conviction into the details of the proposed eucharistic rite.

Two roles are differentiated in the rubrics. Those parts usually reserved to the presiding minister are marked *Presiding Minister*. Other parts marked *Assisting Minister* are done either by a layperson or another clergyperson.

The assistant's role might also be divided between two people.

If the parish has two pastors, one may assume some of the assistant's role. But in no case should this preclude lay participation. As a minimum, layperson should read the first and second lessons.

Besides the actions suggested for the assistant, laypersons may serve as acolytes and in other ways. The various utilitarian acts they perform, however, should not be given undue prominence.[2]

This technique of differentiating leadership roles using rubrics that identify the presiding minister and the assisting minister was carried to a new level in *LBW*. It there took on a new level of sophistication and employed a rather elegant typographical character in the text of the book. The designers placed the letter 🅿 for "presiding minister" and the letter 🅰 for "assisting minister." Typographical characters were then printed in red (as a "rubric" would indicate).

Speaking for itself, the introduction to *LBW* identified this differentiation of ministers in the assembly among its "several goals."

An examination of the contents will reveal the several goals toward which the Commission worked in liturgy: to restore to Holy Baptism the liturgical rank and dignity implied by Lutheran theology; and to draw out the baptismal motifs in such acts as the confession of sin and the burial of the dead; to continue to move into the larger ecumenical heritage of liturgy while, at the same time, enhancing Lutheran convictions about the gospel; *to involve lay persons as assisting ministers who share the leadership of corporate worship* [emphasis added]; to bring the language of prayer and praise into conformity with the best current usage; to offer a variety of musical styles.[3]

For Lutherans in North America who had been largely accustomed to the liturgical leadership of an ordained pastor in the liturgy, especially the liturgy of Holy Communion, this move, which was being experimented within some congregations, raised the role of lay leadership to a new level of consciousness. While the dignity of lay readers and lay ministers of communion was growing, and while the ministry of acolytes was a familiar one in many congregations, the partnership of an assisting minister with the ordained pastor changed the shape of the question in many congregations. Those congregations that embraced this ministry in a robust way found patterns of leadership altered. To support the vision, pastors and

Encountering God

worship committees had to begin a new program of gift identification and training for service. Longstanding ministries of ushers and altar guilds also found a new consciousness in this understanding of liturgical ministry and leadership. It may also have encouraged or helped to encourage the vision of the "cantor" as a lay office for musicians in Lutheran congregations.[4]

The vehicle for putting this vision into the hands of congregations was *LBW*, the book itself, its design, as well as its introductory materials and its various supporting volumes.

MINISTERS

The Presiding Minister and Preacher

At the time the ILCW was working, several terms were being employed in various church bodies to describe the liturgical ministry of the pastor of a congregation. "Celebrant" was used in some churches. This usage continues informally among some Lutherans today and in other churches. It is an unhappy choice to describe the ministry of the ordained since it can suggest that one person is active in the liturgy while others are not. A preferable choice was made by the ILCW when it chose to employ the term "presiding minister" as a complementary term to "assisting minister."

These terms are rooted in a vision of the assembly where different gifts and calls result in different service. The ordained minister presides over a liturgical celebration where all present celebrate together. Every participant is in some sense a "celebrant." Like a good convener for a meeting, the presiding minister has certain prescribed functions for the sake of the unity of the assembly. Within the assembly for worship every baptized participant exercises his or her own voice by speaking and singing, standing and sitting or kneeling. The presiding minister is assigned the important task of speaking for all those present—as the voice of the assembly.

Presiding in the Holy Communion in *LBW* means caring for the whole of the liturgical assembly. This ministry comes to expression in speaking the apostolic greeting, giving voice to the assembly's prayer in the Prayer of the Day, announcing and reading the Gospel, preaching the Sermon, concluding the Prayers, announcing the Peace, leading the Great Thanksgiving, and blessing the congregation. When the Brief Order for Confession and Forgiveness is used prior to the Eucharist the presiding minister is the designated leader and pronounces the forgiveness of God to the congregation. All other leadership functions in the rite may be shared or properly belong to other members of the assembly.

In some contexts the preaching of the sermon will be given to another ordained minister. Occasionally, and under the close supervision of the pastor, other persons who are not ordained may also be invited to preach. The richest vision of presiding ministry holds these tasks of preaching and presiding to be aspects of the same ministry. Dividing these ministries may help to increase the number of leaders in a given liturgy. It does so by making a division between the leader to whom the congregation looks for leadership in the liturgy and the leader to whom one looks for exposition of the Word of God. Since these are not separable in the liturgical context, preaching and presiding are most congruent when the same leader exercises leadership in both of them.

There are prudential exceptions to this principle, but they are exceptions. A pastor visiting in a congregation might be invited to preach rather than to preside and preach—allowing the congregation's pastor to preside as usual, allowing the guest not to have to come to terms with the local customs and practices that might be complicated or unfamiliar. In a similar way, congregations with several pastors on staff may choose to assign the preaching task to a pastor different from the pastor presiding, thus allowing a responsible use of preparation time among staff. Clergy from other churches who cannot be expected to be practiced in the leadership of a liturgy from a church other than their own, might also be invited to preach.

The commitment to the presiding role of the ordained minister is consistent both with long custom in the Western church and with the special emphasis given to called and ordained ministry in the Lutheran confessions. "It is taught among us that nobody should publicly teach or preach or administer the sacraments in the church without a regular call."[5] It is certainly no manifestation of "clericalism." On the contrary, by specifying the presider's role clearly, the *LBW* rite invites a vigorous and responsible partnership with many other leaders.

For the *LBW*'s vision of shared and differentiated leadership to come to fullest expression, the commitment to leadership which always involves laity cannot be over stated. Rather than parceling leadership roles out among several clergy (as *Contemporary Worship* had suggested as an interim measure) the partnership between ordained liturgical leaders and lay liturgical leaders, including musicians, needs careful, unwavering, and systematic support. Such support undercuts fears that laity are somehow devalued by liturgical worship. It also helps, on a practical level to overcome the false dichotomy that is often pointed to between ordained ministry and the priesthood of all baptized believers.

Leadership at the Daily Prayers of the Church

The vision of differentiated and shared leadership also comes to expression in the Divine Office: Morning Prayer (Matins), Evening Prayer (Vespers), and Prayer at the Close of Day (Compline) in *LBW*. Ordained leadership is not required for these offices. Rather than finding rubrical indicators for presiding and assisting ministers, in these offices the indicators are for a leader and the congregation. These are indicated in the typographical style noted above, using an Ⓛ rather than a Ⓟ. When an ordained minister is the leader for these services the final blessing takes a different form. Lay leadership is consistent with the origins and long monastic practice of the Divine Office.

VESTURE

The Holy Communion

When it comes to the exercise of presiding ministry there are tools which can complement and support the vision of presiding ministry which is so important to *LBW*. Vesture, the place from the presiding minister leads the assembly, ceremonial, musical intonations, are all important resources. The primary purpose of all these resources is to serve the identification of leaders and enhance the participation of everyone in the assembly for worship. They are techniques of communication on several levels.

These supporting resources can serve to shape the stylistic aspects of the liturgy of Holy Communion. It is important to recall that the logic of *LBW* does not wed it to any one liturgical or ceremonial style.

The services of the *Lutheran Book of Worship* embody the tradition of worship which received characteristic shape during the early centuries of the church's existence and was reaffirmed during the Reformation era. As such, they are an emblem of continuity with the whole church and of particular unity with Lutherans throughout the world. At the same time, the services are adaptable to various circumstances and situations. Freedom and flexibility in worship is a Lutheran inheritance, and there is room for ample variety in ceremony, music, and liturgical form.[6]

The *LBW* has contributed to the recovery of historic usage in many respects. The use of vesture is one example of this recovery. The 1960s and 70s, the period of development, were a time of experimentation with vesture among North American Lutherans. The older pattern of vesture had largely become a cassock and surplice as the basic vesture with a stole (in the color appropriate to the day or seasons) added for the ordained minister. This had come to replace the use of a black "preaching gown" or "academic gown" among North American Lutherans—though these had, strictly speaking never been considered vestments in the classical sense. The use of the alb and cincture came to replace the cassock and surplice in many contexts. Choirs, lay readers, assisting ministers, lay ministers of Holy Communion, servers and acolytes all found the alb (and cincture) a congenial vestment. The stole continued to be used to identify the ordained minister. Alb and stole are now clearly the dominant form of vesture for liturgy among Lutherans in North America.

This return to the foundational Western eucharistic vestment (the alb) also made it possible to consider recovering the chasuble as the vestment for the presiding minister at the Eucharist. While this usage had continued among many European Lutherans it was not in general use in North America prior to the introduction of *LBW*. Today it is a common, though not universal, form of vesture among Lutherans. The use of the chasuble is perhaps the most visually powerful way to designate the presiding minister at the Eucharist. Wearing the chasuble from the beginning of the liturgy or vesting in it at the offertory, just prior to the Great Thanksgiving, are both patterns of use that are practiced by Lutheran presiding ministers today.

Since the introduction of *LBW*, intensive discussions and church-based studies of ministries have further complicated the use of vesture. Building on the tradition of deaconesses and lay professional ministers, several kinds of lay ministry have been affirmed in the Evangelical Lutheran Church in America and the Evangelical Lutheran Church in Canada. How to designate these ministries when they come to expression in the church's liturgy has become a common question. The presumed "easy" answer to the question, the use of a "deacon's stole" (a stole worn over the left shoulder and across the chest and crossed at the waist on the right side) is a novelty that does not contribute to clarity. Since Lutherans have used the stole to designate ordained ministry of Word and Sacrament, and since Lutherans in North America have declined to make the ministry of deacon or diaconal ministry an ordained ministry of the whole church, the use of a stole in this context makes a very confused and inconsistent witness. Ecumenically, the usage can easily give offence by presuming that ordained deacons from traditions that ordain them are no different than the carefully designated lay ministries of Lutherans embracing this usage. The use of a dalmatic or tunic, which does not carry the same connotations as the stole for Lutherans, may be a better course to pursue. These are sleeved vestments, usually in the color of the day or season and coordinated but distinguished from the design of the chasuble worn by the presiding minister at the Eucharist.

Vesture for lay ministers is most appropriately the alb. Because of its association as a baptismal garment, and as its name suggests (alb is the Latin for "white"), it should be white. The use of colored "albs" as choir vestments seems to undercut this association. Lay assisting ministers are best vested in white at the Holy Communion.

The Daily Prayer of the Church

Vesture for Morning Prayer, Evening Prayer, and Prayer at the Close of Day follows two traditions. The use of cassock and surplice as the basic vesture is rooted in the use of the surplice as a climatic accommodation of the alb to the temperatures in Northern Europe. Its use continues in Anglican/Episcopal usages in many places. The Anglican/Episcopal use of a tippet for choir offices did not generally find a use among Lutherans. The use of an alb as the foundational vestment is also common today and is reflected in modern Roman usage in North America. Additional solemnity is often added to festival celebrations of the Divine Office by vesting the leader (whether ordained or lay) in a cope of the color of the day or season. A cope designates the leader in a dramatic fashion. A sense of solemnity is heightened when a cope is worn by each having a leadership role.

THE PRESIDING MINISTER'S CHAIR

The placement of the chair from which the presiding minister will lead the assembly is another important tool for supporting that leadership. Deciding from where the presiding minister will lead necessitates careful attention to the architectural realities of the worship space. Placing the presider's chair to one side of the chancel facing the altar is a traditional location. This has the advantage of keeping the presiding minister out of the major sight lines. It can have the weakness of making this minister difficult to see, thereby compromising the leadership which it should enhance and serve.

Roman Catholic usage today tends to locate the president's chair directly behind a freestanding altar on a platform or off to one side of the altar or the other facing the congregation. The chair needs to be located so that the presiding minister does not have to move to some other place in order to be seen or heard by the assembly. Movement to the altar for the presiding minister's spoken leadership prior to the Great Thanksgiving is not desirable. It confuses the relationship of the altar to the meal with an older usage that identified the altar as *the* place for leadership.

Presiding from the chair also helps to build on the sense of place for everyone in the assembly. This is not a rigid issue but one that honors the whole assembly and all its various members within the space for worship. Locating the chair so that the presiding minister can be seen clearly, and heard with no difficulty and so that motion to and from the pulpit or ambo and the altar can be made with grace and a minimum of distraction, all contribute to graceful presiding. Chairs for the assisting minister and an acolyte to hold the presider's book should also be considered in the placement of the presiding minister's chair. The traditional pattern for such seating is to place the presiding minister in the center chair with the assisting ministers on either side.

When daily prayer is celebrated, the location of the leader's chair is also an important concern. Again, the architectural shape of the space and the way in which the congregation's seating is configured need to be prior concerns. Cues for the congregation to stand and sit can easily be given by the leader with no spoken requests ("Please stand"; "The congregation may be seated") if the congregation can clearly see the leader simply stand or sit. This also allows the leader to tend to the pace of the office and to safeguard the silences that are so important to its meditative nature.

THE PRAYERS

Among the most important roles assigned to the assisting minister in the *LBW* is the leadership of the Prayers in the Holy Communion. This leadership means reading or speaking the intercessions clearly. It may mean singing the prayers from time to time if that is what the planning process has indicated. The fullest expression of this ministry is not only to speak the prepared words of the prayers but also to prepare them for the assembly. This preparation should ideally arise out of the relationship which the assisting minister has with the community in its daily life and ministry. This relationship of the leader of prayer to the concrete and specific needs of the community recovers for the church the ancient model expressed in the ministry of the deacon in the early church. A person assigned by the church to deal with the needs of the community and of strangers and others in need is the ideal voice for those needs when the church assembles for worship.

This vision of prayer and the voice of prayer necessitates that the assisting minister be an integral part of the preparation of prayer texts and overall liturgy planning and decision making if the content of the prayers is to ring true before God and in the life of the assembly. The persons preparing the prayers will need to consult with social ministry committees, education committees, those who care for the sick and dying, and any other parish leaders who address real human needs in the community.

The Prayer of the Day is a prayer common not only to the local community but is rooted in the calendar and lectionary and the relationship of a local assembly to the church catholic, the intercessions, however, should not be from a book. They should come from the lived experience of the local community. Persons should be invited to communicate needs for prayer to a reliable place where this minister will have access to them in plenty of time prior to the liturgy. They should be filled with names to recognize and needs to address. They should ring with joys shared and sorrows borne in common. They should be the living voice of the assembly lifted earnestly before God in common. The privilege of caring for, crafting, and giving voice to this aspect of the Christian life is an awesome ministry.

The *LBW* again models shared leadership between the presiding minister and the assisting minister who speaks the prayers of the assembly. It models a form of prayer where the needs of the church and the world are invited by the assisting minister and then summarized and concluded by the presiding minister. Decisions to collapse these roles into one by having the presiding minister prepare and offer all of the individual intercessions undercuts the vision of shared leadership.

CEREMONIAL

Among Webster's definitions of "ceremonial" is this useful characterization: "stressing careful attention to form and detail." Ceremonial is a neutral technical term to describe a coordinated use of form and detail in the service of an idea or an event or assembly. It need not denote a particular style of ceremony. A Quaker meeting where all wait upon the Spirit exhibits a particular ceremonial. Without skilled and practiced use of ceremony the possibilities of the meeting could easily be lost in chatter and distraction. All liturgy needs to attend to ceremonial.

Planning liturgy means attending to every detail including ceremonial. Unfortunately, ceremonial has a negative connotation in some parts of North American culture today. The cultural expectation that informality is the antithesis of ceremony is a serious mischaracterization. Providing an informal liturgical experience for worship which still allows their fullest and most engaged participation in prayer and praise takes just as many careful ceremonial decisions and as much planning as preparing and leading a very ceremonially rich and formal celebration, it is just that the choices and their consistent implementation will be different.

The keen and often scathing observer of Christians, Annie Dillard, describes this situation with great power.

> It is the second Sunday in Advent. For a year I have been attending Mass at this Catholic church. Every Sunday for a year I have run away from home and joined the circus as a dancing bear. We dancing bears have dressed ourselves in buttoned clothes; we mince around the rings on two feet. Today we were restless; we kept dropping onto our forepaws.
>
> No one, least of all the organist, could find the opening hymn. Then no one knew it.
>
> Then no one could sing anyway.
>
> There was no sermon, only announcements.
>
> The priest proudly introduced the rascally acolyte who was going to light the two Advent candles. As we all could plainly see, the rascally acolyte had already lighted them.
>
> A high school stage play is more polished than this service we have been rehearsing since the year one. In two thousand years, we have not worked out the kinks. We positively glorify them. Week after week we witness the same miracle: that God is so mighty he can stifle his own laughter. Week after week, we witness the same miracle: that God, for reasons unfathomable, refrains from blowing our dancing bear act to smithereens. Week after week Christ washes the disciples' dirty feet, handles their very toes, and repeats, It is all right—believe it or not—to be people.
>
> Who can believe it?[7]

The vocabulary of Christian ceremonial has its origins in several different settings. Roman court ceremonial of the fourth century and later influenced the ceremonial of much of the Western church. In the East, the ceremonial of the Byzantine court was a depository from which to draw. Both of these were cultural sources which had understandable civic connotations in these cultures. They made cultural sense to people. In Northern Europe, the liturgical standardization of Charlemagne became the important source of ceremonial ingredients. These too were often drawn from civil practices and royal or imperial practices. The Reformation preserved many of these ceremonial elements, and it simplified or did away with others.

The *LBW* reopened and recast many ceremonial questions by drawing from early church sources which predated many of the ceremonial decisions and formulas of the Middle Ages. By choosing pre-Constantinian establishment models to guide the shape of the rite, especially of the Eucharist, it was able to add a new and clear and constructive alternative to the Reformation polemics about ceremonial in worship. Healthy and confident worshiping communities following the *LBW* embrace a variety of ceremonial options depending upon the decisions made in the careful planning of Sunday, seasonal, festival, weekday or occasional liturgies. Some will be ceremonially rich. Others will be ceremonially spare. All will be carefully planned and evaluated.

While good ceremonial speaks clearly and obviously it can easily be overlaid with layers of obscure and stipulated meanings. The vesting of the altar as though it were Christ's body is one example of this. Here the paraments take on connotations of Christ's seamless garment and the fair linen become associated with his burial shroud. Ceremony that is congruent does not have to tell people repeatedly what things mean—it is apparent to them. The modern view of church ceremonial is less allegorical and overlaid with meanings and more interested in the functional rootage of particular practices. The altar is seen as a table from which to serve and around which to gather. The paraments are a calendrical and artistic device to communicate the character of particular festival days or Sundays. This approach to ceremonial also seems less arbitrary to the mind of this current time.

What constitutes ceremonial in a Christian liturgical context? Perhaps the simplest characterization is to say that it is "the way we do things together." Ceremonial is a set of recognizable, repeated, conventional behaviors. These can be chosen to distance the worshiping assembly from the surrounding culture or to identify with the surrounding culture. They can be chosen by a community and its worship planners and its educators and catechists to mark off the assembly for worship as a transcendent time and place. The use of vesture and incense are examples of the former. They can be selected to identify with the immanence of Christ in the culture and world. The ceremonial washing of feet or the gesture of shaking hands during the exchange of peace in the Eucharist would be an example of embracing this immanence.

The vocabulary that makes up this ceremonial is ever changing. A few examples of ceremonial in our time would include:

- Postures: standing, sitting, kneeling, bowing
- Gestures: making the sign of the cross, shaking hands at the exchange of peace
- Movement: entering and leaving the worship space: procession and recession; moving to the altar the altar to receive Holy Communion; passing among the congregation to collect an offering; moving to the altar with gifts of food for the hungry, versus collecting those same gifts in the narthex of the church prior to the service
- Treatment of physical objects and persons: carrying a Bible or lectionary book; bowing to the altar or processional cross; presenting gifts of bread and wine; presenting offerings of money; distributing the Holy Communion to the baptized.

INTONATIONS

Singing together is among the most powerful ways of inviting the Spirit to form human community in the worship context—and in other contexts as well. Congregational singing in unison or harmony is a bedrock part of the Christian liturgical experience. Lutherans, since the founding of the movement in the 16th century, have been serious and effective proponents of the power of the church's song. The singing of hymns is one expression of this song. Congregational singing of liturgical music, generally in unison, is another expression of it.

In the context of liturgical song, the role of the presiding minister and assisting ministers also comes to expression in the use of intonations that constitute a kind of sung dialogue between the congregation and its leaders.[8] Perhaps the most important of these moments of musical dialogue are associated with the Great Thanksgiving. From the time of Justin Martyr[9] in the second century this great prayer has begun with a dialogue. The *LBW* continues this ancient practice. The dialogue looks like this:

> ℗ The Lord be with you.
>
> ℭ And also with you.
>
> ℗ Lift up your hearts.
>
> ℭ We lift them to the Lord.
>
> ℗ Let us give thanks to the Lord our God.
>
> ℭ It is right to give him thanks and praise.

Encountering God

This dialogue between the presiding minister and the congregation is the beginning of the Great Thanksgiving. It is followed by a proper preface. It is called "proper" because it changes with each season or festival. It speaks of the particularity of time. It is called "preface" because it precedes the proclamation of the text of the eucharistic prayer.

Virtually every presiding minister should be encouraged and helped to sing this dialogue. It is both a historical witness of great antiquity and an ecumenical witness of great power. The simple intonations here are based more on patterns of speech and the proclamation of the word than on a complicated musical form. Most every person who can speak these words can also learn to intone them.

These are not the only intonations in the *LBW*. Another example from the Holy Communion is the salutation that may precede the Prayer of the Day.

ℙ The Lord be with you.
ℂ And also with you.
ℙ Let us pray.
(Prayer of the Day)

This sung dialogue introduces and invites the congregation to attend to the Prayer of the Day. It is not a sung conclusion to the Hymn of Praise as some congregations seem to assume by their practice of singing this dialogue but speaking the prayer. The integrity of the relationship between leaders and congregation is best maintained when these intonations are sung by the presiding minister and responded to by the congregation. As with other dialogical elements in the liturgy, if they cannot be fully sung by both presiding minister and congregation, they should be spoken by all.

Learning to chant these simple dialogues is a manageable project for virtually all presiding ministers. The foundational skill for chanting is public speech. The simple music supports that. If the presiding minister cannot (or will not) chant these intonations then, for the sake of the logic of the dialogue, everyone should speak them—presider and congregation. In the very rare event that the presiding minister is not able to intone this dialogue, then the congregation should speak its parts as well to preserve the sense of dialogue on which this part of the liturgy is based. A spoken invitation invites a spoken response. A sung invitation invites a sung response.

Presiding ministers can go the next mile and use simple intonations for the full text of the prayer of the day.[10]

The presiding minister is not the only leader invited to lead sung intonations in *LBW*. An assisting minister (understood in the broadest sense) may intone the parts indicated by **A** in the *Kyrie* in the eucharistic rite, for example. The assisting minister chosen for this intonation may be serving with the presiding minister at the altar, another assisting minister from the choir, or the cantor designated during the planning process to lead these parts of the liturgy. There are many intonations provided for the leader in Morning Prayer and Evening Prayer.

PRESIDING AND PLANNING

If the relationship between the presiding minister, the assisting ministers, and the congregation is to reflect the real dynamics of making shared choices that affect common prayer in the assembly, then the presiding minister needs to be involved in the planning process for the liturgical celebration where those choices are made. Simply being ordained is not adequate for this ministry. While that is indispensable, it is not a substitute for actual involvement in decision-making. Planning and decision-making as well as teaching all those involved in the liturgical celebration is also an important aspect of presiding ministry.

This planning/teaching process works most effectively if it includes as many persons involved in the liturgy and its support as possible. Ushers, acolytes, altar guild members, readers, musicians all need to be working together in the planning process. Those who cannot be personally involved in the planning process need to be carefully briefed and trained so that they may interpret and answer questions about the decisions that were made in common. Several guides for planning together are available.[11] This supports and encourages the vision of the *LBW* for shared leadership which is participatory.

THE MINISTRY OF HOSPITALITY

In the last few years of the twentieth century Christian communities in North America have recovered a more robust sense of the need for welcome and hospitality to the assembly for worship. This turn toward the visitor or stranger is eminently consistent with the vision of Christian leadership that is so important to the *LBW*. Leaders in the assembly are not only those who serve in the chancel and at the altar and the place of reading but also those who serve in the entry space.

Persons engaged in the ministry of caring for those things used in worship, sacristans and altar guild members, also exercise a ministry which serves God in the assembly for worship and those assembled. Few things are as disruptive to the assembly's life together as lacking what is needed for each and every celebration of Holy Communion, daily prayer, services of the Word, or other liturgies of the church. The altar guild or sacristan will steward these requirements for the assembly. Their work often happens before or after the liturgy itself. It is, nonetheless, a gracious and indispensable ministry.

The ministry of ushers is on the front line of hospitality. Helping persons to find their way in the church building, providing appropriately planned and printed service folders, answering questions, expressing welcome through a confident smile—genuinely offered—is an important place for people to see the church close-up. Genuineness is the key to this ministry. As with all ministries associated with worship not every person has every gift needed for every ministry. Careful effort should be made to identify the gifts needed for the ministry and then to find them in the individuals in the community. Support through personal encouragement and training is important.

If the congregation asks ushers to provide physically demanding work such as the ringing of church bells, the moving of furnishings, etc., then care should also be taken to see to it that persons are not taxed beyond their physical capabilities.

IN CONCLUSION

Few if any privileges compare with the call to lead public worship in a Christian congregation. Thanks to the *LBW* and its vision of leadership we enjoy a broadened and deepened expression of Christian leadership in the assembly for worship. The vision of differentiated and shared leadership opens congregations to a rich and wholesome experience. *Lutheran Book of Worship* and its framers and the generation of worshipers formed by it all owe it a debt of gratitude for this.

NOTES

1 *Contemporary Worship 2: The Holy Communion* (Minneapolis: Augsburg Publishing House; Philadelphia: Board of Publication, Lutheran Church in America; St. Louis: Concordia Publishing House, 1970), p. x.

2 Ibid., p. x.

3 *Lutheran Book of Worship* (Minneapolis: Augsburg Publishing House; Philadelphia: Board of Publication, Lutheran Church in America, 1978), pp. 7-8. Hereafter *LBW*.

4   Paul Westermeyer, *The Church Musician,* revised edition (Minneapolis: Augsburg Fortress, 1997).

5   Augsburg Confession article XIV, *Book of Concord*, Tappert et al. eds. and translators (Philadelphia: Fortress Press, 1959).

6   *LBW*, Introduction, p. 8.

7   Annie Dillard, *Teaching a Stone to Talk: Expeditions and Encounters* (New York: Harper Collins, 1982), pages 37-38.

8   Note that this use of "intonation" is broader than the more technical use which identifies the cantor or organist providing and "intonation" which signals the pitch, pattern, and tempo for congregational singing or singing by a choir.

9   Justin Martyr (c. AD 100-c. AD 165) describes this dialogue in his *First Apology.*

10 See directions for intoning this prayer in *Manual on the Liturgy* (Minneapolis: Augsburg Publishing House, 1979), pages 215-217. Additional helps for practicing all of the intonations in *Lutheran Book of Worship* are available on a audio cassette tape, *Singing the Liturgy: Building Confidence for Worship Leaders.*

11 See for example, *Sundays and Seasons* (Minneapolis: Augsburg Fortress). This is an annual planning guide which includes alternate texts and background materials.

MUSICAL LEADERSHIP

Paul Westermeyer

LOOKING BACK FROM THE FUTURE

The year is 2198. You are a historian writing about church music and musicians in the late 20th century. You have found a rare-book room devoted to the 20th century where several shelves of books are related to worship, hymnology, and the church's music. Among them you discover the spate of hymnals and worship books that began to appear in 1978 with the *Lutheran Book of Worship*[1] (*LBW*) and continued to the end of the century, eventually encompassing virtually every denomination. You line them up in chronological order and decide to make notes about their contents. For the *LBW* you write the following:

Introduction
>   stands in continuity with Christian worship "across the ages"
>   details about Lutheran groups

Calendars and occasions
>   seasons, commemorations, prayers, psalms, lessons

Athanasian Creed
>   (Apostles' and Nicene Creeds appear in services at appropriate places)

Services and propers
>   four Holy Communion services
>   three the same texts with different music
>   Baptism
>   Word

Daily prayer offices
  Morning Prayer
  Evening Prayer
  Prayer at the Close of Day
  Responsive Prayer
Litany
Propers and Psalms for daily prayer
Daily lectionary
Confession
  corporate, individual
Affirmation of Baptism
Marriage
Burial
Psalter (with some omissions)
Hymnal (569 canticles and hymns — wide variety)
Acknowledgments and indexes
permeated with music
presumes a singing congregation and a musical leader

You are impressed that this full round of liturgical and musical materials is compressed between the covers of a book that measures about nine by six inches and is about an inch and a half thick. You discover its contents spill out into and are complemented by other related books. In a Ministers Edition[2] you find further notes, Holy Week services, additional indexes, and the complete psalter. You also find a manual[3] with longer essays; a companion[4] with still more essays plus detailed commentaries on each hymn, author, and composer in the hymnal; a concordance[5] to the hymn texts; and commentaries.[6] Later you notice a paperback supplement called *With One Voice*[7] *(WOV)* and a worship wordbook[8], both published when the *LBW* was 17 years old. A shelf full of resources seems to have been prepared to go with the *LBW*.

Musical Forces

You are particularly interested in learning about musical leadership in churches at the end of the 20th century, especially as revealed in the rites and hymns of the *LBW*. You set out to determine what kind of musical leadership the *LBW* presumed. As you begin your analysis you realize that you must first sort out the music and musical forces that are expected before you can decipher who might have led them. You delineate the following.

The Congregation's Song. The congregation's song appears to be a central component in the churches for which this book was prepared. Hymns take up the largest part of the book, and the psalms are pointed for singing

    Encountering God

by the congregation as well. The Holy Communion services, Morning Prayer, Evening Prayer, Prayer at the Close of Day, and the Litany all provide congregational music in the services. With the exception of Individual Confession, all the other services make provision for canticles, psalms, or hymns to be sung by the congregation. At virtually every point the congregation is assumed to have a role as important as those in liturgical and musical leadership, and it seems to be expressed most often through musical participation. That participation includes a wide variety of styles from across the church's history—strophic hymns and metrical psalms, poetic but non-metrical texts such as the *Gloria in excelsis* of the ordinary (those invariable texts in the eucharistic liturgy), and psalm singing of all sorts with ten psalm tones provided. Obviously, the people and their song were matters of great importance to the framers of this book.

Choirs. You notice that the proper verse and the offertory for the Holy Communion liturgy are assigned to a choir, and you assume such a group must have been envisioned to lead the congregation in its singing. You look in the manual and find your expectations confirmed. "The choir," it says, "gives vocal leadership to the congregation in the people's part of the liturgy."[9] You read a little farther and discover that the choir not only leads the congregation, but may also alternate with it on stanzas of hymns—the choral stanzas might be more elaborate than the congregational ones. A few paragraphs later the proper Verse and Offertory are referred to as assignments for the choir, plus numerous possibilities for singing the psalms with the congregation. A few pages later[10] even more choral possibilities and responsibilities are discussed. On occasion, the choir could sing a setting of the ordinary on behalf of the congregation. Introits, entrance songs, and processional hymns suggest numerous opportunities for choral involvement. During the communion the choir can help the congregation sing hymns, but may also sing pieces by itself. Motets, cantatas, and anthems all find their place in the choir's liturgical responsibilities. These grow out of the singing of the appointed Gospel and its proclamation in cantatas that may surround the sermon and the hymn of the day.[11]

So, while the congregation's song seems central, choirs have both a supporting and an independent role. How these roles are carried out varies from what is quite simple to what may be quite complex, and seems to admit all sorts of possibilities for choirs of various capacities and skills. A one-person choir—a vocal soloist or cantor—is even envisaged.[12] The range that is possible for choral song is very wide — from a complex polyphonic cantata with multiple voices and instruments to one unaccompanied singer.

Organs. As you finish the section on the choir, you notice that organs are immediately mentioned. Historically the organ came late, according to the manual, but it developed rapidly after the Reformation "to its present position of eminence as the premier instrument for leading worship in the liturgical church."[13] By it the organist leads the people in their singing, introduces hymns, varies accompaniments, alternates with the congregation as the choir does, and plays preludes, postludes, and other voluntaries.

Other Instruments. Though the organ may be regarded as the most important liturgical instrument, other instruments are also welcomed.[14] They can be combined with the organ, or may be used in the same way as the organ. The range of instruments seems to encompass all the orchestral ones plus bells, guitars, percussion, and by implication whatever makes sounds. Sound amplification that does not overwhelm congregational singing is also included in the list of possibilities.[15]

Vesture and Ceremonial .You know that Luther retained the traditions and practices of worship he inherited and that the Introduction to the *LBW* reflected that position when it said the book stands in continuity with Christian worship "across the ages." You also know that Luther thought some things in worship were essentials, some were non-essentials and that the Lutheran tradition freely employs a wide variety of non-essentials, or chooses to use but a few. You notice that vestments for the ministers are discussed in an ecumenical context,[16] though there seems to be no comparable discussion regarding vestments for the choir. You learn that lectors need not be vested,[17] therefore you conclude that the choir may or may not be vested. The implication would appear to be that, should choir vestments be worn, they would be similar to those worn by the clergy—that is, white albs, though without a stole. They would not be calculated for show. Their point seems to be that leaders do not get to show off their secular finery at worship, but are liturgically vested to represent humanity standing sacramentally before God.

A similar logic seems to hold for gesture. It appears to be taken seriously,[18] but does not seem to be prescribed. The importance of Baptism in the book implies a pilgrim people who could easily symbolize their pilgrimage by movement in worship, led by the choir, instruments, and their music since music spins itself out in time just the way worship and ritual actions do. Rubrics for movement throughout the book suggest this possibility, as in a procession for the reading of the Gospel, but a minimum of movement would appear equally as possible. Again, you conclude that the book reflects Lutheranism's tolerant attitude toward practices that are regarded as non-essential.

Quality. You notice in the Ministers Edition[19] that a statement about music at weddings and funerals seems appropriate for every other service as well. It says music is to be of high quality, not trite or sentimental; and it is to be within the capacity of the given community to do "with assurance." This matches what you know of the Lutheran tradition, that it seems to hold together the finest music and the people's abilities, treating the people with the utmost respect. That apparently is why this book's framers were willing to use what may not always have been the easiest music at first blush.[20] You are reminded that you found something of this same idea in the Methodist hymnal that followed the *LBW* by a few years. In that Methodist publication, John Wesley is quoted as encouraging the congregation to sing even if "it is a cross to you." It will, he said, turn out to be a blessing.[21]

Musical Leader

You begin now to sort out what the music and musical forces require for leadership. Musical leaders have many tasks. They could be delineated to include the following: The musician

- leads the congregation
- conducts choral and instrumental groups
- rehearses them
- needs to know about the voice, possibly as a trained singer
- possibly plays the organ
- teaches
- needs to be sensitive to movement which, especially if employed extensively, requires careful preparation
- may need to be concerned about vestments for the choir
- has to engage in substantial planning[22]
- embodies in the planning a concern for quality and treating people well

You begin to sense that the musical leadership implied could easily require a lifetime of training. As you feather this out you realize that the musicians

- would have to study the voice and instruments as the finest music educators or conductors do
- must conduct well and rehearse well
- need to play the organ with a high degree of skill
- are expected to know a wide range of literature for various seasons of the church year

- apply that literature to the community being served on its behalf,
- develop the skills of a fine teacher
- improvise well
- compose well
- practice
- study and plan well with the kind of resources that go with the *LBW* so that over time a coherent whole develops.

You also sense, however, that the *LBW* does not only suggest all the activity of weekly rehearsing that the preceding lists would require. It also presumes an equally valid expression in a community that might have no choirs or instrumentalists, where the musician may not be highly trained. Presumably such a musical leader would enable the congregation to engage in a high quality of musical response, but one that is not so complex. It might employ voices alone without any instrumental accompaniment or choirs at all. The same shelf of resources would be available, but applied in a different context.

A wide range of congregations seems to have been envisaged. In some the eucharistic assembly on Sunday morning could have been one of the few gatherings for the week. For the rest of the week the members of that community of faith could have been dispersed vocationally in their rural, suburban, or urban settings. In other congregations a highly developed musical life might have required rehearsals during the week and many groups who would come together to rehearse. Between these two extremes wide varieties of possibilities seem to suggest themselves. You realize now that you have come upon matters that are more than musical. You have to ask what is the point of all this? The musical leader is obviously not simply a musician, but is a church musician. What might that mean?

You remember seeing a book called *The Church Musician*. You pull it from the shelf and discover that Lutherans wrote it and its foreword. While the writers, Paul Westermeyer and Martin Marty, had nothing to do with forming the *LBW*, you sense that they in no way contradict it, but affirm its spirit and counsel. You discover that Westermeyer defines the church musician as the "cantor"—the chief singer or leader of the people's song that includes the potential for all the choral and instrumental activity the *LBW* presumes to be possible. Then, getting to what he calls "the heart of the matter," Westermeyer defines the church's song as praise, prayer, proclamation, story, and gift. That gives clues to the dimensions of the cantor's task.[23]

Leading the People's Praise. The cantor is the leader of the people's praise. The congregation's vigorous response to God's grace, to be expressed through the rich medium of music, needs form and shape. The cantor's role is to take responsibility for that forming and shaping. Musical leadership of the people's praise means understanding the capacities and resources of a particular congregation, then writing or choosing music which expresses the praise of God with those capacities and resources in mind. Once the music is composed and chosen, the cantor must then lead the people in it, singing this song of praise.

The song of praise is preeminently vocal. Words are the means by which praise is articulated, and music is the means by which the articulation is carried aloft. Song gives wings to the words. But not only humanity sings this song of praise. The whole creation is called to join in, including "angels and archangels." Instruments are to play their part as well. Their part is not only to accompany the voices, but also to sound alone where fitting and appropriate. The cantor is the one who co-ordinates this and even plays as talents warrant, so that instrumental music also relates to the people's song of praise. Neither instrumental music nor any other music is to be treated as an afterthought or an unrelated addendum.

Leading the People's Prayer. The cantor aids the presiding and assisting ministers in leading the people's prayer. The presiding and assisting ministers bear the primary responsibility for the prayers and petitions of a particular service, and the pastor bears the ultimate responsibility for the prayer life of the congregation. The cantor assists in this responsibility in the following ways.

First, the cantor provides the leadership for the people's litanic responses, spoken and sung. Corporate responses to the bids, even when spoken, are incipiently musical — that is, elated forms of speech. The cantor through his or her direct leadership, and through training the choir, shapes this response and thereby helps to shape the prayer life of the people.

Second, since some hymns are themselves prayers, the cantor sometimes leads the people in prayer by leading hymns. The choir also sings some texts that are prayers. In this case the cantor leads a group who prays on behalf of the people just as the presiding minister does. This is obviously not a performance before the people, but an act of intercession for and with the people.

Proclaiming the Word. The cantor aids the readers in the proclamatory work of reading the appointed lessons. This may sometimes involve the use of more or less complex choral or solo settings of lessons that are sung rather than read. Though such a worthy practice may not be normative, it deserves to be considered from time to time. When lessons are sung by the lectors, the cantor should train those who do the singing. Similarly when lessons are read, the choral musician helps readers read clearly and meaningfully. Such musicians know about phrasing, diction and enunciation, as well as the most effective ebb and flow of words. Musicians can help lectors read in ways that gain the reverent attention of the hearer.

The preacher obviously has the primary proclamatory task of publishing the good news of God's grace and love. By careful application to the biblical word and the daily news, the preacher speaks human words in the hope that they will be received and heard as God's Word, so that the love of God in Christ through the Holy Spirit will be known and shared among the congregation.

The cantor cannot and should not attempt to "preach" in the same way as the preacher for at least two reasons. First, the time required for composition of text and music and the preparation of music by musicians cannot match the sermon's relevance to the moment. Second, the preacher can examine texts and relationships in spoken prose in ways not possible for the musician.

On the other hand, a polyphonic piece of music or the simultaneous juxtaposition of two texts gives the musician an opportunity to proclaim relationships in a way that is not available to the preacher who must communicate in a single stream of words. And, while the relevance of the moment is not the responsibility of music which of necessity demands preparation that often begins many weeks before a given service, music has the capacity for breaking open a text in a way spoken words cannot. In singing a hymn or hearing a Schütz motet or a Bach cantata, many people have shared William Cowper's experience.

> Sometimes a light surprises
> The Christian while he sings;
> It is the Lord who rises
> With healing in his wings.[24]

Telling the Story. The cantor helps the people sing the whole biblical story and thereby helps them tell the story. The preacher also tells the story, of course, as does the teacher. Some understandings of preaching would even argue that it is at heart storytelling. There is a sense in which that is true: Proclaiming the good news is telling the story of God's love. But the preacher is always compelled to apply the story in the moment so that the searing edge of God's love can burn its way into the people's hearts. This requires the context of the whole story as it is celebrated and proclaimed through the full Sunday liturgy; preaching can only give that context over time or in an ancillary way. The cantor, more than the preacher, is directly responsible for the context and the fullness of the story all the time.

This means that the cantor tells the story by seeing to it that the whole story is sung. The readings, prayers, and sermon for a given service are likely to have a similar focus. The hymnody, psalmody, and anthems ought to relate to that focus also, but in addition they flesh out the rest of the story and remind the hearers of other parts of the plot. Over the course of a year the whole story needs to be sung, from creation to last things. Doing the same six or ten hymns over and over does not serve the people well, for it prevents them from singing the whole story and omits much of the context the preacher needs for her or his words.

Music is related not simply to the story, but to time. This gives the musician a peculiar and remarkable responsibility. The church musician tells time for the people. In part that is true in singing the story. But in part it is true in direct relation to a service of worship and its music, since music spins itself out in time just the same as worship does. Music accompanies processions, either of all the people or of some of the people for everyone else. This processional nature of the pilgrim people on the move takes place in time. Music articulates that time, as in music that accompanies processions. Beyond that, music articulates worship itself. That is, the church musician is the one who controls the pace and flow of a service. Points of beginning and ending—an entrance rite, the reading of lessons and Gospel followed by sermon, and during the distribution of Holy Communion—almost invariably have musical components that accompany them. This includes silence, which is music's backdrop. The sensitive church musician handles this responsibility with great care and with a genuine sense of concern for the people.

The Steward of God's Gift. The cantor is the steward of God's gracious gift of music. Since this gift is so effective and persuasive, the steward receives an impressive degree of power as its deputy. This power, unfortunately, can be easily misused for such selfish ends as ego gratification and domination over others. The cantor is called, therefore, to the paradox of using the power that is granted, and of using it with restraint on behalf of God in Christ from whom all blessings flow.

That paradox brings with it another. The cantor knows that the lector or preacher can stumble over a word here or there and yet the message will have its impact. To stumble over a musical note is much more consequential. The impact of the message will dissipate much more quickly when there is a musical error, constraining the cantor to press for an excellence and perfection that is ultimately never humanly possible. That drives the church musician to rehearse and practice every detail until it is right, for without practice there is the certainty that the necessary perfection and excellence will never be achieved. The paradox is that even with disciplined rehearsing there is no guarantee. The musician who is at all sensitive knows that when she or he finally gets it right, that too is a gift for which the only appropriate response is thanksgiving.

Approaching the Task. Having determined what to do is not quite enough. Three additional components of the cantor's role need to be stated. They fit under the heading of how to approach the task.

First, the cantor is serving a specific people. That means the cantor needs to allow the song of the people of God in a given place to find expression. That is not done by superimposing an unattainable ideal and then scolding the congregation for failing to reach it. The realistic ideal is found in the congregation, the choir, and the instrumentalists a cantor works with and serves. That's because God is present among them with the song. The cantor's responsibility is to allow that song to find expression. That is the ideal.

This is not to suggest that there are no standards. Indeed, there are standards for music just as the Ten Commandments are standards for living. The church as a community of grace, however, begins with grace, not with the law. Likewise, the cantor begins with God's gracious gift of music among a given people and not with arbitrary legal constructs and rules of constraint. The incipient song must find expression. Essentially, this means selecting durable music that is worth the people's time and effort, then doing things musically so that the people are invited to sing. The example of a beautifully shaped phrase, organ playing that breathes with the people, rhythm that pulsates, and melodies that sing — these all do more to give the song expression than heavy-handed rules and legalistic constraints, as musical people instinctively know.

Second, the cantor's craft is exercised with kindness and compassion. Some musicians are allowed to be temperamental because artists are often thought to be naturally short-tempered and need to be humored. Humoring such musicians includes, unfortunately, permitting them to throw temper tantrums and to treat people shabbily.

Church musicians ought not to imitate their example. The responsible cantor knows another reality: That all people are to be treated with respect because God loves them all. Music is for people. People are not for music.

This is not to suggest that cantors can be expected to be more perfect than other groups of people. Cantors, like all musicians and all people, will sometimes get angry, lose their tempers, and be temperamental. Rather, it is to suggest that the ideal is kindness and compassion and that we gather around the song God gives and not around the personality of the conductor, no matter how able he or she may be.

Third, the leadership of the song is a complex matter that needs great sensitivity. There are times, such as Easter Sunday morning on a triumphant hymn of resurrection joy, when the organ can appropriately drive the congregation with a powerful rhythmic punch. Generally the organ should lead — sensitively, but lead. There are other times, however, such as the singing of responsorial psalms or prayers, when neither organ nor conducting seems appropriate, as the community finds its own tempo with only a breath from the cantor to set things in motion. George Black, former president of the Hymn Society in the United States and Canada, is credited with saying that a community of love will sing together, that to tamper with the people's prayer is a tricky business, and that sometimes the people should be free to set their own tempo. Cantors need to ponder such matters and experience them with their communities of faith. Church musicians need not always conduct nor overtly control everything with the voice or organ or other instruments. That is not leadership so much as an exhibition of insecurities and an unwillingness to allow the people's voice to find expression.

Leadership, then, involves a balance of many items. The style of music is one. A rhythmic chorale from the sixteenth century, for example, has a different "ideal" tempo from a nineteenth century tune. The nature of the text is another. The place the text and its music are located in the liturgy is yet another. Then there are matters such as the time of the year, the time of the day, the weather, the size and acoustics of the building, the traditions and backgrounds of a congregation (ethnicity, language, geography), the nature of the community (young or old, good or ill health), the size of the group, the pacing of the pastor, and the cantor's own tendencies. All of these things have to be considered. They need thoughtful attention before the service, but they also require responses in the moment to the music making itself. Wonderful surprises happen when cantors are sensitive and allow them to occur.

A Brief Summary. That is the way Westermeyer expresses the vocation of the church musician. A similar statement on the role of the cantor has been produced by the Association of Lutheran Church Musicians, an organization which was formed after the *LBW* was completed. Again, there seems to be no explicit connection with the *LBW*, but one senses that the statement expresses the sentiments of that book, this time in a concise way that looks as if it were prepared for use on a poster. It reads like this.

The Role of the Cantor

When Christ's people, the baptized, gather for worship,
   they receive God's love in Word and Sacrament,
   and through the gift of music,
     praise, pray, proclaim, and recount
     the story of God's grace in song.

The cantor—the historical term among Lutherans—
   is the leader of the people's song.

The cantor is responsible for leading the musical expression
     of the people—
   the assembly, choral groups, solo singers, and instrumentalists,
   among whom organists have been especially important
     for Lutherans.

The cantor uses whatever musical resources are available,
   in a manner appropriate
     to the talents of those serving
     and the needs of those being served.

The cantor leads the earthly assembly
   in a foretaste of John's vision of the heavenly assembly
     in which all creatures give
     praise, honor, glory, and power
     to the Lamb.

The cantor's work is worthy service
   to God,
   God's people,
   and the world.
     It is a high and holy calling.

NOW

So far you have analyzed the *LBW* and the music and musical forces it assumed. From that analysis you derived the nature of the musical leadership that was required. Your next step is to ask how much of what you discovered received actual historical embodiment. Did late 20th century church musicians actually do what was implied and live out their callings in the spirit of the *LBW*, or did that book set up a theoretical construct which never took shape? That is the question with which we take leave of your alter ego in the 22nd century and return to the 20th century to ask it of ourselves.

An Overriding Reality

Church musicians have not controlled the answer themselves so much, because they have been controlled as much by the communities they have served as by their own conscious choosing. That suggests multiple answers to the question and a far bigger context than the *LBW*. Before getting to those matters, however, one overriding reality must be noted, namely, that the majority of Lutherans in North America is using the *LBW*. Admittedly, it is probably a rare congregation that has sung all 569 of its hymns and canticles, although it's not unusual to hear of those where between 400 and 500 are fairly well known and used with some regularity.

The liturgical music is also being sung. Many congregations know the first two settings of the Holy Communion virtually from memory. *LBW*s in pew racks are well thumbed at those service settings, and when Lutherans from various congregations come together they sing the liturgy vigorously.

In this overriding sense, musical leaders have lived out the central feature of their vocations: They have led the people in their song and done it well. True, there may be musicians who have worked in the church but are not committed to being church musicians. They may have been more interested in developing choirs or instrumental groups that served as performers.

It is also true that a far greater number of Lutheran church musicians have been committed to their role of leading the people and have done it as well as their abilities allowed. They have also developed the choral and instrumental groups in an amazing array of shapes and forms. Vocal choirs, instrumental ensembles, and bell choirs have been recruited and rehearsed week after week. Some of them fit the spirit of the *LBW* by contributing to the flow of worship in an unobtrusive and lively way. Others have intruded and turned their music-making at worship into concertizing. Musical leaders have reflected these tendencies as much as the congregations they have served. By and large, however, church musicians have sensed their vocation and have tried to live it out, very often precisely in the spirit of the *LBW*. They have practiced, learned, attended conferences, studied, searched out suitable music, taught, and sought to practice in their communities a compassionate living out of their musical responsibilities. There are exceptions, to be sure, where musicians have allowed their egos to ride roughshod over their serving, but these are exceptions rather than the rule.

Multiple Answers

When one probes a little deeper, the overriding reality breaks into three or four smaller answers to the question posed above regarding the impact of the *LBW*. They group themselves not so much according to individual church musicians, but to the responses parishes or groups within parishes have made. These responses merge into one another in various combinations, though they are distinct enough to be separated.

1. Warm Embrace. One response has been to embrace the *LBW* fully and work out its implications. The group that responds this way has used most of the hymns. Here it is also likely that most if not all of the services will be known and used fully, and the Easter Vigil and the Triduum are being observed as well.

Congregations who have made this response not only know the *LBW*, but they have added to it. They may pass out new hymns with their bulletins and are likely to have the *Hymnal Supplement 1992*,[25] *With One Voice (WOV)*, or both of those paperbacks in their pew racks. They will use hymns from those books and possibly settings of the liturgy as well. They experiment, always in search of the finest craft. For example, they may know all four settings of the Holy Communion in the *LBW* plus "Now the Feast and Celebration" by Marty Haugen in the GIA *Hymnal Supplement*. They may also know a couple settings in pamphlet form such as the ones by Gary Cornell[26] and Dale Wood.[27] They may know Evening Prayer in the *LBW* plus the Holden Village setting by Marty Haugen.[28] The number of settings and styles available boggles the mind.[29] Congregations cannot possibly keep pace with all of these, but those in this group nevertheless have assimilated an amazing number of texts and music, in many styles and from many times and places. They keep adding, replacing, growing, and finding new insights in the *LBW* itself, which has opened them up to a wider world of possibilities. They have perceived its structures and spirit and have pursued them creatively. Strong preaching, a vigorous sacramental life, faithful Bible study, and a deep concern for the world may be found in this group of congregations.

The musician in such a parish as this, if she or he is responsible, does live in the spirit of the *LBW* and is generally challenged by the congregation to do so. There may be disputes. People may disagree about details in the *LBW*, about musical styles, hymn texts, what the musician does, what the pastor does, or any number of other things. But where a situation exists as described above, a collegial spirit between the pastor, people, and musician, who decide to figure things out as creatively as possible, generally characterizes it. The *LBW* suggests such collegiality, by such things as its emphasis on planning and by the presence of assisting ministers from the congregation itself.

2. Qualified Support. A continuum moves gradually to a second group. At the end of this continuum one still finds support for the *LBW*, but with qualifications. Here there is less likelihood to employ such a wide array of hymns as the first group, and choices may well be restricted to those that are known well. Only selected stanzas of a hymn may be sung rather than all of them. The use of the worship book parallels the approach to the hymnal. Services may be treated the way churches in the Reformed tradition of the Westminster Directory are apt to do—as directories of suggestions rather than liturgies of whole cloth. Here, parts of services may be chosen and other parts omitted.

Once chosen there is a tendency to fasten on a single setting of a service or a single psalm tone as the only one that is used. Congregations in this group may well have strong preaching traditions and active Bible study groups, but they may also be nervous about an emphasis on sacraments.

There may be some tension between the *LBW* and those who characterize this second response. The tension may spill over to the musician who, in such a church as this, may not be free to do many things the *LBW* implies. The choir may not sing the propers, for example. Organ introductions and harmonizations may be restricted. This congregation may also be more adamant about introducing new things than the first group. The central matter, however, leading the congregation in their song, remains constant and strongly affirmed.

3. Conflict. Though the second group may not feel quite so much at ease with the *LBW* as the first one, it also may stiffen more sharply when its tradition and worship book are maligned. A third group assumes a more aggressive stance. It has chosen to write off the *LBW* (and worship books generally) altogether and to use none of it. In its place rewritten services are substituted which may or may not follow the forms and traditions of Christian worship "across the ages." It veers toward music written since 1970, usually in a popular idiom, as being more relevant and Spirit-driven. Historic liturgies, organs, choirs, and the whole tradition of "classic" music are regarded as outmoded, not user-friendly for seekers, and not geared to evangelism. Bands and singers with microphones are substituted, worship books and hymnals are dismissed, and in their place words are projected on screens in the belief that people will then move and express their emotions freely.

4. Drift. The three groups just described above have thought out what they are doing. Those who feel strongly about one or another of their respective postures often pursue it with fervor.

A fourth group tends to drift. This fourth group has not thought things out very clearly or at all. It goes through the motions of its tradition, which may bear a similarity to any one of the other three, but it's not quite sure what it does and why. Lest this be misinterpreted as a criticism, let it be said that people in congregations of this sort do not find their worship meaningless. Conversations with these people indicate that what may appear to the observer to be deadly and dry often has deep meaning for them.

They are always in danger, in a divisive context like ours, of being pushed and pulled by forces they do not understand. Curiously enough, however, they can also represent a current of continuity that simply stands outside the conflicts of the period. At the moment that stance is difficult to maintain and certainly does not work forever, but it often has considerably more stamina than may be expected.

The Larger Context: A Divided People

Let the obvious be stated: our context is divisive. We are a divided people, in and out of the church, fighting what have been called "culture wars." Lutherans in this regard are in the same condition as other denominations. Among virtually every one of them—Baptists, Methodists, Presbyterians, the United Church of Christ, Episcopalians, Roman Catholics, Unitarians, Mennonites, etc.—there is a narrative comparable to the Lutheran one. We are all part of a cultural climate that divides us.

In the church where we confess our oneness in Christ we have often allowed the world's divisions to control us instead. The *LBW* stands squarely where the Christian church and its worship have stood about this matter for two thousand years. It calls us to repent. It greets us with the good news that God in Christ through the Spirit is at work among us, justifies us, and gives us new life. We are compelled to fall on our knees and repent our sinful divisions. However, neither we nor any generation before us has done that very well.

While evil remains constant, the nature of its network that ensnares each generation changes. Conflicts earlier in our century were between communities of faith where some coherent internal position gave people a home. As the century progressed we became more and more nomadic as people left their home communities, moved often, and joined churches of traditions other than the ones in which they grew up. We have also experienced mergers where formerly separated denominations are now forced to live with each other. While this situation has much to commend it, pain and new divisions attend it too. Earlier in this century the various postures described above would have been characteristic of separated churches. Now they are equally as likely to live together in one church. We have played fruit basket upset. Then, rather than learn from one another, all too often we have chosen not to talk with each other and to go our separate ways — as the introduction of various styles of worship services in the same denomination indicates.

Church Musicians

Church musicians are as much a part of the divisive fractures of our world as others, but there are times when some professions are more at the mercy of our sinful conflicts than at other times. At the moment it is the musician's turn to be targeted. Especially the second and third groups, as described above, have split themselves into "traditional" and "contemporary" or "traditional" and "alternative" camps, with worship services for each set of tastes. Musicians have been caught in the crossfire and marked as the cause of many of the church's problems. The first group has not escaped the pain, but it is less likely to split its worship in parts and more likely to embody in one community the wide variety of musical styles and possibilities the rubrics the *LBW* suggest.

Trying to live out their vocations has turned into a nightmare for many church musicians. In addition to the personality conflicts that musicians often experienced with their pastors and parishioners, they now have to confront a situation where what they thought was their faithful service — whether that was in the spirit of the *LBW* or not —has been denounced. They have spent their lives trying their best to serve their churches, resolve their conflicts, and put up with little or no pay only to discover that their service is now regarded as having been misguided.

In response, some musicians have simply bailed out. They have left their vocations and now worship in churches where they will not be recognized or abused. Others, finding themselves fired or mistreated without cause, have formed support groups. Others have elected to "hang in there," whatever the cost to their health or families. Still others, in the midst of the pain they share with their colleagues who have been hurt, happily serve churches where their vocations and gifts are affirmed.

So, have church musicians lived out their callings in the spirit of the *LBW*? Some have. Some have not. Some have tried and found their attempts affirmed. Some have tried and found their attempts unacceptable. To the extent that they have led the people's song and sought to do so to the best of their abilities, they have indeed lived out the spirit of the *LBW*. Most Lutheran church musicians probably fit into this category. To the extent that such worthy efforts have been thwarted and scorned, they have failed.

Irony

The *LBW*, when it is rejected now, is usually perceived as related to a dead past. There is a curious irony in this, for when it was published it was criticized for just the reverse—for language that was too inclusive, harmonizations that were not traditional enough, a baptismal emphasis that was too radical and prophetic, and making too big a break with the past. Its prophetic spirit opened the way for the spate of hymnals and service books that succeeded it. In so doing it set in motion successive publications which felt free to stand in judgment on the ones that spawned them. In a sense, the very prophetic character of the book set it up for future criticism.

There is nothing new about that. The church, especially in its Lutheran version, is always critical of itself in a prophetic way. Furthermore, the church is in mission. Its faithful hymnals and worship books reflect that. They are not missionary documents—they are prepared for the baptized — but they stand broadly with the mission of the church against the principalities and powers. Such a stance makes enemies. We should not be surprised at attacks on the *LBW*.

But, with 20 years of history, it may be that the more recent critics have it right—or half right. The *LBW* is related to the past, and in that sense it may be most prophetic. The past is not dead, as our generation wants so desperately to believe. It stands in judgment on us and comes back to haunt us when we forget it. Christians not only know that, but know they confess the holy catholic church which God has sustained. Since the church has a history where God has chosen to be present with the people through Word and Sacrament even when we are (always!) disobedient, we have no choice but to attend to that history and be advised by our sisters and brothers in the faith who have gone before us. What they have bequeathed to us is no imposition, but the sifting of centuries of Christians who have learned from their mistakes and would not have us repeat them. The *LBW* is related to the past because it is equally related to and for the sake of the present and the future.

At the moment, perhaps it is church musicians who are called to voice this prophetic reality—not only in their music making—but also by their tenaciousness in the face of so much malevolence. Musicians are especially primed to know how reliant they are on the past and how important our heritage is to them and those they serve. They study with teachers who have studied with teachers who have studied with teachers, who impart a stream of knowledge and technique they could never have access to on their own. They sing and play music from past composers, which opens their ears to insights they could never have gleaned from only their own generation.

The *LBW*, like all responsible worship and music books, lives with the wealth of the church's traditions imbedded in it and implied by it. It pushes forward to the finest new compositions in the spirit of the church's confessions and the deep structures of Word, Sacrament, and daily prayer. It lives over centuries of time, not single generations or parts of them. The church musician knows perhaps better than others this depth of meaning and vitality, and is called now to embody it on behalf of a church and world which wants to forget it. It is a most prophetic reality because it forever reminds us that we in our generation have no corner on the Word of God, but that the Word has come to others in words other than ours, borne in musical syntaxes other than ours—and will continue to do so. The *LBW* probably did not envision this sort of prophetic role for the church musician, but "new occasions teach new duties."[30]

Perspective

The conflicts in which the church and the church musician live are not new. If H. Richard Niebuhr is right, they can be found throughout the church's history.[31] The first three responses delineated above do not simply represent culture wars in our time—they are classic responses as the church has sought to work out the relation of Christ and culture. The first of the three, not unexpectedly the most sympathetic to the *LBW*, has the characteristics of Christ and culture in parado. The second veers toward the Reformed position of Christ transformer of culture and, not unexpectedly, has a good deal of resonance in the North American context where Reformed motifs have been strong. The third moves toward Christ of culture and finds considerable support in our current cultural moment.

One could also find evidence for Niebuhr's two other motifs, Christ against culture and Christ above culture. The latter, however, while it may appear to be embraced by Lutherans because they retain catholic forms and often appear very "catholic," never really finds a Lutheran home. While nature surely bears grace for Luther and Lutherans, it never leads to grace. Lutherans always take the world's disease with the utmost realism along with an alien Word of God which, like a hammer, smashes the rock in pieces and grants genuinely new life.

None of these responses is going to go away, and each response needs the other ones. We would be well advised to learn from one another and to repent our unwillingness to live in charity with each other. But that is a lesson we human beings seem reluctant to learn. Meanwhile, the *LBW* with its cantor continues to live among the people with a historic and unceasing admonition, no matter what cultural wars swirl around it:

"Then let us sing, for whom he won the fight: Alleluia."[32]

And somehow by God's grace we still sing the song of God in Christ loose and active in our world through the Spirit, in spite of all our attempts to stop it.

NOTES

1 *Lutheran Book of Worship* (Minneapolis: Augsburg Publishing House and Philadelphia: Board of Publication, Lutheran Church in America, 1978). Hereafter *LBW*.

2 *Lutheran Book of Worship:* Ministers Edition (Minneapolis: Augsburg Publishing House and Philadelphia: Board of Publication, Lutheran Church in America, 1978). Hereafter *LBW* Ministers Edition.

3 Philip H. Pfatteicher and Carlos R. Messerli, *Manual on the Liturgy* (Minneapolis: Augsburg Publishing House, 1979).

4 Marilyn K. Stulken, *Hymnal Companion to the LBW* (Philadelphia: Fortress Press, 1981).

5 Robin R. Hough, comp., *Concordance to Hymn Texts LBW* (Minneapolis: Augsburg Publishing House, 1985).

6 Philip H. Pffateicher, *Commentary on the LBW: Lutheran Liturgy in Its Ecumenical Context* (Minneapolis: Augsburg Fortress, 1990); Philip H. Pfatteicher, *Commentary on the Occasional Services* (Philadelphia: Fortress Press, 1983); Philip H. Pfatteicher, *Festivals and Commemorations: Handbook to the Calendar in LBW* (Minneapolis: Augsburg Publishing House, 1980).

7 *With One Voice* (Minneapolis: Augsburg Fortress, 1995).

8 Ralph R. Van Loon and S. Anita Stauffer, *Worship Wordbook: A Practical Guide for Parish Worship* (Minneapolis: Augsburg Fortress, 1995).

9 *Manual on the Liturgy*, p. 93.

10 Ibid., pp. 100-102.

11 *Manual on the Liturgy*, p. 101. *LBW* Ministers Edition, p. 39, gives a briefer statement about many of the issues in this paragraph.

12 *Manual on the Liturgy*, p. 102.

13 Ibid.

14 Ibid., pp. 105-106.

15 *LBW* Ministers Edition, p. 39, gives a briefer statement of these same issues.

16 *Manual on the Liturgy,* pp. 158-159.

17 Ibid., p. 159.

18 Ibid., pp. 160-161.

19 *LBW* Ministers Edition, p. 39.

20 *Manual on the Liturgy,* p. 79.

21 *The United Methodist Hymnal* (Nashville: The United Methodist Publishing House, 1989), p. vii.

22 See the *Manual on the Liturgy,* pp. 106-107.

23 The following twenty-two paragraphs quote and paraphrase Paul Westermeyer, *The Church Musician,* Revised Edition (Minneapolis: Augsburg Fortress, 1997), pp. 37-43.

24 This text by William Cowper (1731-1800), while exclusive to our ears, nonetheless points to a recurrent experience of the Christian church at song.

25 *Hymnal Supplement* (Chicago: GIA Publications, Inc., 1991).

26 Gary Cornell, *Holy Communion Musical Setting* (Minneapolis: Augsburg Fortress, 1981).

27 Dale Wood, *Holy Communion Musical Setting for Lent* (Minneapolis: Augsburg Fortress, 1991).

28 Marty Haugen, *Holden Evening Prayer* (Chicago: GIA Publications, Inc., 1990).

29 A few of the published ones include Jay Beech, *One Body Alive: Holy Communion for Contemporary Christians* (Minneapolis: Augsburg Fortress, 1994); Marshall Bowen, *Holy Communion Musical Setting for Pentecost Season* (Minneapolis: Augsburg Fortress, 1991); Michael Burkhardt, *A New Song: A Musical Setting of the Liturgy of Holy Communion* (St. Louis: Morning Star Music Publishers, 1995); Stephen P. Folkemer and Beth Bergeron Folkemer, *Of Land and Seasons: A Quarterly Observance of Prayer and Holy Communion Drawn From Life on the Farm and Orchard* (n. p.: Chantry Press, 1990); John Ylvisaker, *Holy Communion Musical Setting* (Minneapolis: Augsburg Fortress, 1992). The list of communion settings published by GIA take up ten pages of small print, Morning and Evening Prayer about four pages more.

30 "Once to Every Man and Nation," *Service Book and Hymnal* (Minneapolis: Augsburg Publishing House and Philadelphia: Board of Publicatiion, Lutheran Church in America, 1958), hymn 547. This hymn is not without its problems, but there is much about it, like the line cited, which is true.

31 See H. Richard Niebuhr, *Christ and Culture* (New York: Harper & Row, Publishers, Incorporated, 1951).

32 "When in Our Music God Is Glorified," *LBW,* hymn 555.

LITURGY:
AN EVANGELISM
ADVANTAGE

David Paul Gleason

Evangelism is a matter of understandable concern among North American Lutherans. Twenty years after the publication of *Lutheran Book of Worship* (LBW), we are still witnessing a decline in church membership which began nearly 20 years prior to the book's publication. The fact that such declining membership is shared by other mainline denominations is of little comfort. So, too, is the preponderance of explanations for this decline that have been advanced.

It is interesting and challenging to consider the possible effect on church membership during periods of social and political unrest. These include the shift from local industrial economies to a global service economy, the suspected liberal biases in mainline churches countered by a rise in conservative evangelicalism, the broad implications of efforts to insure the equality of races and sexes, the emergence of models for domestic life that are dramatically different from the traditional nuclear family. Also included in this roster of change are breakthroughs in medical technology, lower birth rates among middle class Christians, religious television, and virtually all significant developments and events of the past 40 years. Yet, while such considerations may be interesting and even offer some insight into what is happening on the North American religious landscape, it is equally interesting to note that the historic liturgy of the Western church has been conveniently assigned a disproportionate share of the blame for both the loss of church members and the apparent inability to attract new ones. The liturgy is under fire. It has become a lightning rod for the church's failure to sustain and increase its membership. What is more important, the liturgy is also blamed for failing to satisfy the spiritual hunger of Americans who feel overwhelmed, rootless, and unable or unwilling to cope with or accommodate themselves to societal changes taking place around them.

In the opinion of some, both within the mainstream of North American Lutheranism and outside of it, the historic liturgy of the church, as set forth in LBW, is perceived as hopelessly antiquated. Some insist that its structure, ritual actions, aural and visual signs and symbols, no longer possess the power to move the human heart. It fails to provide the necessary guidance and support for Christians in turmoil, nor does it meet the needs of Christians battered by all manners of upheaval in the daily pattern of life. The liturgy does little, these critics say, to capitalize on the potential for people to make the best of any situation if only they were equipped with the appropriate guidance and tools for doing so. The liturgy does not offer the encouragement or cultivate the skills necessary for people to be the best they can be. Such critics assert that the historic liturgy does not make persons feel good about themselves or God.

Thus, some congregations are willing and eager to abandon the historic liturgy in favor of newly created rites designed to meet the expressed needs of religious consumers, capitalize on human potential, boost the sagging human spirit and, thus, bring in new members. If those were the goals of a Christian community, gathered to worship, and if the intended outcome of evangelization were simply to bring newcomers into such a congregation, one could hardly take issue with the abandonment of the liturgy. Indeed, a consumer-oriented approach to churchly life, giving people whatever they want or *feel* they need, would appear to demand it.

However, evangelism seeks to invite those who believe and those yet to come to faith into the gracious presence of Jesus Christ. Moreover, it seeks to bring them together in a community which has as its goal and its life a regular, transforming encounter with this same Christ. Worship is where the Lord of the church most assuredly and decisively meets his followers to offer a correcting word of judgment, to shower them with mercy and love, and to equip them for discipleship. It is not where believers are to be offered whatever they seem to want, but what they need to live faithfully as God's children and disciples of Christ.

HISTORY AND TRADITION

Lutherans have rightly maintained that a decisive encounter with the Lord of the church happens as God's Word is proclaimed and the Sacraments are celebrated within the community of faith. They have done so in the realization that these are the means through which Christ chooses to be present for his people, offering them what they must have to live faithfully, offering them himself. These are the givens of worship. They are not activities shaped by desires of the moment or by universal longings. Nor are they convenient tools for maximizing human potential. Word and Sacraments are Christ present for his people. They are the received tradition of the gospel and of the community of faith which bears witness to it. They are, of course, not new. Neither is the liturgy in which they are embodied.

This very lack of newness appears to be a crucial factor in the current disdain for liturgy. To many of those caught up in sweeping societal change, a steady stream of scientific discoveries, and always facing new challenges and problems, the notion of an ancient liturgy possessing contemporary significance and power seems absurd. Yet only by inviting believers and newcomers to faith into a shared life with the Christ who is the ancient of days can the people of God discover the object of all hope and receive the grace needed to live in this chaotic world.

The Christian faith is not new. It has its origins in a time before creation when there was but God. Its history is one that is shared with the Creator and marked by God's acts on behalf of the created order and, especially, by his acts on behalf of human creation. God's crucial act in Jesus of Nazareth does not qualify for what is commonly regarded as "current event." Nearly two millennia of theological reflection and debate, of ecclesiastical rule and misrule, of inspired art and architecture, of sacred music, of liturgical renewal movements, of reformation and counter reformation, separate us from the Jesus of the first Christian century. Presumably, Christians know that. They know this holy religion is not new. So do most inquirers into Christian faith and seekers of spiritual truth. Indeed, it is difficult to imagine anyone, even those who have never actually encountered a Christian community, laboring under the impression that the Christian faith is of recent invention and possesses no delineated history.

Therefore, endeavoring to present it as new by stripping it of its antiquity, ridding it of its ancient rites and ceremonies, eliminating its rituals and customs, quieting its authentic song for the sake of enticing unbelievers, becomes a denial of the church's historic integrity and the integrity of its received tradition in the gospel. If the Christian claim for the truth of its witness is to be heard and received by an unbelieving world, that witness must be honest and must be perceived to be such. At the very least, the unchurched are aware that Christianity has a history. They realize that it owns a rich heritage of sights and sounds that are unique to itself.

The point here is that the historic liturgy of the church, as faithfully preserved and presented through the LBW, is not an obstacle to evangelism nor to the growth of church membership. It is, instead, a distinct advantage. The advantage lies principally in the integrity of its authentic historicity, of its connection to and compatibility with the church throughout all generations. The current shape of the liturgy, with its origins in ancient Judaism, our Lord's own institution of the Holy Supper, and the fairly ordered structure of worship from the earliest days of the Christian community, bears testimony to its durability and stability. In the midst of a culture which regularly and rapidly amends itself and leaves its people breathlessly behind, the historic liturgy of Word and Sacraments provides a sure testimony to the constancy of God's care through encounters with the risen Christ. To generation after generation of believers, struggling to order their lives in a chaotic world of sin, the liturgy has spoken and embodied the grace of God for all people through the gift of Christ. Worshipers discover the order they seek in an orderless world through gatherings around the book, bath, and meal, by which they are invited into the life of God in all of its eternal constancy.

In and of itself, the liturgy is not an obstacle for evangelism. However, a liturgy that is not done well may become such an obstacle. That can happen when the liturgy is not valued and cared for as a received treasure of the church, when its historic structural integrity is compromised by incessant tinkering, when the holy things of God are handled without reverence. Liturgical evangelism is blocked when preachers and presiding ministers insinuate themselves and their personalities into the encounter of the risen Christ with his people and when the goal of music is simply to set toes to tapping rather than to render God the praise that is his due. Under such circumstances, badly planned and led liturgies weaken the church's witness.

For the sake of evangelism, as well as for the sake of preserving true Christian faith, doing liturgies well requires that we, first and foremost, humbly acknowledge that worship is about the triune God. It is about meeting the Creator in the particular place where we are and allowing God to draw us into God's presence. It is about Christ, the Christ of the book and font and table, coming to us and inviting us to share his risen life. Liturgy is allowing the Spirit, the Spirit of the Creator and of the Christ, to move us to trust in God's promises and empower us for discipleship. Liturgy is about God, and liturgy that is faithfully and well-done points us to the triune God: Father, Son, and Holy Spirit. It points us to the ongoing story of

God's involvement with all creation by pointing us to the holy things which embody God's living presence among us.

THE CHURCH YEAR

The liturgical year provides us with an annual re-presentation of his story. It anchors our worship in God's mighty acts throughout the history of God's people and in God's decisive act on our behalf in Christ. In recounting, again and again, the events of our Lord's birth, life, passion, death, resurrection and ascension; in presenting the accounts of his teaching, preaching, and powerful signs; in relating the witness of the early Christian community—the liturgical year allows us to focus clearly on the object of our faith and of our hope. The message of the church, of the gospel, is given. We are simply to speak it faithfully in truth. We are not to devise or conjure up a cheering word for weary souls awash in a chaotic world. We are not to speculate piously about the possible solutions to society's ills. We are not to hammer personal prejudices into the heads and hearts of God's children. It is not our responsibility to proffer pop psychology and helpful hints for coping with the daily stress of life. We are to proclaim Christ.

Adherence to the movement of the liturgical year provides some assurance that we will. Through it, we will regularly move from hope and expectation for the Lord's final coming to the celebration of his first coming in the Child of Mary and to receiving him humbly as he comes to us, day by day, in the bread and cup of his kingdom. With the magi, we will behold his manifestation as the Christ through the guiding of a star and move on to contemplate the mission of making him known to the world. We will move with Christ through temptation, self-denial, suffering and death to resurrection, new life, and return to the Father. Our journey will be marked by ashes, palms, the agony of the cross, the awe of an empty tomb, and alleluias. We will join with the church of all the ages in rejoicing in the gift of his abiding Spirit and will find ourselves, thereby, empowered to be his witnesses in the world. We will be instructed by his wisdom, admonished by his call to obedience, and encouraged by his tender care.

Along the way, the message of his life, death and resurrection and the truth of his limitless love for us will be reinforced by his self-offering in the bread and cup of the Holy Eucharist. It will also be reinforced through the signs, symbols and ritual actions that have been passed on to us through centuries of faithful devotion. The story, clarified and illuminated and enacted as it has been throughout Christian history, will be alive. We will

Encountering God

discover again and anew the profound truth of the gospel that life is born in death and that eternal peace and security emerges from suffering. Through faithful observance of the liturgical year, we will be pointed to truth. We will be pointed to the truth of God and to the holy things which communicate his living presence with his people.

Too often, God and the holy things of God are inadvertently obscured by well-intentioned but ill-informed liturgical practice. Desiring to speak a word of good cheer to disheartened seekers, preachers sometimes abandon the liturgical year and its re-presentation of the Christ event to preach topical sermons based on personally selected passages of Scripture which may underscore some theme of self-help. The operative assumption seems to be that feeling good about oneself and about God is equivalent to the gospel's truth and that God's divine intention for humanity is happiness rather than its salvation.

WORSHIP PLANNING

Likewise, in efforts to be liturgically creative, presiding ministers and worship committees sometimes attempt to modify the shape and content of the historic liturgy only to result in confusing worshipers and drawing attention away from the God who has gathered them. Worship assistants who are unrehearsed, ill-prepared, and ill-informed about their roles in the liturgy do not provide a bold witness to a shared ministry. Instead, they inevitably draw more attention to themselves than to the God addressed in the prayers they offer, or to the Lord whose Word they read, or to the Christ who comes to his people in and through the holy things they handle. Recorded music, piped through a labyrinth of technologically sophisticated electronic gadgetry, is an affront to the authenticity and integrity of songs raised by God's people in praise of God's love and draws attention away from offering the pure praise and worship that belong only to God. While electronically produced music and staged lighting for dramatic effect may be established elements of popular musical culture, the church must strive to offer its songs and shouts of praise and thanksgiving with authenticity.

The integrity of the church's gathering in the presence of God is gravely diminished when there is a lack of care for the holiness of the encounter or by insinuating artificiality into it. Worship deserves honesty—the honesty of believers caring for the treasure of the gospel and caring for the manner by which it has been transmitted to us. Worship, therefore, also deserves an excellence that is not mandated by liturgical snobbery or elitist desires for ceremonial artistry or by misguided efforts to repristinate a golden age of liturgical purity. It is mandated, instead, by the need for honesty and integrity before God and the people of God. Achieving and maintaining such excellence in worship is demanding. It necessitates and deserves hard work.

Some of that hard work lies in the ongoing, judicious decisions which need to be made to support the focus of a particular liturgy or liturgical season. Variations of the rite, in keeping with standard rubrics, are to be considered. Hymns are selected wisely to support the message that is proclaimed through the liturgy and to accommodate the musical proficiency of the congregation. Other music, intended to serve the proclamation of the Word, will be rehearsed and presented skillfully. The actions and logistics of the liturgy will be thought through and planned.

Then, too, worship leaders will strive to establish a pattern for how the liturgy normatively will be done. They need to determine the various ministries that will be fulfilled, who will fulfill them, and how they will be carried out—for example, where ushers will be stationed, where acolytes will be seated, how and when the gifts of bread and wine will be presented, where the altar guild will place vessels, and other such important details. A host of logistical decisions is made and implemented to establish a normative pattern. The pattern is allowed to become familiar through repeated use and, thereby, comfortable for all involved, with the possible exception of newcomers. The normative pattern, however, may express greater concern for expedience than excellence. Periodically, worship leaders need to revisit such logistical decisions, not only for the sake of evangelism but especially so. They need to step back and ask whether the manner in which liturgy is done actually facilitates the invitation to enter into the life of God. Does that manner of celebration keep the holy things of God central and the people fully involved in their encounter with God? Are the expectations of worshipers clearly set forth? Do the people, both members and visitors, know what to do and how to do it? Are rubrics clear? Do people know how to approach the altar to receive the sacrament and the means by which it will be administered? Are directions for standing, sitting, kneeling, speaking, and singing unambiguous? Are the ritual actions of those who serve as worship leaders deliberate, visible and graceful? Does the placement of people and candles and banners and flowers obfuscate or point to the holy things of God?

Stepping back from the familiar, comfortable, normative pattern of how we do the liturgy and reexamining it with a critical eye is very instructive, especially when accompanied by the question: What is being communicated by the way we do the liturgy? Such a critical view helps us understand that we may have unintentionally done more to obscure the God who deigns to dwell in our midst than to point to God. Such a review will also aid in developing the excellence that a clear and unambiguous encounter with God expects and will serve to assist believers and inquirers in fully entering into the encounter.

DOING LITURGY

Worshipers learn to value and appreciate the integrity, beauty, and meaning of the liturgy as they involve themselves fully in its words, prayers, songs, and actions. Much of what is currently promoted as contemporary or alternative worship is not intended to be interactive; it seems to assume that worship expects no profound, transcendent encounter with the risen Christ. "Entertainment evangelism" may offer a good deal of semi-professional showmanship and may even be truly entertaining but it is not effective evangelism. While unchurched seekers may enjoy it and receive good feelings from such entertainment, they will not, thereby, be invited into the life of God. They will not meet Christ, crucified and resurrected, in entertainment. Instead, seekers will encounter the Lord as he chooses to make himself known through Word and Sacraments. They will acquire a greater knowledge of God's mighty acts and an appreciation for the liturgical heritage of the church by actually engaging in worship than by any other means. Moreover, this knowledge will be imparted and this appreciation gained as much from fellow worshipers as from the clergy who preside.

People learn to do the liturgy and learn what is communicated through it by doing it and by observing how others involve themselves in it. When visitors and inquirers are welcomed into an assembly that is alert to the central things of God and practiced in the ceremonial and ritual of a eucharistic community, they quickly learn the profound character of liturgical worship. Seeing the attentive and devout care given to the reading of sacred Scripture, the proclamation of the Word, and the blessings over bread and cup enable all to know that they are in the presence of the holy and to respond with appropriate awe and reverence. Witnessing the devotion with which believers approach the table of the Lord announces to all that here an uncommon gift is offered in common bread and a common cup. Watching as an entire congregation orients itself toward the cross—as it is carried in procession—prompts even the seeker to know that they, too, are to turn and, at least momentarily, see themselves as pilgrim people following the way of Christ and of his cross. Hearing a collection of volunteer, nonprofessional musicians raising their voices in hymns and songs encourages even the unchurched inquirer to know that they, too, should add their voices to the strains of praise.

The liturgy is learned in the doing of it, and so is faith. Even more than expressing the faith we have in Father, Son and Holy Spirit, liturgy shapes our faith. That is an especially important consideration for evangelism. Believers come to know the object of their faith and the content of a received tradition of the apostolic witness through worship, through the doing of liturgy.

This is, perhaps, most apparent in the lives of those young believers, the children. Children who are brought regularly into the worshiping assembly, beginning in infancy, demonstrate remarkable understanding and liturgical facility at an early age. Through exposure to and witness of the worship practices and devotional piety of older siblings, of parents, and of other adults, they quickly learn the actions and nuances of liturgical worship. They verbalize liturgical responses, add their voices to familiar liturgical songs, and ritually enact signs of the great truths of faith, such as tracing the sign of the cross. Even more significantly, they quickly and almost effortlessly learn the content of Christian faith. They absorb the stories of faith, become acquainted with the leading characters in the stories, and come to know the story of God's activity in the world simply by hearing and hearing again. They become accustomed to the vocabulary of "God talk" and recite much of it for themselves. At only four or five years of age, we hear them joining the liturgical exchange between God and God's people, confessing the faith of the church in the words of ancient creeds, and making the "Our Father" their own address to God. To be sure, in years to come, other opportunities must be made available for them to deepen their understandings of the faith and answer the perplexing questions that are sure to arise. The same is also true for adults new to the faith or seeking to grow in faith.

At the very least, the liturgy has set young or new believers on the path to godliness by allowing them to be placed in the presence of God. It has done so with no artificial concession to youth. It has not been adapted to their level of intellectual development. No alterations have been made to accommodate their admittedly brief attention spans. The liturgy has simply been allowed to stand, in all of its inherent integrity, with all of its words and sounds and actions, as the worship of God's people gathered in God's presence. It does its own work of imparting the faith of the church, of continually shaping faith, and of allowing God's people to express the trust and devotion which they share. In short, the full, reverently celebrated liturgy is catechetical. It teaches the faith. The church's historic liturgy is, therefore, a vital and highly effective advantage in the evangelization of new believers and in the ongoing evangelization of those already within the fellowship of faith.

This advantage, however, needs to be fully utilized. It cannot be perceived as an advantage that is exhausted when the Sunday morning gathering is dismissed. There is more to the received liturgical heritage of the church and more that is helpful to the task of inviting believers and those who do not yet believe into the life of God. But just as there are many who seem quick to write off the weekly liturgical gathering around book, bath, and supper as hopelessly antiquated, there are also those who dismiss other treasures of our liturgical heritage.

THE DAILY PRAYER OF THE CHURCH

It is baffling and disappointing to note the frequency with which para-liturgical orders of devotion are concocted to mark special emphases of the church year, or the beginning of the day or the end of the day or the start of a meeting of churched people engaged in planning or carrying out some task of ministry. Observing the use of such newly invented "rites," one is tempted to conclude that the life of the Christian community has been woefully impoverished by an absence of received orders of devotion or traditional forms of communal prayer. It appears that these must now be provided through the constant labor and creativity of worship leaders. Rarely is the Daily Office (Morning Prayer, Evening Prayer, Prayer at the Close of the Day) given more than limited use in the church. Its rich juxtaposition of the themes of light and darkness, work and rest, death and resurrection, is lost among believers unacquainted with its rhythms. Its focus on the devotional praying of the psalms and quiet reflection on Scripture seems to be painfully uncomfortable for believers unaccustomed to even a moment of silence. Its character of corporate address to the Almighty struggles to find a place among those who have somehow reached the conclusion that the life of prayer is purely an intensely personal and private matter.

Not only does the Daily Office afford a devotional resource for God's people that is infinitely more rich, rhythmic and clearly centered in the mystery of God than any para-liturgical rite we may devise, but it also addresses a fundamental concern both of believers and of newcomers to faith. People long to deepen their devotional life. They long for a genuine spirituality that is centered objectively on the divine and not subjectively on their own musings. They want to know how to pray. They repeatedly voice their discomfort in addressing God. They say, and say again, in times of jubilation and distress, "I don't know how to pray."

The Daily Office, with its focus on God's Word to God's people in the normal cycles of living and on their prayerful response, teaches us how to pray and how to pray well. In company with others, we open ourselves to the voice of the Lord and consider his Word for us. We speak forth our own joys and sorrows, hopes and disappointments, praise and doubt, to the one we believe hears and answers. Thus, we learn to pray. We learn first to listen, then to contemplate, and finally to speak. We learn from quiet reflection on the prayers of the psalmist, and the words of prophets and apostles, and prayers of God's people through generations before our own. We, then, can add our prayers to theirs and to those of the Lord who prays with us and intercedes for us.

The devotional life of believers is deepened and the faith of new believers affirmed by doing the discipline of prayer as it has been handed onto us. Pastors, committee members, church school teachers, and the officers of women's or men's groups need not be left to their own devotional devices. The devotional resources of the church should not be reluctantly dragged out for an annual series of midweek Lenten services or for a once-a-year retreat. The Daily Office is a *daily* office. As presented in the *LBW*, it is easily adapted from congregational use to family and/or personal devotion. The faith of newcomers will be enriched and the uncertainty of inquirers will be assuaged by Christian communities and individual believers who take seriously the discipline of prayer, who are daily in communication with God, and who maintain the integrity of the church's received tradition of devotion.

Responsive Prayer 1 and 2, The Litany, Psalms for Daily Use, and the Daily Lectionary also affords individual believers and communities of faith resources for deepening genuine spirituality and the life of prayer that are grounded in the prayer and devotional life of the church. The use of such resources should be fostered in every community of faith seeking to draw new believers into the life of God.

God's encounter with his people which regularly happens in the liturgy of Word and Sacrament, and which is deepened through the devotional practices of a Christian community grounded in the tradition of the church catholic, at times takes on very particular significance: as when God makes a new believer in Baptism, when he binds a man and woman together in the covenant of marriage, when he affirms his promise of new life for one who has died in faith, when he offers forgiveness to a tortured conscience, when he extends a healing touch to the sick or despairing.

Such particular encounters accentuate God's involvement with human life in all of its fullness. They afford both believers and inquirers opportunities to know the Lord as he initiates followers into life and guides them to faithful discipleship through all the passages of life.

LITURGY ALIVE

The liturgical richness of the rites associated with these encounters provides believers and inquirers a view of and an invitation into the life of the God who became incarnate for them in Jesus. As God's Word for them is proclaimed and ritually enacted, they are drawn in by the power of the promise clothed in the earthiness of human utterance, common elements, powerful symbols, and ritual gestures.

The unchurched we strive to reach for Christ are children of an age that is often characterized by highly sophisticated aural *and* visual communication. Seeing is as important to learning and understanding as hearing. They are enticed by the graphic and the colorful, by action and movement.

The very nature of the historic liturgy of the church as ritualized encounter with God is, likewise, characterized by verbal *and* visual communication. It is the liturgy of Word and Sacraments, of the spoken and enacted Word, of the Word preached and made visible in earthy elements. It is filled with the color of churchly vesture and with the movement of ritual action. Inquirers to faith find the visual and enacted communication of the Word something to which they can readily relate. It draws them in and encourages them to join with believers in actively doing worship. The realization that the sounds and sights of the liturgy belong to a tradition passed on through generations of witness to apostolic faith, grounds their doing of the liturgy in faithfulness to that witness. They discover a sense of belonging, of belonging to a community of believers which transcends the moment by being intimately tied to the entire heritage of the church catholic, of belonging to the reality of God alive and at work among his people. They come alive—alive in the beauty and truth of a holy encounter between themselves and the God who loves them. They enter into the presence of the divine.

Assertions that the liturgy of the church is hopelessly antiquated and is an obstacle to doing the work of evangelism are groundless and unsettling. It may, of course, be true that more currently popular and marketable techniques could be employed to entice people into a church building. But once they are in, can such trendy measures lead inquirers into faith in the triune God and discipleship for him? Will those new, slick techniques offer an encounter with the living Christ or simply an entertaining diversion from the responsibility of living faithfully as his followers? Will they invite inquirers into the presence of the Lord and discipleship for him or offer them a moment's amusement and a bit of self-affirmation?

Many of those who cherish and value the liturgical heritage of the church and seek to use the *LBW* fully and well preside over or participate in actively growing communities of faith. Such congregations center their work and mission in robust celebrations of the liturgy. Their faithful ministries of education, service, care, and outreach flourish and expand. They grow out of an encounter with the God who most assuredly meets his people in the midst of their chaotic lives, who meets them in Word and Sacraments—just as promised.

The spiritual lives of individuals who comprise these communities are deepened by attentive devotion to the holy things of God. Their relationship to him and to one another is nurtured by his self-giving love so evident in the liturgy of the church. They are formed into a community of Christian faith in unity with their Lord and with one another. And they are, thereby, equipped and empowered to evangelize faithfully.

WHAT LANGUAGE SHALL I BORROW?[1]

Susan Karen Hedahl

"Therefore, every scribe who has been trained for the kingdom of heaven is like a householder who brings out of his treasure what is new and what is old" (Matthew 13:52).

INTRODUCTION

The lectionary texts for the festival of Pentecost leave no doubt that the sources of salvation, frustration, disbelief, and conversion all have to do with language! What is God's creative Word doing? What are the people's languages of response to God's power and presence—both as individuals and as communities of the faithful?

Clearly, one thing is certain: In the texts and subtexts of our various communities, language still continues as the simultaneously rewarding and problematic center of our faith lives.

It is this reality which this chapter discusses and does so with worship leaders and planners in mind; their responsibilities are crucial regarding choice of texts (meaning hereafter, the printed word) as well as music in connection with *Lutheran Book of Worship* (*LBW*).

There is no question that of the issues raised in this volume, language is perhaps *the* most difficult one to address. The significant cultural wars of the last two decades since the printing of *LBW* have not raged largely around music, but language. Thus, any discussion about the *linguistic* texts of the *LBW* will undoubtedly affect readers and worship planners in a variety of ways both positively and negatively. Neutrality seems not to be an option!

In the closing decades of the 20th century language usage has become a central focus in all venues. Business, government, the arts, and education struggle with that reality and so, inevitably, this means that our worship life is affected as well.[2] Given that fact, what does it mean that most Lutherans use a worship book that is now two decades old? What can we use and celebrate with *LBW*? What do worship leaders and planners need to consider regarding the language *LBW* presents and the language we speak today? With the publication of more recent Lutheran worship materials, what role does *LBW* play? These questions only raise others.

In order to shape a comprehensive discussion, three questions are discussed in the following pages. They focus on the pressures and possibilities of current *LBW* usage.

1. What basic *traditions* of worship language—biblical, liturgical, and hymnodic—have Lutherans inherited?
2. Which *changes and challenges* in language usage and texts now affect *LBW* usage?
3. Finally, what does it mean to provide *liturgical leadership* amidst these changes when using the *LBW* today?

It is no accident that these matters are stated in interrogative form. This indicates that any given worship community must answer these questions in ways which are like other communities but also unique to themselves.

The values and assumptions which inform this chapter are derived from the author's ministry of the past 27 years in serving as a parish pastor, interim pastor, and now seminary professor. Explicitly stated, they are: The tension between tradition and the current workings of the Spirit in the present is the primary way to think of language usage in worship; current worship contexts vary widely and must be taken seriously; language is subject to change; images of God and the human are interwoven with one another; language usage in worship should serve the dual functions of both affirming and challenging community values, thus clearly establishing a need for vigorous leadership in worship planning.

LUTHERANS AND TRADITIONS OF WORSHIP LANGUAGE

With its compact historical survey of Lutheran worship, the Introduction to *LBW* centers on language usage. Language-oriented words used to refer to both historical and contemporary concerns—"vernaculars," "translations," "language of the people," "speech and culture," and "language of

Encountering God

prayer and praise." This Introduction shows that Lutherans have been sensitive to the cultural patterns which determine language in worship in both spoken and printed forms. It is this intuitive flexibility which gives a predictable, stable vector to Lutheran language use regardless of place and to some extent, time. For example, a reading of Luther's *Deutsche Messe* (German Mass) from the 16th century is not unfamiliar to us at the end of the 20th century.[3]

Luther understood, however, both the blessings and pitfalls of language usage among the faithful. The following quote expresses his awareness of the quicksilver nature of language, its ability to lose meaning, its susceptibility to misinterpretation, the tendency to become outdated, its limitations in containing and expressing fully human thought and feeling, particularly when committed to the printed page:

> In the New Testament, preaching must be done orally and publicly, with the living voice, to produce in speech and hearing what prior to this lay hidden in the letter and in secret vision. . . . However, the need to write books was a serious decline and a lack of the Spirit which necessity forced upon us.[4]

Luther's observations about the fluctuations in language usage raise the question of what suits the worship of God in any given assembly; the "good old days" of language standards have, in fact, never existed. In some sense the Tower of Babel, the Pentecost experience, and contemporary worship texts are not separated by time; the same issues of meaning, accuracy, intentionality, and compassionate usage exist and have created problems wherever the faithful worship.

The only two certainties with which we are confronted then are the worshipers' needs to be in relationship with God on the one hand, and on the other, unstable and evolving patterns of language to express that.

In planning worship, Luther also had to work with a variety of worship planners in his own day. They, as well as we, encounter the same realities and problems in the arena of liturgical revision. Luther advises a particular group of worship planners in words which are fitting for today's work by those charged with worship leadership.

> Now even though external rites and orders—such as masses, singing, reading, baptizing—add nothing to salvation, yet it is unChristian to quarrel over such things and thereby to confuse the common people. We should consider the edification of the lay folk more important than our own ideas and opinions. Therefore, I pray all of you, my dear sirs (sic), let each one

surrender his own opinions and get together in a friendly way and come to a common decision about these external matters . . . lest the common people get confused and discouraged.[5]

The continual shifting of the linguistic foundations is something Lutherans both accept and with which they struggle. As Luther's Small Catechism states in the explanation of the Third Article of the Creed, the Spirit continually, "calls, gathers, enlightens . . ." —something that certainly applies to our use of language.

This can happen both to the dismay or joy of the worshippers. Thus, it should be no surprise that an appraisal of *LBW* at its 20th anniversary elicits mixed feelings from its users. Our faith history, our linguistic make-up tells us this is inevitable! A biblical statement about the importance of language—God's Word—states it even more impressively: "Is not my word like a fire, says the Lord, and like a hammer that breaks a rock in pieces? (Jeremiah 23: 29).

CHANGES AND CHALLENGES

Language changes are continuous in the church. Its worship life is continually affected both by the church and the influences of culture. (Separating the interaction of two realities is impossible to some extent.) Whether the faithful agree with these changes or not, the major linguistic ones in the last two decades impacting *LBW* hymnal use and liturgy planning are:
- the *umbrella* issue of what changing language means;
- attention to inclusive language;
- changes in the lectionary and its connections with ecumenical dialogue.

Changing Language

The ambiguity of this heading is intentional. It can be understood in two very different ways and should be: First, language undergoes changes constantly. Second, there is also another meaning which implies instrumentality—individuals and/or groups are actively changing the language. This can happen by substitution of one word for another, coining new words and phrases, omitting words, or placing words in new contexts to elicit new meanings. In any event, both dynamics are always happening simultaneously. Language users can maintain some control over their use of language but in other ways are part of a larger communal use of language that functions beyond personal control.

Thus, if individuals and worshiping communities experience a dissonance with *LBW*'s printed text(s), what are their options and choices for using it or abandoning it? This question has been sharpened by the following two developments.

Inclusive Language

The emphasis on and definition of inclusive language has created significant changes throughout the church and culture. *Inclusive* began with efforts to see that women, as well as men, were reflected linguistically in descriptions of community. However, the word has also expanded to mean inclusion of others based on ethnicity, physical ability, sexual preference, and rank. Inclusivity is not simply an optional linguistic mechanism, but truly an essential means of seeing to it that the gospel's address to all people is noted in the worship language of any given worship community.

Several denominations have released statements on inclusive language over the past two decades, including the Evangelical Church in America (ELCA). The statement published in 1989 by the Office of the Secretary of the ELCA, *A Guide to the Inclusive Use of the English Language*, was removed from publication in the early 1990s due to pressures and disputes over some of its contents. The statement has not been replaced with any other at this writing.

The absence of such a statement can be interpreted in two ways: First, what does the church say about language now? Second, what freedom do worshipping communities have, with no official statement in place, to adjust the language of various texts?

Regardless of whether or not worshipers choose to engage the reality of inclusive language or ignore it, it remains a constant in the production and use of linguistic texts. A recent book on stewardship and ecology includes an example of reverse noninclusiveness showing that today it is insufficient, inaccurate, and simply bad theology to speak noninclusively. This particular vignette can be used as a significant discussion-starter relating to issues of inclusivity and worship planning.[6] Many church texts have been rewritten to demonstrate concerns for inclusion. These include church constitutions, hymn and liturgical texts, biblical translations, sermons, and educational materials. The use of any one set of texts reveals how deeply interwoven one is with other types of texts. This raises the question as to whether or not a congregation's worship reflects the inclusionary language of its other basic documents of governance and authority.

Two issues are raised with the matter of inclusion. First, inclusion means leaving no member of the human family out of the circle. James Joyce rendered this in a delightful phrase when he said, "'Catholic' means here comes everybody!"

The debate intensifies, however, when it focuses on a related and second issue not of anthropology but theology—that is, how do we speak of God? Is there a direct line from speaking inclusively of the human to speaking in a multiplicity of images regarding God?

The issue has centered particularly on the continuing usage of the trinitarian formula in *LBW*, found in the baptismal service, invocations, and prayers. While the theological issues attached to these arguments pro and con are too lengthy to include here, a suggested approach to this discussion on the naming of God should not only include the traditional statements but also expand to include readily available images and names of God from biblical sources. An inclusionary spirit rather than dismissiveness or substitution serves better than other approaches.[7]

Another issue peculiar to the English language and involved in the discussions on inclusionary language is that pronominal usage distinguishes between "he," "she," "it" in ways other languages, more context-dependent for definition, do not. It is possible to make significant statements both either for or against inclusiveness in relationship to people and to God in the way pronouns are used.

Since images reflect, determine, guide, and order communities, thoughtfulness in planning worship must be given in order to balance *LBW*'s predominantly male pronominal usage written in a time prior to current sensitivity to this issue. The task is not impossible. For example, one of the major hymns of the tradition, "Holy, Holy, Holy," (*LBW* hymn 169) uses no pronouns! A choice of such a hymn, in due season, along with other such hymns, can go a long way in offering a balanced worship service regarding language use.

Worship committees, musicians, and pastors are sometimes called upon to rework, rewrite, or redefine the traditional texts before them. Some groups are more proactive than others in this regard. At stake is the issue of quality and the theological aptitude of leadership not only in worship but in planning worship. What can worship planners do to enhance the spiritual growth and development of their people?

Several other resources now apply to their work.

Lectionary Changes

One of these is the recent wide-spread adoption and use of the *Revised Common Lectionary* (RCL).[8] The adoption of the RCL as an option for choice of readings has made *LBW* listings outdated in many parish settings. Often the publication of a new lectionary for use in several denominations had been made to coincide with the publication of new worship books. This has not happened in the case of the Lutheran lectionary being used today.

Care must be taken with the use of the RCL, however, since denominational differences at some points of the church year can be very confusing. Yet, the benefits of the RCL far outweigh its disadvantages. Text choices and language of the RCL clearly set out some new models of language use. Behind this lectionary stand new translations of the Bible, and human inclusion and God-talk are heard in ways which differ from the *LBW*'s wording to some extent.

Buttressing these translations is over three decades of extensive work in biblical studies, some of it done by notable female biblical scholars, which has reopened and deepened the discussion on inclusivity in significant historical terms.[9]

Inevitably connected with the use of the RCL, is the fact that it raises issues of ecumenical dialogue and can necessarily prompt new attention to worship forms as well as to the use of biblical texts. A history of ecumenical documents marks the current ecumenical statements which have been voted upon recently in several denominations. Crucial theological and communal issues are at stake in these statements which will have enormous and longterm implications for worship planning as an extension of the use of biblical texts now shared in common by many Christians.

This challenge is open to succeeding decades of hard work in liturgical and hymnal texts. It will mean judicious use of the many worship resources which will be produced in the years ahead as a response to the decisions made by different denominations. Yearly planners of the typical community Thanksgiving and Lenten services will welcome these possibilities!

LBW AND WORSHIP TODAY

If the riches of *LBW* are appropriately valued and used, what role remains for Spirit-engendered change? At what points can language be changed without creating a radical dissonance with *LBW* printed texts? And if the dissonances are felt, what is their value and purpose?

> Several points of change are possible and necessary. First, which *general* areas of resources and planning must liturgical leaders attend to and, second, what *specific* areas of worship can reflect appropriate linguistic changes?

Liturgical Planning in General

Formatting a worship service each Sunday based on the patterns of what the computer or bulletin files contained a month or a year ago is inadequate. Mindless repetition of what was sung, said, or done at parish worship during previous years, with no consideration of changing current context, is not worship which respects the people and God. Thus it becomes important to work with both general considerations and particular points of change within the order of *LBW* services.

First, in general terms, one unique way of planning worship should include educational settings outside of worship to instruct believers in the rich liturgical history of *LBW*. Such courses should be repeated every two or three years. Using the basic resources—the Bible, *LBW*, *Occasional Services, LBW* Ministers Edition, and *Manual on the Liturgy*,[10] worshipers can gain new and exciting insights into the rationale behind the liturgy's construction and meaning.

Some sample questions and areas for studying the language of *LBW* are: What biblical quotes are used in the liturgy? What do the Latin words mean (e.g., *Sanctus*)? Where do the prayer(s) of the day come from? What are the "may rubrics?" What is the most basic form of a worship service for Sunday morning? What do the listings of texts at the beginning of *LBW* mean? What is a moveable feast? What is the *Revised Common Lectionary?*

While worship planners may take the answers to these questions for granted, do not be surprised to see how uninformed and thirsty for information parishioners are in this regard.

A second key factor in using *LBW* is the judicious use and incorporation of music and texts from other sources. These have undoubtedly made a significant impact on worship planning and cannot be ignored. If worship leaders ignore them, parishioners will, in fact, find ways of bringing such resources to their attention.

Several reasons for this influx of materials present themselves: advances in desktop publishing, increased parish use of such resources, available music licenses for reprinting large numbers of songs and hymns, an increasing number of hymnals, music reprinted on bulletins (such as psalm responses), alternative services, and the excellent music created by Lutheran composers such as Nancy Galbraith and Marty Haugen, whose particular ministry settings have shaped their music and texts.[11]

Finally, consider ways to use a variety of people in worship planning outside the regular staff of the congregation. Children, adolescents, and adults otherwise unengaged with worship are valuable resources—either

Encountering God

on an ongoing basis, or as contributors to brainstorming sessions prior to the beginning of a particular church year season.

Changes within Worship

Specific changes can be made to some parts of *LBW* services in order to ensure proper contextualizing of worship regarding language use.

First, there are the announcements! Here the use of language, coincident with contemporary usage and spiritual insight, can be explicitly discussed and implicitly modeled. What is said and not said about people, worship, and God in the announcements is substantial. It is also during this time where, in the interests of evangelism, the visitor will form many impressions and may even draw some conclusions about whether or not this congregation is worth a return visit.

Next, the role of the assisting minister is significant in relationship to those freely-constructed parts of the service. Here the writing of the prayers offers another opportunity to model a community which is inclusive and expressive of both tradition and change. Periodic workshops on the history, meaning, language, and construction of liturgical intercessory prayers can lend courage to those who have not attempted such a task, and also encourage the gifts of the community.

Another place in which language changes can be highlighted is in the use of biblical translations for the readings and reference in preaching. Texts read by the lector should reflect language which is inclusive and ecumenical to the best possible extent of both issues. Obviously lector training should always be provided so that language usage can be demonstrated publicly as an act of worship in the assembly.

One primary part of the liturgy in which language most freely and forcefully manifests its capacity to change and influence a community is through the sermon. By both reading and commenting on text and daily life, the preacher's language demonstrates vividly in a representative way what a given congregation is about and the mission to which it is called.[12]

Undoubtedly the entry of women into many pulpits has influenced the language of proclamation. One recent and thorough study of women preachers has shown that women indeed use language differently.[13] Their approach to the biblical texts, their use of a different cache of experiences and anecdotes, their use of narrative—all profoundly influence the way congregations hear and think about language. To what extent then, does female leadership today in liturgy and preaching affect a congregation's use of a worship book that is two decades old? Do persona and text clash or come to terms?

Another linguistic issue which is affecting many congregations in worship is directly linked to evangelism. With the shifts in religious life in North America, attention has turned to what are generally called "seekers." Views and assessments of the seekers are multiple. Seekers may be Christians who are "shopping" for a more stable tradition. They may be lapsed Christians or without Baptism. Whatever their background, all seekers are searching for acceptance and the new life.

In any case, language usage in worship is often reflected in using complete bulletin-contained orders of worship. Here the spirit rather than the actual presence of *LBW* occurs. And at this juncture, several key questions come to the fore for thoughtful study and discussion.

First, what linguistic changes are signaled to both the visitor and member as a result of the two printed formats? Are the compromises felicitous or only a resultant jumble of styles (not to mention paper)? What symbolic value do the use of books have—the lector's Bible (not the bulletin insert), the *LBW* (not the printed-out service in a bulletin)?

There is also significant study in the area of graphics to indicate that the way language is literally choreographed on the printed page says a great deal about a person, a community or, in this case, the theology and life of a congregation! Upper case or lower case, italicized print or roman print, black letter and the older rubrics—all give or delete certain messages to the worshiper.

Finally, is the printed *LBW* bulletin format inclusive—not only of gender and ethnicity but also of both traditional and contemporary usage?

The question is an interesting one in that bulletin-contained orders of worship do not replace *LBW*, but a genre signifying transition and thus, to what?

CONCLUSION

Clearly, the use of *LBW* texts from two decades ago raises substantial questions about their effectiveness today. However, the dual gifts which the church has—tradition and contemporary context—offer ways to address both when planning worship.

The linguistic issues attached to *LBW* today are not easily solved without recognition and acceptance of the fact that its contents reflect language of both needed tradition and seemingly outmoded elements from the North American context of two decades ago. Repeating those elements with the assumption that it is *all* tradition and not subject to change is inappropriate and naive.

If anything, the question of how we use language within the church has intensified over the last two decades. Worship planners must engage this reality or only repeat the past without the Spirited realities of the present context. As this chapter has demonstrated in several ways, there are a number of factors which must figure in linguistic realignments in worship.

The first of these is basic and attitudinal in nature. *Compromise* is obviously a key reality in all worship planning. As the earlier Luther quote made clear, discussion and consensus must rule as the path to the overall goal of the edification of God's people. A congregation's mission statement and church constitution can serve as starting places to speak of who is responsible for worship and in which ways. This is not merely a defensive posture but can be an exciting way of drawing in an entire congregation to think of worship more deeply!

Education is another component of effective worship planning. It is not sufficient for worship committee members to educate only themselves. Careful and sometimes extensive educational work in a congregation is the only way to effect language changes in worship. Change moves at many different paces throughout the church. In some places, linguistic change is needed and eagerly sought and created.

In other places, the responsibility and hard work of worship leaders and planners must include continual efforts to educate worshipers as to the rationale for changes in worship language and model that clearly without embarrassment or hesitation.

Readily available means to do this are the bulletin, the parish newsletter, audio and audiovisual materials, the training of worship leaders, church school classes for both adults and children regarding worship, ecumenical worship services, and synod worship resources. Consider presenting a series of Sunday forums with the entire worship committee present to discuss liturgical history and practices as well as emerging plans for parish worship. Possibly a special piece of choral or instrumental music could be commissioned to designate a year-long focus on worship.

Finally, *openness* is the primary factor in introducing worship changes—a basic openness to the work of the Spirit, an openness to the changes in parish life caused by worship changes, and an openness to new and different ways of reflecting the traditions of faith which will enrich the life of God's people in any place and time. Especially needed is an openness to receiving the sometimes-hidden gifts of worship planning which reside in the members of all congregations.

Poised on the edge of a new millennium, the colors of worship certainly include green! The presence of *LBW* accompanies us as we continue new adventures of faith, seeking words to express our thanks and praise to the one who has brought us to this time!

NOTES

1 "O Sacred Head, Now Wounded," *LBW* hymn 116.The phrase is completed this way in the hymn: "What language shall I borrow to thank thee, dearest friend . . . ?" The phrase is a poignant summary of the on-going work of all worship planners regarding the use of linguistic texts.

2 See Deborah Tannen, *You Just Don't Understand* (New York: Ballantine Books, 1990). Tannen is a professor of linguistics and has done extensive work in the area of language and gender. This book is "must" reading for those who need to be convinced gender makes a different in female/male interactions. The book has significant implications for understanding gender and worship.

3 See "The German Mass and Order of Service, 1526" in *Luther's Works,* Liturgy and Hymns, Volume 53 (Philadelphia: Fortress Press, 1965), p. 51 ff.

4 "The Gospel for the Festival of the Epiphany," from *Luther's Works,* Sermons II, Volume 52 (Philadelphia: Fortress Press, 1974), pp. 205, 206. In a similar fashion, the core of the faith can also be projected through time in a fairly predictable manner. In an experiment in a preaching and worship class at the Lutheran Seminary at Gettysburg in 1997, students created a wedding service set in the year 2700. LBW hymns with creation themes and the human issues at stake in a marriage service startled students by their similarities to contemporary worship, despite the "Star Wars" setting!

5 "A Christian Exhortation to the Livonians Concerning Public Worship and Concord," 1523, by Martin Luther. From *Luther's Works,* Liturgy and Hymns, Volume 53 (Philadelphia: Fortress Press, 1965), p. 47. This volume contains several short and excellent works on liturgy that have to do with both regular Sunday worship and materials for occasional services such as Baptism and marriage. These materials are excellent not only for their historical value but their typically sound Lutheran advice on worship matters!

6 Anne Primavesi, *From Apocalypse to Genesis: Ecology, Feminism and Christianity* (Minneapolis: Fortress Press, 1991), pp. 138-139. Primavesi's powerful vignette of language reversals strongly makes the case for the need to speak inclusively in worship, e.g. "You have heard only feminine words used for yourself and your fellow worshippers. You have been assured that these are intended to be inclusive of both sexes; that whenever the officiating woman says 'womenkind' she means all humanity."

7 Two excellent books on the inter-connected topics of language, inclusive speech, gender and the naming of God are: Johanna W. H. van Wijk-Bos, *Reimagining God: The Case for Scriptural Diversity* (Louisville: Westminster John Knox Press. 1995). This volume, by a Reformed theologian, is exceptionally well documented, including information on

both biblical texts and references to hymns. The second work is by Ruth C. Duck, entitled *Gender and the Name of God: The Trinitarian Baptismal Formula* (New York: The Pilgrim Press, 1991). This book contains excellent historical information related to the earliest baptismal texts and what implications they have for the current discussions over the necessity of using one phrase alone for Baptism. Whether one agrees with the conclusions of these books, they are essential for those who are unfamiliar with these issues is worship planning.

Two ELCA documents regarding baptismal terminology are useful resources for worship planning. First is the March 8-11, 1991, statement by the Conference of Bishops: "'In the name of the Father, and of the Son, and of the Holy Spirit' is therefore the only doctrinally acceptable way for a person to be baptized into the Body of Christ. ...'" Second is the statement, *The Use of the Means of Grace*, adopted by the 1997 Churchwide Assembly. Principle 24 declares that "Holy Baptism is administered with water in the name of the triune God, Father, Son and Holy Spirit...."

8   A new resource which is excellent for use with the RCL is the *Indexes For Worship Planning* (Minneapolis: Fortress Press, 1996). Each Sunday is given approximate dating, such as Sunday between July 24 and July 30th inclusive, texts and prayers of the day, along with the verse, the offertory are listed for all three years. Suggestions are also given for the hymn of the day, hymns related to the readings, and additional suggestions. Worship planners will find this an indispensable tool. It can also be used for comparative purposes with the lectionary in the front of *LBW* to see which texts have been omitted, included, and in what fashion.

9   Two names which are especially notable are New Testament scholar Elisabeth S. Fiorenza and Old Testament scholar Phyllis Trible.

10 All these resources were published between 1978 and 1982 by Augsburg Publishing House, Minneapolis, and Board of Publication, Lutheran Church in America, Philadelphia.

11 Nancy Galbraith is a Lutheran organist and choir director at Christ Lutheran Church in Pittsburgh. She is also an Associate Professor of Composition at Andrew Carnegie Mellon University. She has published and recorded both secular and sacred choral and instrumental works. Her source of liturgical compositions stems directly from her work with her parish choir and is based on LBW texts. Marty Haugen first began publishing and using his works through the Holden Village Community near Lake Chelan, Washington. His settings of liturgical music are available in written and recorded form and his work is included in *With One Voice*.

12 One of the best books on preaching that takes community and context seriously is by Leonora Tubbs Tisdale, *Preaching as Local Theology and Folk Art*. Minneapolis: Fortress Press, 1997.This book speaks clearly about what it means to be a local congregation and the resources available to and generated by its members for ministry.

13 Carol M. Noren, *The Woman in the Pulpit* (Nashville: Abingdon Press, 1991). This study of women preaching deserves a reading by worship committees as well as congregations who have called or are thinking of calling a woman to serve as their pastor. The book is written by a professor of preaching and contains information on the way women use language in relationship to authority, biblical work, doing theology, and leading worship. It is the only available work on women which adequately covers all the major realities associated with ordained women in the pulpit.

THE CULTURAL PATTERN OF CHRISTIAN WORSHIP

Language, Order, Song

Thomas H. Schattauer

Two broad purposes resonate in the preface to *Lutheran Book of Worship* (*LBW*) and throughout its liturgical services and hymnal.[1] The first sounds out from "the liturgical tradition," which bears "the gestures, songs, and words by which Christians have identified themselves and each other."[2] This liturgical heritage is understood to include a rich historical and ecumenical inheritance as well as a distinctive Lutheran legacy. The second purpose sounds out from the contemporary cultural situation and the pastoral need for liturgical adaptation, with implications for language, ceremony, leadership, musical style, and flexibility of forms.[3] This latter commitment carries forward and expands upon the Reformers' commitment to a vernacular liturgy capable of faithful and understanding participation. Both purposes—to reclaim tradition and to adapt it to present circumstances—have characterized the modern liturgical movement, and they reflect the fundamental aims of ecclesial reform and renewal in the modern period. The catchwords *ressourcement* (French: "returning to the sources") and *aggiornamento* (Italian: "bringing up to date") used to describe the reforming impulses at work in the Second Vatican Council also articulate the dual purpose of liturgical reform and renewal at work in *LBW*.[4]

The two intervening decades since the publication of *LBW* have affected the two parts of this double trajectory disproportionately. The pressures to update and adapt liturgical practice have steadily increased. These include the expanding influence of American popular culture as well as the heightened awareness of cultural diversity both within American society and around the world. The relation of the church and its liturgy to the present cultural moment has become a matter of urgency for all concerned about the mission of the church in the North American context. These concerns have raised questions about the sources of liturgical practice: Are the historic patterns and traditional materials of Christian worship adaptable to present need? Do they not derive from cultural contexts distant from our own, and as a result, are they not a hindrance to faithful and understanding participation by contemporary Christians? Furthermore, is "the liturgical tradition" as univocal, even in the earliest sources, as it has sometimes been presented by the proponents of liturgical renewal? These questions have complicated and, at times, diverted the trajectory of return to the sources. It remains to be seen whether postmodern sensibilities, which favor communal particularity in the midst of cultural pluralism, might give renewed persuasiveness to historic liturgical patterns and traditional materials, or whether the experience of fragmentation in contemporary life might give renewed impetus to the appropriation of liturgical practice rooted in the Christian past.

What follows in this essay is not primarily about liturgical *aggiornamento*, although such questions are not far from its horizon of interest. It is rather an extended reflection about an approach to liturgical *ressourcement*, one that searches for the patterns in worship peculiar to the church as community existing in time and space. It explores the usefulness of looking at the communal life of the church as a culture and seeks to identify some of the cultural patterns indigenous to the liturgical assembly, especially in relation to the language, order, and song of Christian worship. Such an approach moves liturgical *ressourcement* beyond naked appeals to authoritative historical sources and grounds it in the nature of the church as a historical community that bears the gospel to the world and, through ritual and symbol, enacts the gospel for the world.

GOSPEL MESSAGE AND GOSPEL COMMUNITY

The Russian Orthodox theologian Georges Florovsky has written provocatively about the church's message in relation to its existence as a historical community:

> Christianity entered history as a new social order, or rather a new social dimension. From the very beginning Christianity was not primarily a "doctrine," but exactly a "community." There was not only a "Message" to be proclaimed and

delivered and "Good News" to be declared. There was precisely a New Community, distinct and peculiar, in the process of growth and formation, to which members were called and recruited. Indeed, "fellowship" (*koinonia*) was the basic category of Christian existence.[5]

Christianity is not only a message—the proclamation of God's saving deed for all in the death and resurrection of Jesus Christ—but also a "distinct and peculiar" community that exists within and for the sake of the larger human community.

In the first chapters of the book of Acts, the correlation of gospel message and gospel community are clear from the start of the early Christian movement. As a result of the outpouring of the Holy Spirit upon the apostles and those gathered with them in Jerusalem at Pentecost, Peter preaches a sermon that proclaims Jesus of Nazareth, crucified, raised up by God, exalted at the right hand of God; the one crucified, God has made both Lord and Messiah (Acts 2:14-36). The claim of this message upon Peter's hearers calls them to repentance and to a baptism in the name of Jesus Christ for the forgiveness of sins and a share of the Spirit poured out (Acts 2:38). The result is a new community and the patterns of its life together: "So those who welcomed his message were baptized, and that day about three thousand persons were added. They devoted themselves to the apostles' teaching and fellowship, to the breaking of bread and the prayers" (Acts 2:41-42). The gospel *and* the church, the message *and* the community, characterize the Christian movement. These two things cannot be separated. There is no church without the gospel, and no gospel without the church. The message and the community stand together as the hearable and visible realities of God's purposes in Jesus Christ. The right understanding of Christianity—and its worship—must always correlate these two things.

It is necessary to insist upon the correlation of gospel and church, because Lutheran Christians have in general been clearer about the significance of the gospel message than they have about the gospel community.[6] And our lack of clarity and insight into the place of the church as a distinct and peculiar community in the encompassing reality of the gospel is the source of a good deal of liturgical confusion in Christian congregations seeking to engage contemporary North American culture.

Easter Sunday 1995, the front page of the *New York Times* featured an article on the ferment in contemporary Christian worship, and it included this description of worship at the Community Church of Joy:

The 10:30 A.M. service at the Community Church of Joy, a Lutheran congregation in Glendale, Ariz., earlier this year . . . opened with a trio of vocalists, backed by a rock quartet, singing a "praise chorus," a contemporary pop-style hymn of perhaps 25 words. The lyrics were printed in the church bulletins passed out at the door so the congregation could sing along.

After the final chord died away the senior pastor, the Rev. Walther P. Kallestad, clad in a blue blazer and holding a cordless microphone, urged everyone to greet one another, "the most fantastic people in the world."

The music surged again, another praise chorus. A staff member read two verses of the New Testament and recited a brief prayer. Then two other staff members, dressed as schoolchildren, acted out a skit about sharing one's faith.

After another pop-style hymn, Pastor Kallestad preached a sermon titled, "You Can Change the World," about how the church's mission, to draw in people unconnected with organized religion, had succeeded so well that the Community Church of Joy would soon move to a larger location. The offering plate was passed as the band played again.

A few minutes later the 50-minute service was over. It was the third of the morning. A fourth would begin in 15 minutes.[7]

The advocates of church growth, including its Lutheran adherents, are urging a reorientation of worship for the purpose of outreach to persons steeped in the ways of a highly secular culture. They are busy shaping worship events that have the feel of the contemporary marketplace and the liveliness of popular culture. The aim is to provide worship accessible, in style and content, to the unchurched and the irreligious, who are purported to be uncomfortable with and put off by formal, "churchy" liturgies.

From the perspective of church growth, worship is principally a means for communicating the Christian message, and therefore, the current task of reform is to accommodate Christian worship to the forms and practices of mass communication and popular culture. The sacred liturgical space becomes an auditorium dominated by a stage surrounded by theater-style seating with few if any historic markers of Christian identity; the sound of choir and organ are replaced by the electronic acoustic of a rock band and miked singers; and the minister or worship leader takes a role akin to the talk-show host and entertainer, with the cordless microphone as the principal symbol of authority. The church as an institution and its communal traditions, including its inherited patterns of worship, are viewed primarily as obstacles to the proclamation of the gospel to modern, secular persons.[8]

The contemporary worship movement is about finding the most effective means available for communicating the gospel message. The gospel message here incarnates itself in the forms of contemporary culture. Those who advocate this approach have, to their credit, recognized and made others take note of the new missionary situation of the church in North America. They are acting on the pressing need to engage this cultural moment with the Christian message. What is missing from this picture, however, is a deeply theological appreciation of the church as historical community, with its own distinctive patterns of life and ways of worship, some of which are functions of the gospel in the church and not merely the forms of a passing cultural inheritance.

On the one hand, Christian worship is thoroughly conditioned by culture. Christian worship is a matter of human behavior, and consequently, it cannot take place apart from the physical and artistic, the linguistic and conceptual material of human culture. As Aidan Kavanagh has often remarked, "The liturgy did not drop from heaven in a Glad Bag," hermetically sealed off from the contamination of contact with human things. Christian worship is inevitably shaped by the local cultural milieu. Participants bring the culture with them in their ways of thinking, speaking, and acting, and worship makes use of cultural materials—language, music, and all the arts; the architectural arrangement of space and the calendrical organization of time; ways of movement and gesture.

On the other hand, Christian worship is a function of the gospel, the message of God's salvation in the death and resurrection of Jesus Christ, which redirects the material of human culture to serve God's saving purposes. Although deeply enmeshed with the material of human culture, worship is not determined primarily by the worlds of meaning constructed by human beings but rather by God's ultimate purposes for the world revealed in Jesus Christ. Furthermore, because the gospel message constitutes a new community, Christian worship is also a function of this visible, historical community. Christian worship and specifically the worship of a local assembly is thus a complex interaction of the gospel message in the gospel community within the context of a local culture.[9]

My point is this: Authentic Christian worship is not simply a communication of the gospel message with whatever cultural instruments are most effective. Authentic Christian worship also involves the distinctive inheritance of the gospel community, its own patterns of speech and action—that is to say, its own cultural patterns. Anscar Chupungco, a Roman Catholic theologian with long experience in matters of liturgical inculturation, puts it this way: "The liturgy is a ritual action which has developed a cultural pattern distinctly its own."[10]

CHURCH AS CULTURE

To say that the liturgy exhibits its own cultural pattern is to imply that the church can be compared to a culture. What might it mean to view the church not only as a community in the midst of human culture and specific cultures but also as itself a kind of culture? And what is the relation of liturgy to the church as culture? The reflection on these questions will focus on three statements:

1. As a way of life, the church is like a culture.
2. Liturgy stands at the center of the "culture" of churchly life.
3. Liturgy exhibits patterns that are distinctive or "indigenous" to the "culture" of churchly life.

1. As a way of life, the church is like a culture. "Culture" here refers to a whole way of life among people in a place. It encompasses all the things that together construct the social environment in which people live—language, ways of thinking and belief, the use of space and physical artifacts, literature, music, the arts, institutions, customs, and practices of all sorts. The materials of culture not only sustain a common life but also form a web of significance. Culture, then, is a way of life that constitutes a more or less comprehensive world of meaning. If the church not only carries a message to be proclaimed, taught, and believed but also embodies a way of life within a visible community of persons inhabiting space and a historical community extended in time, then the church can be compared to a culture. The church, like a culture, is a way of life that constitutes a world of meaning.

A number of authors have adopted the model or metaphor of culture to talk about the church today, and we might ask why the notion of culture seems to have illuminative power for the contemporary understanding of the church and its worship.[11] One important reason is that it helps us to make sense of the church's place in a post-Christian society. For roughly 1500 years, the church in the Western world lived under what is sometimes called the Constantinian arrangement. With the conversion of the Roman emperor Constantine early in the fourth century of this era, Christianity was legalized, lavishly patronized, and eventually endorsed as the religion of the state. No longer did the church exist as a separate community cultivating its own life and pursuing its own mission under the umbrella of empire; now it was itself a part of the structure of society. The collapse of empire furthered the church's influence and its identification with the structures of society and the whole way of life in what we call Western culture. In the minds of many, Western culture became a Christian culture.

The Constantinian arrangement has collapsed, and with that the church is increasingly unable to understand itself as an extension of society or to identify itself with the culture. Rather, many are beginning to understand the church as a distinct and peculiar community, existing within the larger cultural framework of a secular society, in which it cultivates its own life and pursues its own mission amidst a host of competing claims to truth and a variety of ways of life (which is what we mean by pluralism, in both its religious and cultural dimensions). In this new and somewhat confusing context, it makes sense to underscore the nature of the church as a community and to speak of the church as something like a culture.

It is important, however, to note that we are speaking of the church as something *like* a culture. The community of the church does not provide us with the food we eat or the clothes we wear; it does not generate all the ideas we discuss or all the music we enjoy; it is not the source of most of our habits; it does not determine every political choice. There is no need for a Christian Yellow Pages (as some have tried), where we can obtain anything we might need from a Christian source. The church as a community is not a complete way of life, an enclosed world in which one can find all the things that make for life. To this way of thinking, the church is not a sectarian community that desires to remove itself from the surrounding culture or cultures. As such, it is only *like* a culture.[12]

This "like" is extremely important, because it points to the eschatological nature of the church and the symbolic character of churchly life. The church as a visible community in the world orients us (and seeks to orient all people) to the ultimate communion with God and the perfect community of life in the kingdom of God that Jesus proclaimed. The church is not the world (and therefore only like a culture) and it is not the kingdom of God. It is a third thing that exists between the creation and its consummation. It is a visible sign in the midst of the world that manifests God's purposes for the world, purposes revealed in the death and resurrection of Jesus Christ, purposes that will that will be perfected in the fullness of God's promised reign over all things. What the church is and everything it does, then, is symbolic, because it points beyond itself to the kingdom of

God.[13] We might say that the "culture" of churchly life refers us to the "culture" of the kingdom of God.[14]

2. *Worship is at the center of the culture of churchly life.* Worship, and specifically the Sunday eucharistic assembly, is at the center of the culture of churchly life because that is where the church as a visible community in the world assembles to enact in a symbolic way what it means to live in a world redeemed. There, it playfully rehearses life in the kingdom of God, which is fundamentally a *communio*—a communion with God in the community of a redeemed humanity. Worship is at the center because that is where the church most fully realizes its own nature as sign to the world in the *communio* established by the death and resurrection of Jesus and where it most fully carries out its mission to orient people to God's purposes for the world.[15]

3. *Liturgy exhibits patterns that are distinctive or "indigenous" to the "culture" of churchly life.* At the center of churchly life, the liturgy exhibits patterns of speech and action that are indigenous to the way of life within the Christian community. These patterns are the result of the interaction of the revelation of God in Jesus Christ with the materials of human culture. Consequently, these patterns are not devoid of the influence of culture (and indeed specific cultures, especially Hebrew culture and Graeco-Roman culture of late antiquity), but they are specifically the product of the Christian community. And consequently, these patterns function to identify and define this community in its relation to God and God's purposes for the world.

PATTERNS IN THE CULTURE OF CHURCHLY LIFE

The language, order, and song of the church's liturgy offer good examples of patterns distinctive to the culture of churchly life, specifically the trinitarian language of liturgical prayer, the fundamental *ordo* of the liturgy (i.e., the essential components of word and action), and the priority of song in the music of worship. Each of these presumes an even more basic pattern: the vary pattern of gathering together or assembly.

The Sunday assembly of Christians is itself a distinctive pattern in the life of the Christian community.[16] In the middle of the second century, Justin Martyr offered a report of the Christian assembly in the city of Rome. It begins and ends in this way:

> And on the day called Sunday an assembly is held on one place
> of all who live in town or country.

And we all assemble together on Sunday, because it is the first day, on which God transformed darkness and matter, and made the world; and Jesus Christ our Savior rose from the dead on that day; for they crucified him the day before Saturday; and the day after Saturday, which is Sunday, he appeared to his apostles and disciples, and taught them these things which we have presented to you for your consideration.[17]

Two things distinguished the early Christians in their cultural environment: the peculiar message of salvation for all through God's action in Jesus Christ, crucified and risen from the dead, *and* this distinctive assembly of the community. The Sunday assembly of Christians around the scriptures and a meal was, as Justin reports, a gathering of all who lived in a place. This very manner of gathering was distinctive in the ancient world, so argues John Zizioulas, precisely because it was for all the people in a place.[18] It was not an assembly based upon race (as among the Jews) or one based upon social status (as among the pagans in their professional *collegia* or associations). It ignored the markers of human identity. In the words of the apostle Paul, "There is no longer Jew or Greek, . . . slave or free, . . . male or female; for all of you are one in Christ Jesus" (Galatians 3:28, NRSV).

In the unity of Christ, local assemblies of Christians in their make-up overlooked the things that separated people from one another, things like—to use the jargon of contemporary social theorists—age, race, gender, ethnicity, and social location. "The eucharistic assembly," according to Zizioulas, "was in its composition a *catholic community* in the sense that it transcended not only social but also natural division, just as it will happen in the kingdom of God of which this community was a revelation and a real sign."[19] The Sunday assembly of all Christians in a place is the context for the three "cultural" patterns of Christian worship under examination here.

The Trinitarian Language of Liturgical Prayer.[20]

The first thing to note about the language of prayer is something we can hardly conceive otherwise: that we address God directly as "you." Prayer, of course, presupposes this personal address to God. That Christians regard such address to God in prayer as a basic form of worship is an inheritance from Judaism.[21] This pattern of personal address characterizes worship, and consequently, the relation to God, in the most fundamental way. Christian worship is constituted not by a third person description of a distant God, but by the act of personal address to the living God.

The language of prayer in the Christian assembly is further character-ized by its address to God *through Christ*. The prayers of the day in *LBW*, for example, terminate either simply "through your Son, Jesus Christ our Lord" or in the elaborated form "through your Son, Jesus Christ our Lord, who lives and reigns with you and the Holy Spirit, one God, now and for-ever." The proper prefaces of the eucharistic liturgy address prayer to God "through Christ, our Lord," and the doxological termination of the first eucharistic prayer in *LBW* declares "through him (i.e., Christ), with him, in him, in the unity of the Holy Spirit, all honor and glory is yours, almighty Father, now and forever." This pattern of prayer to God through Christ can be seen in the earliest Christian formulas for prayer that we know (in the *Didache* 9 and 10, from as early as the first century)[22], and it is evident as well in the New Testament (e.g., Romans 1:8, 2 Corinthians 1:20).[23] There are many examples in the tradition of Christian prayer and in *LBW* of prayers that directly address Christ, for example, the "Stir up" prayers appointed for the First and Fourth Sundays of Advent ("Stir up your power, O Lord, and come . . . for you live and reign with the Father and the Holy Spirit, one God, now and forever"),[24] but the dominant pattern is prayer addressed to God through Jesus Christ—through Christ to God, who is at times explic-itly called upon as Father, just as Jesus called this one "Abba." This pat-tern, as Josef Jungmann has persuasively argued, is the classic structure of Christian prayer.[25]

The "through Christ" pattern of prayer points to the christological cen-ter of Christian faith and practice. It refers us to the gospel, to the procla-mation of Jesus' death and resurrection as God's saving deed through which we have been restored to life with God. The "through Christ" is a form of shorthand for the message of salvation that "in Christ God was reconciling the world to himself" (2 Corinthians 5:19, NRSV), that "we have peace with God through our Lord Jesus Christ" (Romans 5:1, NRSV). In the terms of Lutheran theology, the "through Christ" is a summary of the foun-dation of Christian existence in justification by grace through faith in Jesus Christ embedded in the very pattern of prayer. We come to God in prayer in the only way possible for us: through Jesus Christ, the mediator of our prayer and of all that we are.

And where is the Holy Spirit in the pattern of Christian prayer? In the simple termination "through your Son, Jesus Christ our Lord," there is no reference to the Spirit. The elaborated termination adds "who lives and reigns with you and the Holy Spirit, one God, now and forever," which declares in a doxological fashion the living God as a unity of the three persons of the Trinity. The most revealing reference to the Spirit as concerns the pattern of Christian prayer, however, comes in the traditional western doxology of the eucharistic prayer, already mentioned above: "Through him, with him, in him, in the unity of the Holy Spirit, all honor and glory is yours almighty Father now and forever." The "in the unity of the Holy Spirit" refers to the unity of the praying assembly in the activity of the Holy Spirit as the agent of prayer.[26] The Holy Spirit prompts and guides the prayer of the assembly; the Spirit unifies the assembly in its praying and draws its prayer through Christ to God. Whether or not it is explicitly stated, the deep structure of Christian prayer is this: the assembly prays in the Spirit, through Christ, to God.

This pattern of prayer is trinitarian, not because prayer is addressed to the triune God, but rather because the whole movement of prayer has a trinitarian shape, "in the Spirit, through Christ, to God." In the trinitarian shape of Christian prayer, we see a picture of prayer that is quite different from an understanding of prayer as a response to God "out there," an activity that bridges the gap between the human creature and the transcendent God. It is rather a picture of prayer as a communion with God in the dynamic relation of the Trinity. In the Spirit and through Christ, God embraces the assembly's speech and action and draws it into the communion of God's very being. This is a pattern of prayer that is possible only for an assembly of the baptized, for those who live in Christ and in the Spirit-filled community of God's people.

The pattern of prayer addressed to God through Christ in the Spirit-filled assembly is a linguistic pattern distinctive of speech within the church's worship.[27] As such, it exemplifies a pattern indigenous to the culture of churchly life.

The Fundamental *Ordo* of the Liturgy.[28]

The basic shape of words and actions in the liturgy (the *ordo*) also exhibits a pattern distinctive to the culture of churchly life. Justin Martyr's description of the Sunday assembly of Christians at Rome in the mid-second century sets out a pattern that has persisted, more or less clearly, through the centuries in local assemblies of Christians:

> And on the day called Sunday an assembly is held in one place
> of all who live in town or country, and the records of the
> apostles or the writings of the prophets are read as time allows.

Then, when the reader has finished, the president in a discourse admonishes and exhorts (us) to imitate these good things.

Encountering God

Then we all stand up together and send up prayers; and as we said before, when we have finished praying, bread and wine and water are brought up, and the president likewise sends up prayers and thanksgivings to the best of his ability, and the people assent, saying the Amen; and the (elements over which) thanks have been given are distributed, and everyone partakes; and they are sent through the deacons to those who are not present.

And the wealthy who so desire give what they wish, as each chooses; and what is collected is deposited with the president . . . [who] takes care of all those who are in need.[29]

An outline of Justin's description would look like this:
Gathering of the assembly
Reading of scripture
Preaching
Prayers of intercession
(Peace—attested elsewhere in the same document)

Collection of gifts for those in need
   (precisely where in the order is not clear)
Presentation of bread and wine
Prayer of thanksgiving over bread and wine
Communion in the elements of bread and wind

(Dismissal), with distribution of elements
   to those absent and of gifts to the needy

With remarkably few adjustments, Justin's description provides a basic outline for most any eucharistic rite in Christian churches both East and West, including Luther's *Formula Missae* (1523) and *Deutsche Messe* (1526) as well as the liturgy for Holy Communion in *LBW*. When we look at the liturgy not so much as a sequence of texts, but rather as a pattern of action, what becomes evident is the common structure exhibited by Christian liturgies of different times and places.

Gordon Lathrop has offered an instructive and illuminating analysis of this pattern of action at the Sunday assembly.[30] The Sunday *ordo* is made up of pairs of actions, most fundamentally that of word and meal, which we see already in Justin's description and even in some New Testament texts (e.g., Acts 20:7-11; Luke 24:13-32). The Word component is itself also a pair of actions: the reading of Scriptures and the preaching; and so, too, is the meal component: the prayer of thanksgiving over bread and wine and the eating and drinking of these things. This pattern is christological because the word proclaimed in Scripture and preaching and the meal celebrated in thanksgiving and communion are about Christ and our participation in him. This pattern is biblical not because the Scriptures specifically describe it or mandate it, but because it resonates with the way the Scriptures themselves reveal God's activity: as Lathrop observes, in the pattern of the word "ancient texts are used to speak a new grace" and in the pattern of the meal "old words and actions are made to speak a new grace" in the same way that the scriptures themselves use "the old to say the new by means of juxtaposition."[31]

There is one more thing to say about *ordo* of word and meal. Each pair of actions generates a third, so that Scripture reading and preaching yield the prayers of intercession, and thanksgiving prayer and communion yield a collection for the needs of all.[32] In this pattern, we see that the assembly drawn to Christ in word and meal turns to the world and its need in prayer and self-giving. The *ordo* of word and meal is not an enclosed sacred precinct in which Christ and his people are the only actors; rather, the *ordo* embraces the world and its need. Indeed, God's ultimate purposes for the whole world are the point of the assembly's pattern of action.

This *ordo* of word and meal is another distinctive pattern in the culture of churchly life. It is a pattern of action (including many words) connected to the biblical witness and focused on setting the things of Christ in relation to the participating assembly for the sake of the whole world. It is a pattern that has been enacted and will continue to be enacted in diverse forms of cultural expression.

The Priority of Song in the Music of Worship.[33]

In most every religious or cultural tradition, ritual action and music have an integral relation. This is also true for the Christian community. What is significant about the pattern of music in the Christian assembly for worship, however, is not the use of music in general, but rather the priority of song, most especially the song of a singing congregation, the song of the assembly in its prayer and praise. There are times in the past when this has been obscured, and it is not always evident today. The extent to which and the way in which the priority of song and a singing congregation distinguishes the Christian assembly from other religious or social gatherings lie beyond the scope and competence of these reflections. Nonetheless, the significant place of song in Christian worship suggests its inclusion among the things characteristic of the cultural pattern of Christian worship.

Encountering God

What are some of the indicators of the priority of song? In his letter to the church at Ephesus, the apostle Paul identifies the church's song as something that sets Christians apart from the corruption of their cultural environment:

> Be careful then how you live, not as unwise people but as wise, making the most of the time, because the days are evil. So do not be foolish, but understand what the will of the Lord is. Do not get drunk with wine, for that is debauchery; but be filled with the Spirit, as you sing psalms and hymns and spiritual songs among yourselves, singing and making melody to the Lord in your hearts, giving thanks to God the Father at all times and for everything in the name of our Lord Jesus Christ (Ephesians 5:15-20; NRSV).

The extraordinary variety of this song throughout the centuries—variety in text, musical form, and performance practice—is certainly one indication of the significant place of song. Another is the resistance to instruments in preference for the unaccompanied human voice in the earliest Christian communities. This was initially an inheritance from the Jewish synagogue and a marker of resistance to paganism, but its persistence for many centuries in Western Christianity and in the churches of the East to this day suggests that singing is congruent with the purpose of the Christian assembly.[34] And none should forget that the priority of song and the nurture of a singing congregation were at the heart of the Lutheran reform of liturgical practice.

By no means should this be taken to imply that authentic Christian worship will do without organs and other instruments, or that it will eliminate the rehearsed voices of a choir. The significance of song and a singing congregation—not just music *per* se—is, however, worthy of exploration.

In Luther's preface to *Geistliches Gesangbüchlein* (1524), he writes: "That it is good and pleasing to sing hymns is, I think, known to every Christian." Luther reminds his readers of the place of song in the Old Testament and of "the common and ancient custom of the Christian church to sing Psalms . . . instituted . . . so that God's Word and Christian teaching might be instilled and implanted in many ways." Luther's interest in this hymnal has a similar purpose: "that the holy gospel which now by the grace of God has risen anew may be noised and spread abroad."[35] Christian song serves God's Word; the singing assembly participates in a common proclamation of the gospel in such a way that those who sing and hear the song are themselves attuned to God's Word. This is the first reason for the priority of song. In song, music carries the proclamation of God's Word, and music also instills and implants the Word in those who sing. Music serves the divine Word and its human appropriation.

Luther also understands that singing serves the human expression of faith created by the Word. In his preface to the *Babst Gesangbuch* (1545), Luther writes:

> For God has cheered our hearts and minds through his dear Son, whom he gave for us to redeem us from sin, death, and the devil. The one who believes this earnestly cannot be quiet about it but must gladly and willingly sing and speak about it so that others also may come and hear it.[36]

In Luther's view, faith overflows in song, and this expression of faith is in turn a witness that invites and encourages others into the hearing of the Word that is the source of faith. This is the second reason for the priority of song and a singing congregation.

The final reason for the priority of song is that it serves the bond of love in the Christian assembly. On this point, the 4th century bishop and theologian Basil the Great is our conversation partner:

> A psalm creates friendships, unites the separated and reconciles those at enmity. Who can still consider one to be a foe with whom one utters the same prayer to God! Thus psalmody provides the greatest of all goods, charity, by devising in its common song a certain bond of unity, and by joining together the people into the concord of a single chorus.[37]

In this way of thinking, singing is a vehicle of the Spirit that unites the assembly in its act of prayer and praise. The Greek word for "spirit" is *pneuma*, which also means "breath." Our common breathing in the act of singing images the unity of the assembly in the Spirit (breath) of God— "through him, with him, in him, *in the unity of the Holy Spirit*, all honor and glory is yours, almighty Father, now and forever." Singing together manifests this unity and offers an experience of the fellowship of the assembly that is the basis for its common prayer and praise to God.

The priority of song and a singing congregation, evident in the musical patterns of the liturgical assembly, is another mark of the culture of churchly life. This identifiable pattern in the use of music in Christian worship can help to define the proper role of the church musician as the leader of the assembly's song (thus, cantor or chief singer), the proper use of instru-

Encountering God

ments in Christian worship, especially the organ, as an encouragement to song, and the proper place of the choir as the rehearsed voices of the assembly.[38] It may also help to focus the contemporary debates about music in worship. From the perspective of the culture of churchly life, the fundamental question is not about musical style but about what serves the priority of song and a singing congregation.

These patterns of language, order, and song together with the pattern of assembly itself are part of the way the gospel of Jesus Christ is embodied and enacted in the gospel community. They are indigenous to the culture of churchly life. Pastors, lay ministers, church musicians, indeed all who participate in worship are the stewards of these patterns in local assemblies, amidst all the complexities of contemporary life. In the engagement with the present cultural moment, it is critical that we recognize, understand, and properly cultivate the patterns that are distinctive to the Christian community and its worship. We can fail in two directions. Some will be tempted to resist change and to close themselves off from the contemporary cultural environment in the failure to recognize the adaptability of these distinctively Christian patterns to both new and changing contexts. Others will be tempted to abandon these patterns as obstacles to the growth of the church in a desperate attempt to secure a place for the Christian message. In my estimation, neither strategy will serve the life and mission of the church today.

The 19th century German Lutheran pastor Wilhelm Löhe, whose liturgical work had profound effect upon the shape and spirit of American Lutheran worship, himself had a deep appreciation of the connection between the church as a way of life and the patterns of language, order, and song at worship. Thus, he could write: "The church has put together according to holy orders . . . services of various kinds and esteems them to be understood by all the faithful as the highest harmony of earthly life and not only to be sung and spoken but to be lived."[39] *LBW* has transmitted these holy orders to North American Lutherans in this generation. May the Holy Spirit lead us faithfully to sing and speak and live them, to the glory of God and for the life of the world.

NOTES

1 This essay is a revised version of a paper presented at the 33rd Annual Lectures in Church Music at Concordia University, River Forest, Illinois, October 19-21, 1997. Happily, this annual conference carries forward a lively interchange among all the heirs of the work of the Inter-Lutheran Commission on Worship.

2 *Lutheran Book of Worship* (Minneapolis: Augsburg Publishing House and Philadelphia: Board of Publication, Lutheran Church in America, 1978), p. 6. Hereafter *LBW*.

3 *LBW*, p. 8.

4 I first learned about the significance of these catchwords from my teacher and former colleague George Lindbeck.

5 Georges Florovsky, *Empire and Desert: Antinomies of Christian History*, as quoted in Rodney Clapp, *A Peculiar People: The Church as Culture in a Post-Christian Society* (Downers Grove, Ill.: InterVarsity Press, 1996), flyleaf.

6 For an attempt by a Lutheran to understand the church as a constitutive part of the gospel, see Bruce D. Marshall, "The Church in the Gospel," *Pro Ecclesia* 1 (1992), pp. 27-41.

7 Gustav Niebuhr, "The High Energy Never Stops," *New York Times*, Sunday, 16 April 1995.

8 For further analysis of the contemporary worship movement, see Thomas H. Schattauer, "A Clamor for the Contemporary: The Present Challenge for Baptismal Identity and Liturgical Tradition in American Culture," *Cross Accent*, no. 6 (July 1995): 3-11; Frank C. Senn, "'Worship Alive': An Analysis and Critique of 'Alternative' Worship Services," *Worship* 69 (1995): 194-224. Ruth, Lester, "Lex Agendi, Lex Orandi: Toward an Understanding of Seeker Services as a New Kind of Liturgy," *Worship* 70 (1996): 386-405; for a historical perspective, see James F. White, *Christian Worship in North America: A Retrospective (1955-1995)* (Collegeville, Minn.: Liturgical Press, 1997), pp. 155-172.

9 On these points, see my essay, "How does worship relate to the cultures of North America?" in *What does "multicultural" worship look like?*, vol. 7 of *Open Questions in Worship*, ed. Gordon Lathrop (Minneapolis: Augsburg Fortress, 1996), p. 6.

10 Anscar Chupungco, "Liturgical Music and its Early Cultural Settings," in *Worship and Culture in Dialogue*, ed. S. Anita Stauffer (Geneva: Lutheran World Federation, 1994), p. 111.

11 See, for example, George A. Lindbeck, *The Nature of Doctrine: Religion and Theology in a Postliberal Age* (Philadelphia: Westminster, 1984), which proposes a "cultural-linguistic" model for understanding religion and, in particular, Christianity and Christian doctrine; also Rodney Clapp, *A Peculiar People*.

12 For a sympathetic critique of Lindbeck's use of the culture metaphor, its usefulness and its limitations, see David H. Kelsey, "Church Discourse and Public Realm," in *Theology and Dialogue: Essays in Conversation with George Lindbeck*, ed. Burce D. Marshall (Notre Dame, Ind.: University of Notre Dame Press, 1990), pp. 7-33.

13 On the symbolic and eschatological nature of the church, see Wolfhart Pannenberg, *Christian Spirituality* (Philadelphia: Westminster, 1983), pp. 35-38.

14 For another statement of this perspective see Schattauer, "How does worship relate?," pp. 8-9.

15 On the centrality of the eucharistic assembly, see Pannenberg, *Christian Spirituality*, pp. 36, 38ff.

16 In *LBW*, the focus on the assembly itself is most evident in the encouragment toward a participatory act of worship on the part of the whole congregation, together with the pastor and various lay ministers. "The liturgy is the celebration of all who gather. Together with the pastor who presides, the entire congregation is involved. It is important, therefore, that lay persons fulfill appropriate ministries within the service" (*Lutheran Book of Worship:* Ministers Edition [Minneapolis: Augsburg Publishing House and Philadelphia: Board of Publication, Lutheran Church of America, 1978], p. 25). The book presumes but does not consistently highlight the primacy of Sunday.

17 *First Apology*, 67.1, as translated in R. C. D. Jasper and G. J. Cuming, *Prayers of the Eucharist: Early and Reformed*, 3rd ed. (New York: Pueblo, 1987), pp. 29-30.

18 John D. Zizioulas, *Being as Communion: Studies in Personhood and the Church* (Crestwood, N.Y.: St. Vladimir's Press, 1985), pp. 149-152.

19 Zizioulas, *Being as Communion*, p. 152.

20 In LBW, the trinitarian shape of Christian prayer is evident in many places, most especially in the preservation of the collect form in the appointed Prayers of the Day, in the use of the traditional Western eucharistic preface, and in the provision of eucharistic prayers at the Great Thanksgiving.

21 Joseph Heinemann, *Prayer in the Talmud: Forms and Patterns*, Studia Judaica, 9 (Berlin and New York: de Gruyter, 1977), pp. 13-17, 77ff.

22 Jasper and Cuming, *Prayers of the Eucharist*, pp. 23-24.

23 The classic study of this pattern in Christian prayer is Josef A. Jungmann, *The Place of Christ in Liturgical Prayer* (Collegeville, Minn.: Liturgical Press, 1989). On the *Didache*, see pp. 3-4; on the New Testament, see pp. 127ff.

24 The pattern of address to Christ is especially prevalent in the psalm prayers accompanying the psalter in *LBW* Ministers Edition and appointed for use at Morning Prayer and Evening Prayer.

25 Jungmann, *The Place of Christ, passim*; see also Paul F. Bradshaw, *Two Ways of Praying* (Nashville, Tenn.: Abingdon, 1995), pp. 59-63.

26 Jungmann, *Place of Christ*, pp. 201-206.

27 A complete analysis of the trinitarian shape of Christian prayer and praise would involve an account of the other classic formula of Christian doxology: "Glory to the Father, and to Son, and to the Holy Spirit;" see Christopher Cocksworth, "The Trinity Today: Opportunities and Challenges for Liturgical Study," *Studia Liturgica* 27 (1997), pp. 61-78, especially his comment about "the two classic Christian doxologies" (p. 76).

28 In *LBW*, attention to the fundamental *ordo* of the liturgy is evident most especially in the place given to the Holy Communion as the chief service and in the attention to its basic structure: "The Holy Communion has two principal parts: One centers in the proclamation of the Word through the reading of the Scriptures and preaching; the other centers in sharing the sacramental meal. Surrounded by prayer, praise, and thanksgiving these two parts are so intimately connected as to form one unified act of worship. The Augsburg Confession regards the Holy Communion as the chief act of worship on Sundays and other festivals (Article 24)" (*LBW* Ministers Edition, 25). In the preparation of the Holy Communion liturgy and the controversies over it, the question of *ordo* was

evident in regard to the structure of the rite as a whole, the shape of the eucharistic action, and the provision of eucharistic prayers.

29 Jasper and Cuming, *Prayers of the Eucharist*, pp. 29-30.

30 Gordon Lathrop, *Holy Things: A Liturgical Theology* (Minneapolis: Augsburg Fortress, 1993), pp. 15-53; see also Gordon Lathrop, *What are the essentials of Christian Worship?* Open Questions in Worship (Minneapolis: Augsburg Fortress, 1994).

31 Lathrop, *Holy Things*, pp. 19, 23, 33.

32 Lathrop, *Holy Things*, p. 52; and *What are the essentials?* pp. 14, 16-18.

33 In the *LBW*, the priority of song is evident in the musical settings of the liturgy, in the regular place of hymnody, and in the provision of tones for psalm-singing. Those nurtured by Lutheran traditions of congregational song come to worship expecting to sing, and the *LBW* has sustained local assemblies in that expectation.

34 For an introduction to music in the early church, see Edward Foley, *The Foundations of Christian Music: The Music of Pre-Constantinian Christianity* (Collegeville, Minn.: Liturgical Press, 1996); Andrew Wilson-Dickson, *The Story of Christian: From Gregorian Chant to Black Gospel* (Oxford, Eng.: Lion Publishing, 1992) provides an engaging survey of the historical record and the various traditions of song.

35 *Luther's Works* 55, pp. 315-316.

36 *Luther's Works* 55, p. 333.

37 *Homilia in psalmum* i, 2; as quoted in James McKinnon, ed., *Music in Early Christian Literature* (Cambridge, Eng.: Cambridge UP, 1987), pp. 65-66.

38 For this perspective, see Paul Westermeyer, *The Church Musician*, rev. ed. (Minneapolis: Augsburg Fortress, 1997).

39 Wilhelm Löhe, "Von den heiligen Personen, der heiligen Zeit, der heiligen Weise und dem heiligen Orte" (1859), in *Gesammelte Werke*, vol. 3/1 (Neuendettelsau: Freimund, 1951), p. 570.

FOR FURTHER READING

WORSHIP AND THE MEANS OF GRACE
Walter R. Bouman

Arias, Mortimer. *Announcing the Reign of God*. Philadelphia: Fortress Press, 1984. Emphasizes the significance of the gospel as the announcement of the Reign of God, the coming of the messianic age.

Forde, Gerhard. *Theology is for Proclamation*. Minneapolis: Fortress Press, 1990. A most helpful volume on the Word of God as means of grace.

Girgensohn, Herbert. *Teaching Luther's Catechism*, Vol. II. Philadelphia: Muhlenberg Press, 1959. A fine exposition of Luther's teaching on Baptism, Confession/Absolution, and the Lord's Supper.

Hahn, Ferdinand. *Worship in the New Testament*. Philadelphia: Fortress Press, 1973. One of the best brief books on the topic available.

Jenson, Robert. *Visible Words*. Philadelphia: Fortress Press, 1978. An excellent general introduction to the Sacraments from a Lutheran perspective, with a thorough theological treatment of the Lord's Supper and Holy Baptism.

Kavanagh, Aidan. *The Shape of Baptism*. New York: Pueblo Publishing Company, 1978. A rich volume on the nature of the rite for Holy Baptism and its reform in the light of the Second Vatican Council.

Pfatteicher, Philip. *Commentary on the Lutheran Book of Worship*. Minneapolis: Fortress Press, 1990. Invaluable for attention to the history of the rites in the LBW in comparison with liturgical materials from other Christian traditions.

Senn, Frank. *The Witness of the Worshipping Congregation*. New York: Paulist Press, 1993. An excellent introduction to worship as witness and the way in which non-Christians can be introduced to the authentic worship of God in Word and Sacrament.

Senn, Frank. *Christian Liturgy*. Minneapolis: Fortress Press, 1997. The longest volume in this bibliography, it is a thorough and insightful theological introduction to the rites of the LBW set in historical and ecumenical context.

HOW AWESOME IS THIS PLACE!
Gordon W. Lathrop

Forde, Gerhard. *Where God Meets Man: Luther's down to earth approach to the Gospel.* Minneapolis: Augsburg, 1972. An older but still very important Lutheran reflection on the God who is not at the top of the ladder but at the bottom.

LaCugna, Catherine. *God For Us: The Trinity and Christian Life.* New York: Harper, 1991. A remarkable reflection on the Trinity as God turned toward the world in saving love. Chapter 9, "Trinity, Theology and Doxology," includes brilliant passages on the Trinity in Christian worship.

Luther, Martin. *Luther's Works*, vol 35: *Word and Sacrament I.* Philadephia: Muhlenberg, 1960. This volume of the American edition includes several essays of immense importance for worship, including especially "The Blessed Sacrament of the Holy and True Body of Christ, and the Brotherhoods, 1519," on the way the Holy Communion gives us a community and drives us toward the needy of the world, and "A Brief Instruction on What to Look for and Expect in the Gospels, 1521," on the real presence of Christ in the reading of the Scripture in the assembly. These essays are also to be found in various other collections of Luther's works.

Moore, R. Lawrence. *Selling God: American Religion in the Marketplace of Culture* New York: Oxford, 1994. A reflection that may assist us to think about what "God" may mean when dealt with as a commodity.

Ramshaw, Gail. *God Beyond Gender: Feminist Christian God-Language.* Minneapolis: Fortress, 1995. A passionate and intelligent use of biblical language to reflect upon trajectories of reform in the language of prayer and praise. Chapter 7, "The Language of Trinitarian Doctrine," is especially useful for thought about dynamic trinitarian language in the liturgy.

The Use of the Means of Grace: A Statement on the Practice of Word and Sacrament. Minneapolis: Augsburg Fortress, 1997. Although this is the official statement of only one North American Lutheran church which uses the *LBW*, it represents trajectories into the future in ways that accord with the *LBW* and that all Lutherans could fruitfully discuss.

Welcome to Christ: A Lutheran Introduction to the Catechumenate. Minneapolis: Augsburg Fortress, 1997. This book represents the fruit of years of pan-Lutheran conversation and work. Its essays ought to be seen as a specific development of *LBW* gifts. Parallel to this volume are similar volumes containing rites and a guide. A congregation welcoming adults to Christ will be encountering Christ again itself.

THE BLOOD IN OUR VEINS
Philip H. Pfatteicher

Deiss, Lucien, ed. *Springtime of the Liturgy. Liturgical Texts of the First Four Centuries.* Collegeville: Liturgical Press, 1979. A collection of basic texts with helpful introductions.

Luther, Martin. *Luther's Works.* American Edition vol.53, *Liturgy and Hymns* ed. Ulrich Leupold. Philadelphia: Fortress Press, 1965. The texts of Luther's two masses and his other liturgical work.

The Preface to the Common Service, 1888. Available in *The Common Service Book*. Philadelphia: Board of Publication of the United Lutheran Church in America, 1918, pp. 306-308. Copies of this book may be found in the libraries or basements of former ULCA congregations. An admirable statement of the achievement of the framers of the Common Service and of the Lutheran liturgical heritage.

"Preface to the Liturgy," *Service Book and Hymnal*. Minneapolis: Augsburg Publishing House and Philadelphia: Board of Publication of the Lutheran Church in America, 1958, pp. vi-viii. The "red book" still to be found in many former ALC and LCA congregations. A careful statement of how the Common Liturgy (1958) went beyond the Common Service.

Pfatteicher, Philip H. *Commentary on the Lutheran Book of Worship: Lutheran Liturgy in Its Ecumenical Context*. Minneapolis: Augsburg Fortress, 1990. Traces the development of specific texts in the *Lutheran Book of Worship*; companion to Senn.

Reed, Luther Dotterer. *The Lutheran Liturgy*. rev. ed. Philadelphia: Muhlenberg Press, 1960. Written (1947) as a companion to the *Common Service Book* and in the revised edition (1960) to the *Service Book and Hymnal*, this classic volume is still useful for its history of Lutheran worship.

Senn, Frank C. *Christian Liturgy: Catholic and Evangelical*. Minneapolis: Fortress, 1997. A great compendium of history and theology by a knowledgeable and reliable guide. Companion to Pfatteicher.

Thompson, Bard ed. *Liturgies of the Western Church*. Philadelphia: Fortress, 1980 (originally published 1961). A useful collection of liturgical texts from various Protestant traditions as well as Roman Catholic.

White, James F. *A Brief History of Christian Worship*. Nashville: Abingdon Press, 1993. A succinct and readable history by a Methodist scholar.

WORSHIP: THE CENTER OF PARISH LIFE

Frank C. Senn

Hoffman, Lawrence A. *The Art of Public Prayer: Not For Clergy Only*. Washington, D.C.: The Pastoral Press, 1988. Important for probing the dynamics of the various systems in the congregation that impact on public prayer.

Kavanagh, Aidan, *Elements of Rite. A Handbook of Liturgical Style*. New York: Pueblo Publishing Company, 1982. A collection of aphorisms on the dos and don'ts of liturgical celebration distilled from a solid historical study and experience of the liturgy.

Meeks, Blair Gilmer, ed. *The Landscape of Praise: Readings in Liturgical Renewal*. Valley Forge, PA: Trinity Press International, 1996. A collection of essays by a wide ecumenical array of liturgical scholars and leaders previous published in *Liturgy,* the journal of The Liturgical Conference, that bear on the doing of liturgy in the local assembly (congregation or parish).

Pfatteicher, Philip H. and Carlos Messerli. *Manual on the Liturgy*. Minneapolis: Augsburg Publishing House, 1979. The standard commentary on the rubrics in the *LBW*.

Pfatteicher, Philip H. *The School of the Church: Worship and Christian Formation.* Valley Forge, PA: Trinity Press International, 1995. An extended essay on aspects of the formational character of liturgical worship.

Piepkorn, Arthur Carl. *The Church: Selected Writings of Arthur Carl Piepkorn*, ed. and introduced by Michael P. Plekon and William S. Wiecher. Delhi, NY: ALPB Books, 1993. A collection of essays by an eminent Lutheran confessional and liturgical theologian which projects a solid vision of the church as an assembly for Word and Sacrament.

Senn, Frank C. *The Pastor As Worship Leader. A Manual for Corporate Worship*, 2nd ed. Minneapolis: Augsburg Publishing House, 1977. Written to introduce the vision of the kind of corporate liturgical celebration that would characterize the orders in the *LBW*, it attends especially to the role of ritual in community cohesion and the differentiation of roles in the assembly.

Senn, Frank C. *The Witness of the Worshiping Community. Liturgy and the Practice of Evangelism.* Mahwah, NJ: Paulist Press, 1993. Establishes the theological bases of liturgical and sacramental worship in the service of the mission of God.

Schmemann, Alexander. *For the Life of the World.* New York: St. Vladimir's Seminary Press, 1973. This little classic opens up a breathtaking view of the new humanity in Christ as the restored priesthood of the redeemed world and of the world as a place of sacramental encounter with God.

Van Loon, Ralph R. *Parish Worship Handbook*, ed. by S. Anita Stauffer. Philadelphia: Parish Life Press, 1979. One of the best manuals on the total organization of the parish for the liturgical worship that lies at the heart of parish life.

Van Loon, Ralph R. and S. Anita Stauffer. *Worship Wordbook: A Practical Guide for Parish Worship.* Minneapolis: Augsburg Fortress, 1995. A dictionary of liturgical terms and practices keyed especially to the orders and usages in the *Lutheran Book of Worship*.

THE PRAYERS OF THE COMMUNITY
Mark P. Bangert

Book of Common Worship. Prepared by the Theology and Worship Ministry Unit for the Presbyterian Church (U.S.A.) and the Cumberland Presbyterian Church. Louisville: Westminster/John Knox, 1993. This denominational service book contains a section for Daily Prayer (pp. 491-595) which includes Morning Prayer, Evening Prayer, alternative texts, Midday Prayer, Prayer at the Close of the Day, Vigil of the Resurrection (an expanded form of what appears in the *LBW* as "Paschal Blessing"), additional canticles, and prayers at mealtime. The basic five-fold shape of daily prayer is usefully presented at p. 490.

Bradshaw, Paul. *Daily Prayer in the Early Church.* New York: Oxford, 1982. In this book the development of daily prayer is traced from its Jewish antecedents up to the plan of St. Benedict in the early sixth century. Of particular interest are the chapters on the "Cathedral" office both in the East and in the West.

Madigan, Shawn. *Spirituality Rooted in Liturgy.* Washington: The Pastoral Press, 1988. Spirituality rooted in the history of the liturgy is here juxtaposed with the needs and concerns of the contemporary church. A case is made for finding longed-for community in the spiritual dynamics of experiences connected to liturgical worship and its power to pull us

Encountering God

into what could be. Rich bibliographic presentations make the volume particularly attractive.

Pfatteicher, Philip H. *Commentary on the Lutheran Book of Worship.* Minneapolis: Augsburg Fortress, 1990. See "Daily Prayer," 340-390. As is true of other sections of this informative volume the section on daily prayer provides information on the origin of the *LBW* services, their intended meaning, their relationship to other ecumenical versions, and the process of their development within Lutheranism. Pfatteicher concludes the chapter with a helpful and substantial bibliography.

Pfatteicher, Philip. *Praying with the Church.* Minneapolis: Augsburg Fortress, 1995. Pfatteicher's proven ability at producing helpful scholarly studies is here set aside for a moment in favor of a more pastoral introduction to the need and resources for daily prayer. He writes with loving passion and is convincing. His seven-step program for developing rhythm in one's daily devotional life is realistically beneficial.

The Psalter. A faithful and inclusive rendering from the Hebrew into contemporary English poetry, intended primarily for communal song and recitation. Chicago: Liturgy Training Publications, 1995. To a large extent this translation transcends male dominated language by its thoughtful constructions and by its deliberate forefronting of existing imagery and metaphors. The layout of the book is compelling. With a minimal amount of skill these psalms can be pointed to accommodate *LBW* psalm tones.

Ramshaw, Gail. *Between Sundays.* Daily Bible Readings Based on the *Revised Common Lectionary.* Minneapolis: Augsburg Fortress, 1997. In this volume Gail Ramshaw has assembled daily Bible readings (one per day) which are designed to expound further the Sunday's Gospel reading as arranged in the new three-year Revised Common Lectionary. Each reading has a one sentence summary. In contrast to the two-year lectionary of the *LBW*, this gathering of texts follows the seasonal and Sunday themes.

Schumacher, Frederick, ed. *For All the Saints.* A Prayer Book For and By the Church. Four vols. Delhi, New York: American Lutheran Publicity Bureau, 1994. This four-volume set is intended to assist both lay people and pastors in daily worship. Included in each volume are the full orders (without music) of Morning Prayer, Evening Prayer, and Compline from *LBW*, together with entire Psalter, the two-year lectionary with texts, and all other materials from the *LBW* necessary to use these services on a daily basis. Also the volumes contain a liberal selection of edifying readings and additional prayers.

Taft, Robert. *The Liturgy of the Hours in East and West.* Collegeville: The Liturgical Press, 1986. In some respects this study parallels the book by Bradshaw. Taft, however, extends his survey to include the history of the office in Africa, in the later Christian East, and in the Reformation churches. Final chapters explore the meaning of the office and its theology for today's worshipers.

Welcome Home. Scripture, Prayers, and Blessings for the Household. For each of the years of the three-year lectionary. Minneapolis: Augsburg Fortress, 1995ff. These volumes present materials for individual daily prayer or prayer within small groups. Instructions on how to use the book lead one into thoughts about such rhythms of prayer. Compact orders for morning, midday, evening, bedtime, and bddtime with children are supplemented with nine seasonal collections of special materials such as the blessing of a Christmas tree and daily readings. This is a resource, which attractively implements the principle of daily prayer under various circumstances.

A VISION OF WORSHIP LEADERSHIP
Paul R. Nelson

BOOKS

Hovda, Robert W. *Dry Bones: Living Worship Guides to Good Liturgy*. Washington, DC: The Liturgical Conference, 1973. A collection of essays from *Living Worship* many of which focus on the leadership ministries of the liturgy. This is an ecumenical resource by a Roman Catholic priest.

Hovda, Robert W. *Strong, Loving, and Wise: Presiding in the Liturgy*. Washington, DC: The Liturgical Conference, 1978. A collection of essays that focus on the presiding minister's role in the liturgy. Ecumenical with a Roman Catholic point of origin.

Lathrop, Gordon W. *Holy Things: A Liturgical Theology*. Minneapolis: Augsburg Fortress. An important liturgical theology by one of the Lutheran leaders in the field. More theoretical and reflective than practical in orientation.

Lathrop, Gordon W., gen. ed. *Open Questions in Worship*. Minneapolis: Augsburg Fortress. 8 very small volumes covering the following topics: *What are the essentials of Christian worship? What is "contemporary" worship? How does worship evangelize? What is changing in baptismal practice? What is changing in eucharistic practice? What are the ethical implications of worship? What does "multicultural" worship look like? How does the liturgy speak of God?* Available individually or as a complete set. A valuable resource for engaging current questions related to worship.

Pfatteicher, Philip H. and Messerli, Carlos R. *Manual on the Liturgy*. Minneapolis: Augsburg Publishing House, 1979. A supporting resource for *Lutheran Book of Worship* with many details, directions, and amplifications.

Senn, Frank C. *Christian Liturgy: Catholic and Evangelical*. Minneapolis: Augsburg Fortress, 1997. A major new historical and theological resource from within the Lutheran tradition.

Sloyan, Virginia, ed. *Touchstones for Liturgical Ministers*. Washington, DC: The Liturgical Conference and The Federation of Diocesan Liturgical Commissions, 1978. A helpful resource that is practical and guided by the size of local churches. Roman Catholic in its fundamental orientation, this resource is easily adapted for use by other churches.

Stauffer, S. Anita. *The Altar Guild: A Guide for the Ministry of Liturgical Preparation*. Philadelphia: Fortress, 1978. One of the most practical and popular of several manuals for altar guild members. Very practical in its orientation.

Sundays and Seasons: Worship Planning Guide. (Individual volumes for the Year of Mark–Cycle A; Year of Matthew–Cycle B; Year of Luke–Cycle C). Minneapolis: Augsburg Fortress, 1995-1997. A comprehensive planning guide with supplementary supporting materials as well as "alternate texts" for use with *Lutheran Book of Worship*. This resource is built on the Revised Common Lectionary—not on the *LBW* three-year lectionary for Sundays and Principal Festivals.

Van Loon, Ralph R. *Planning Parish Worship*. Philadelphia: Parish Life Press, 1976. A useful guide to planning which is geared closely to *Lutheran Book of Worship*.

Van Loon, Ralph R. and Stauffer, S. Anita. *Worship Wordbook: A Practical Guide for Parish Worship*. Minneapolis: Augsburg Fortress, 1995. A supporting resource keyed carefully to *Lutheran Book of Worship*. An expanded dictionary of Christian worship that focuses on historical and theological background with "guidelines" for practice in the congregation.

Westermeyer, Paul. *The Church Musician* (revised edition). Minneapolis: Augsburg Fortress, 1997. The longest sustained argument in print for reviving the office of Cantor in Christian congregations.

VIDEOS

The Hardest Joy: Leading a Parish to Live from Its Liturgy. Chicago: Liturgy Training Publications (19 min.). An outstanding video with high production quality that sees the ligurgy and its planning as the key to parish renewal. Roman Catholic orientation, but easily adapted to Lutheran contexts.

The Roman Catholic Mass Today. Chicago: Archdiocese of Chicago, Liturgy Training Publications, 1995. (30 min.). A resource focused on understanding the Roman Catholic Mass in the contemporary context. Some adaptation required for non-Roman contexts.

Training the Parish Lector. Collegeville, Minnesota: The Liturgical Press. (47 min.). Methods of delivery (both right and wrong) are demonstrated in this video. This resource advocates increased preparation for this ministry. Prepared for Roman Catholic congregations, the contents of this cassette can be adapted to other churches.

AUDIO CASSETTES

Lector Training Program. Chicago: Liturgy Training Publications. A workshop recorded on audio cassette for training lectors. A resource designed for training Roman Catholic readers, it is adaptable for other churches as well.

Singing the Liturgy: Building Confidence for Worship Leaders. Chicago: Evangelical Lutheran Church in America, Division for Congregational Ministries, 1996. A resource designed to support the singing of the liturgy as it is found in *Lutheran Book of Worship*. A brief lesson on chanting is followed by all of the sung portions of the liturgies (including all the proper prefaces) in both male and female voices. Ideal for building confidence among those who lead.

CD ROM

Lutheran Book of Worship Liturgies. Minneapolis: Augsburg Fortress. CD ROM and copyright license. A resource which provides copyright license and down-loadable graphic files for congregations and other who desire to print *Lutheran Book of Worship* liturgies in bulletins.

MUSICAL LEADERSHIP
Paul Westermeyer

Association of Lutheran Church Musicians Parish Education Series: *Study Guides Relating to Worship and Music*. St. Louis: Morning Star, 1992.

> Philip Gehring, "The Organ: An Instrument of Worship"
> Carl Schalk, "Psalmody in the Life of the Church"
> Thomas Schattauer, "The Church Year"
> Ralph F. Smith, "Liturgy in the Lutheran Tradition"
> Paul Westermeyer, "Hymnody"

Bangert, Mark. "Dynamics and New World Musics: A Methodology for Evaluation," *Worship and Culture in Dialogue*, ed. S. Anita Stauffer. Geneva: Lutheran World Federation, 1994, pp. 183-203. A helpful attempt to evaluate music for liturgy across cultures, with Alan Lomax as guide and musical event seen as behavioral rather than aesthetic.

Cherwien, David M. *Let the People Sing!* St. Louis: Concordia, 1997. A book about leading the people's song from the keyboard by a skilled church organist and improviser.

"Church Music at the End of the Twentieth Century," *Lutheran Quarterly* VIII:2 (Summer 1994): 197-211. A dialogue between the nineteenth and twentieth centuries.

Dawn, Marva J. *Reaching Out without Dumbing Down: A Theology of Worship for the Turn-of the-Century Culture*. Grand Rapids: William B. Eerdmans Publishing Company, 1995. For the integrity of the church's worship, against collapsing it into easy cultural chumminess and commercial sales pitches.

Eskew, Harry, and McElrath, Hugh T. *Sing with Understanding*, Second Edition, Revised and Expanded. Nashville: Church Street Press, 1995. As Carlton Young says, "the only reliable one-volume work to combine the history and practice of Christian song."

Halter, Carl and Schalk, Carl (ed.). *Handbook of Church Music*. St. Louis: Concordia Publishing House, 1978. Numerous helpful essays about the history and practice of Lutheran worship and music.

"How Shall We Worship?" *Reformed Liturgy and Music* I: 1 (1997), 3-10. Central rhythms of Christian worship.

Leupold, Ulrich S., ed. *Luther's Works*, Volume 53, Liturgy and Hymns. Philadelphia: Fortress Press, 1965. Luther's liturgical reforms, hymns, and thoughts on worship and music, with introductions and commentary.

Lathrop, Gordon, ed. *Open Questions in Worship*. Minneapolis: Augsburg Fortress, 1994). A series of eight pamphlets, each with three essays. One of the essays in the second volume is about what music to use in worship.

Niebuhr, H. Richard. *Christ and Culture*. New York: Harper & Row, 1951. A classic study of the relation of Christ and culture.

Pfatteicher, Philip H. *A Dictionary of Liturgical Terms*. Philadelphia: Trinity Press International, 1991. 133 pages of definitions arranged alphabetically.

Pfatteicher, Philip H. and Messerli, Carlos. *Manual on the Liturgy*. Minneapolis: Augsburg Publishing House, 1979. Interpretive essays to accompany the *LBW*.

Saliers, Don E. *Worship Come to Its Senses*. Nashville: Abingdon Press, 1996. Awe, delight, truth, and hope in worship.

Schalk, Carl. *Key Words in Church Music: Definition Essays on Concepts, Practices, and Movements of Thought in Church Music*. St. Louis: Concordia Publishing House, 1978. A companion volume to A Handbook of Church Music, with lengthy essays as the definitions.

Luther on Music, Paradigms of Praise. St. Louis: Concordia Publishing House, 1988. The best brief single volume summary of Luther's thought about music.

Schattauer, Thomas H. "A Clamor for the Contemporary: The Present Challenge for Baptismal Identity and Liturgical Tradition in American Culture." *Cross Accent* No. 6 (July, 1995), pp. 3-11. A careful and balanced analysis.

Schultze, Quentin J., et al. *Dancing in the Dark: Youth, Popular Culture, and the Electronic Media*. Grand Rapids: William B. Eerdmans, 1991. A series of essays which try to make sense of North American society and culture, by a group of scholars at Calvin College.

Senn, Frank. *Christian Worship in Its Cultural Setting*. Philadelphia: Fortress Press, 1983. A study of the relationship of worship to its culture.

"'Worship Alive': An Analysis and Critique of 'Alternative Worship Services'." *Worship* 69:3 (May, 1995), pp. 194-224. Historical sources with commentary.

Shepherd, Massey H., Jr. *The Psalms in Christian Worship, A Practical Guide*. Collegeville: The Liturgical Press, 1976. An overview of Hebrew poetry, how the church has used the Psalms, and the contemporary renewal of the use of Psalms in worship.

Stulken, Marilyn K. *Hymnal Companion to the Lutheran Book of Worship*. Philadelphia: Fortress Press, 1981. Lengthy essays on hymnody, plus brief studies of every text and tune in the *LBW*.

The Church Musician, Revised Edition. Minneapolis: Augsburg Fortress, 1997. The role of the church musician, an analysis of our current challenges and responses, plus a new Foreword by Martin Marty which addresses the same topic.

"The Future of Congregational Song," *The Hymn* 46:1 (January 1995): 4-9. An analysis of our present by means of the past, looking toward the future.

Van Loon, Ralph R. and Stauffer, S. Anita. *Worship Wordbook: A Practical Guide for Parish Worship*. Minneapolis: Augsburg Fortress, 1995. 186 pages of definitions, historical information, and guidance regarding the rites and rubrics of the *LBW*.

Westermeyer, Paul. "Church Music at the End of the Nineteenth Century." *Lutheran Quarterly* VIII:1 (Spring 1994), 29-51. A look at the musical activity which followed the Common Service of 1888.

With One Voice. Minneapolis: Augsburg Fortress, 1995. A paperback supplement to the *LBW*, with additional settings of services and more hymns.

With Tongues of Fire: Profiles in 20th-Century Hymn Writing. St. Louis: Concordia Publishing House, 1995. Biographies, interviews, and lists of hymns by the finest hymn writers of our period, surrounded by historical and interpretive essays.

LITURGY: AN EVANGELISM ADVANTAGE
David Paul Gleason

Kenneson, Philip D and Street, James L. *Selling Out the Church: The Dangers of Church Marketing*. Nashville: Abingdon, 1997. The title says it well. Here is an account of the inherent danger in sacrificing the liturgy to currently popular trends in marketing the Church, along with a plea for the preservation of its transforming power to create disciples for Christ.

Lathrop, Gordon W. *Holy Things: A Liturgical Theology*. Minneapolis: Augsburg Fortress, 1993. Lathrop provides a phenomenology of Christian worship that is both historical and grounded in contemporary and universal human experience. He sets forth how believers encounter God and respond to him through the "holy things" of liturgy.

Lathrop, Gordon, ed. "How Does Worship Evangelize?" *Open Questions in Worship, Vol. 3*, Minneapolis: Augsburg Fortress, 1995. This is a booklet containing three brief essays. Readers will find help in defining evangelism, seeing how liturgical worship facilitates its intent, and brings believers into the life of God.

Pfatteicher, Philip H. *Liturgical Spirituality*, Valley Forge, PA: Trinity Press International, 1997. At a time when Americans and American Christians are searching for an ill-defined spirituality, Pfatteicher expounds an authentic spirituality grounded in the fullness of the Church's liturgical life. It is a spirituality which transcends subjective feelings of interior contentment and locates itself in the reality of God as he comes to his people.

Senn, Frank C. *Christian Liturgy: Catholic and Evangelical*. Minneapolis: Augsburg Fortress, 1997. This is a marvelously thorough treatment of the liturgy of the Western church, including its history, theology, and practice. It serves as a basic text and reference for a full appreciation of the liturgical heritage. It concludes with a brief section on "Contemporary Liturgical Challenges," including the challenge of "Reaching the Unchurched."

Senn, Frank C. *The Witness of the Worshiping Community: Liturgy and the Practice of Evangelism*. Mahwah, NJ: Paulist, 1993. Senn provides a full treatment of the subject of this chapter, complete with very practical suggstions that are applicable to any parish.

THE CULTURAL PATTERN
OF CHRISTIAN WORSHIP
Thomas H. Schattauer

Clapp, Rodney. *A Peculiar People: The Church as Culture in a Post-Christian Society*. Downers Grove, Ill.: InterVarsity, 1996. Clapp is an evangelical author inquiring about with the meaning of Christianity in a postmodern era. The work provides both an engaging analysis of the contemporary cultural situation and a provocative proposal to view the church as a culture that shapes a people in a particular way of life. It includes a chapter on "The Church as Worshiping Community."

Dawn, Marva. *Reaching Out without Dumbing Down: A Theology of Worship for the Turn-of-the-Century Culture*. Grand Rapids, Mich.: Eerdmans, 1995. Dawn provides much wise counsel in her reflections about how "the culture of worship" relates to "the culture surrounding worship." The book explores the theological and spiritual dimensions of Christian worship in critique of the accommodation to culture in much contemporary worship.

Division for Congregational Ministries, ELCA. *Getting Ready for Worship in the Twenty-first Century*. Chicago: Evangelical Lutheran Church in America, 1996. This resource for congregational study and discussion includes the text of the Nairobi Statement from the LWF study on worship and culture (see below), with an introduction and commentary by Mark Bangert that focuses the issues for North American readers. It comes with questions prepared by Karen Ward to aid in using the material with an adult study group.

Lathrop, Gordon W. *Holy Things: A Liturgical Theology*. Minneapolis: Augsburg Fortress, 1993. Lathrop's book is a sustained liturgical-theological reflection on how the things of the liturgy—its words, actions, materials, and ministries—are juxtaposed to the meaning of Jesus Christ, who alone is holy. Exploring the concept of *ordo*, Lathrop argues that the basic patterns of the liturgical assembly are essential to the church's life and mission, with particular attention to the contemporary cultural situation.

Lathrop, Gordon W., ed. *Open Questions in Worship*. 8 volumes. Minneapolis: Augsburg Fortress, 1994-96. These volumes explore a number of urgent (and open) questions in dialogue with the essential things at the center of Christian worship. The first volume by Lathrop argues for these essential things. Subsequent volumes each include three essays on specific questions in relation to a common topic (contemporary worship, evangelism, baptismal practice, eucharistic practice, ethics, culture, and language about God). Matters of worship and culture are addressed throughout.

Mitchell, Nathan, ed., *Liturgy Digest* 3/2 (1996). This issue available from the Notre Dame Center for Pastoral Liturgy is dedicated to the intersection of liturgy and culture with two essays, a lexicon, and a bibliography that introduce and survey some of the literature on the topic in a most helpful way.

Senn, Frank C. *Christian Worship and its Cultural Setting*. Philadelphia: Fortress, 1983. With insight from the human sciences and examples from the entire course of liturgical history, Senn examines the influence of culture on the development and practice of Christian worship. The fundamental aims of the book are deeply theological and pastoral.

Senn, Frank C. *The Witness of the Worshiping Community: Liturgy and the Practice of Evangelism*. Mahwah, N.J.: Paulist, 1993. Senn's treatment of the relation of evangelism to worship highlights the participation of the worshiping community in the mission of God toward the world and argues that the historic forms of worship are the central means of the church's witness to God's purposes. The book offers a vision and practical help for strengthening that witness in present cultural circumstances.

Stauffer, S. Anita, ed. *Worship and Culture in Dialogue*. Geneva: Lutheran World Federation, 1994.

Stauffer, S. Anita, ed. *Christian Worship: Unity in Cultural Diversity*. Geneva: Lutheran World Federation, 1996. These two volumes are the result-to-date of the on-going LWF study on worship and culture. They include two common statements—the Cartigny Statement on biblical and historical foundations and the Nairobi Statement on contemporary challenges and opportunities—with supporting essays, including a significant series of programmatic essays by Gordon Lathrop and Anscar Chupungco. The bibliographies by the editor are the most comprehensive available.

CONTRIBUTORS

MARK P. BANGERT, John H. Tietjen Professor of Pastoral Ministry: Worship and Music, Lutheran School of Theology, Chicago, Illinois.

WALTER R. BOUMAN, Edward C. Fendt Professor of Systematic Theology, Trinity Lutheran Seminary, Columbus, Ohio.

EUGENE L. BRAND, Distinguished International Professor in Residence, Trinity Lutheran Seminary, Columbus, Ohio. Formerly Project Director for the *Lutheran Book of Worship*; Assistant General Secretary for Ecumenical Affairs, Lutheran World Federation.

DAVID PAUL GLEASON, Senior Pastor, First English Evangelical Lutheran Church, Pittsburgh, Pennsylvania.

SUSAN KAREN HEDAHL, Associate Professor of Homiletics, Gettysburg Lutheran Theological Seminary, Gettysburg, Pennsylvania.

GORDON W. LATHROP, Schieren Professor of Liturgy, Lutheran Theological Seminary, Philadelphia, Pennsylvania.

PAUL R. NELSON, Director for Worship, Evangelical Lutheran Church in America, Chicago, Illinois.

PHILIP H. PFATTEICHER, Professor of English and Religious Studies Emeritus, East Stroudsburg University of Pennsylvania.

THOMAS H. SCHATTAUER, Associate Professor of Liturgics and Dean of the Chapel, Wartburg Theological Seminary, Dubuque, Iowa.

FRANK C. SENN, Pastor, Immanuel Lutheran Church, Evanston, Illinois.

PAUL WESTERMEYER, Professor of Church Music, Luther Seminary, St. Paul, Minnesota.

INDEX

D

Daily Office   86, 97, 145, 146
Daily prayer   44, 54, 73, 74, 83, 84, 88, 90, 92, 93, 94, 95, 96, 97, 103, 105, 106, 113, 116, 133, 145, 184, 185
Deutsche Messe   59, 60, 151, 173
Didache   28, 54, 171, 179

E

Ecumenical matrix   10, 12, 14, 16
Education   49, 77, 107, 148, 150, 153, 156, 159, 188
Emmaus   53
Entertainment evangelism   16, 143
Eucharistia   43, 48, 49
Eucharistic prayer   20, 28, 29, 46, 47, 48, 54, 55, 57, 63, 65, 80, 111, 171, 172, 179, 180
Evangelical Lutheran Church in America   14, 30, 45, 47, 79, 104, 187, 191
Evangelical Lutheran Church in Canada   14, 30, 45, 79, 104
Evangelism   3, 16, 32, 33, 39, 129, 136, 137, 139, 142, 143, 144, 147, 157, 158, 184, 190, 191
Evening Prayer   49, 74, 83, 84, 86, 87, 88, 89, 90, 91, 92, 93, 94, 95, 96, 97, 103, 105, 112, 116, 117, 128, 135, 145, 179, 184, 185

F

For All the Saints   87, 97, 185
Formula Missae   58, 63, 173

G

Geistliches Gesang   175
Gelasian sacramentary   57
General Council   63
General Synod   63
General Synod South   63
Gnosticism   23
Gospel   6, 16, 18, 20, 22, 23, 24, 25, 31, 32, 34, 35, 37, 38, 41, 49, 50, 52, 53, 54, 58, 59, 62, 63, 64, 67, 71, 72, 73, 74, 75, 79, 87, 90, 92, 100, 101, 117, 118, 123, 138, 140, 141, 153, 160, 163, 164, 166, 167, 171, 175, 177, 178, 180, 181, 182, 185
Great Thanksgiving   28, 69, 71, 73, 80, 81, 99, 101, 104, 105, 110, 111, 179
Gregorian sacramentary   57

H

Historic liturgy   63, 136, 137, 139, 141, 145, 147
Holy Baptism   15, 22, 23, 32, 33, 34, 35, 67, 68, 71, 72, 75, 76, 100, 161
Holy Communion   6, 23, 24, 25, 26, 27, 30, 31, 32, 33, 35, 44, 46, 54, 61, 62, 67, 68, 69, 71, 72, 73, 75, 76, 78, 87, 99, 100, 101, 103, 104, 105, 106, 110, 111, 113, 115, 117, 123, 127, 128, 135, 173, 179, 182

I

Incense   54, 86, 89, 92, 109
Inclusive language   18, 152, 153
Inter-Lutheran Commission on Worship (ILCW)   5, 7, 8, 11, 12, 13, 15, 19, 29, 65, 99, 101, 177
International Commission for English in the Liturgy (ICEL)   11, 13
International Consultation on English Texts (ICET)   12, 21
Intonations   103, 110, 111, 112, 114

J

Justin Martyr   28, 110, 169, 172

K

King James English   11

Index   195